CHINA'S SECRET STRATEGY

ARTHUR DEPERIS

R SAMPATH

CHINA'S SECRET STRATEGY

How China's Rise Costs America

Economic History · Human Rights · Food & Drug Safety
Geopolitics · Chip War · Trade War · New Cold War

Arthur Deperis

R Sampath
Contributing Author

CONTENTS

ABOUT THE AUTHORS

—ᴧᴧᴧ—

Arthur Deperis is a respected researcher with over two decades of experience examining major global developments. He holds an MBA from the University of Southern California and brings a strong background in economic development, corporate strategy, and market research, allowing him to blend strategic insight with rigorous analysis. His work in economic development has earned awards and recognition from the State of California and the U.S. federal government.

In *China's Secret Strategy*, Deperis delivers a clear and confident examination of China's rise and its consequences for the United States. Drawing on years of meticulous research and strict fact-checking, he exposes the underlying forces driving this shift in global power.

—ᴧᴧᴧ—

R Sampath is Founder and CEO of Quanta Consulting, Inc. and a strategic advisor with deep expertise in US–India cross-border business strategy, M&A, government policy, and economic development. Sampath has held senior leadership & CEO roles in the US & India. He holds an MBA from USC Marshall.

In *China's Secret Strategy*, his research examines China's state-driven economic model, highlighting the structural challenges reshaping global supply chains and driving multinational companies to diversify toward India and Southeast Asia.

www.QuantaCo.com

ACKNOWLEDGMENT

—◊◊◊—

The creation of this book is a testament to the diligent efforts of numerous esteemed journalists and researchers whose deep expertise and dedication have shaped its content. Their invaluable contributions have been acknowledged with gratitude in the reference section.

ENJOYED THE BOOK?

If so, we would be incredibly grateful if you could take a moment to leave a review on Amazon. Your feedback not only means a lot to us, it also helps other readers decide if the book is right for them. Here's the link to the book on Amazon to leave your review:

https://www.amazon.com/dp/B0DX41Q9S8

Thank you for engaging with this critical topic and for your support!

Arthur Deperis

R Sampath

INTRODUCTION

—◊◊◊—

The rise of China in global politics has been one of the most consequential stories in recent times. Since joining the World Trade Organization in 2001, China has rapidly evolved from a dormant player to a mighty superpower, significantly influencing global economics and politics. However, this remarkable transformation has drawbacks, notably affecting the United States.

Imagine a nation with a rich history, combining ancient wisdom with modern tactics. This is present-day China. The country has used its membership in the World Trade Organization to saturate global markets with inexpensive products, challenge international trade standards, and consistently outperform its rivals. The consequences for the United States have been significant: a decline in manufacturing jobs, increased trade deficits, and revealed economic weaknesses.

As China's influence expanded, so did its willingness to employ ruthless tactics. Intellectual property theft has become a tool of state policy, siphoning off American innovation to fuel its technological advancements. Furthermore, currency manipulation and aggressive export subsidies have distorted global markets, giving Chinese goods an unfair edge and crippling American industries.

The environmental toll of China's rise is equally staggering. The pursuit of rapid industrialization has led to severe pollution, poisoning the air and water within China and across borders. Toxic food scandals and contaminated products have infiltrated global supply chains, endangering the American food supply.

China's economic expansion is mirrored by its strategic investments overseas. Extending its reach into every corner of the globe, China has prompted pushback from the US and its allies. The Belt and Road Initiative (BRI) and the Asian Infrastructure Investment Bank (AIIB) exemplify China's desire for global influence, superseding the United States.

The human rights abuse in China reveals a dark side to its growth. The repression of dissent, mass surveillance, and harsh treatment of minorities paint a chilling picture of a state that values control over liberty. This stark reality sharply contrasts with the nation's image of progress, shedding light on the ethical costs of its ambitions.

China is aiming for dominance through strategic diplomacy and military strength. This includes an alliance with Russia and significant military expansion, leading to new Cold War-like tensions. Competition is also occurring in the technology sector, with a "Chip War" unfolding. China is striving for technological supremacy while the US is working to protect its innovations. Additionally, the US is dealing with economic and logistical challenges as industries return from China. The stakes and implications of these developments are enormous.

China's Secret Strategy explores China's ambitious rise and its significant implications for the United States. This book uncovers the hidden mechanisms behind China's ascent and challenges readers to understand the profound impacts of this global power shift. Ready to find the secrets?

CHAPTER 1

CHINA UNVEILED: A JOURNEY THROUGH THE HISTORY OF POLITICS AND POWER

—⚏—

The chapter comprehensively overviews China's most pivotal historical, political, and power events. It offers invaluable insight into the nation's remarkable transition from ancient dynasties to its status as a global superpower. By exploring crucial moments such as the fall of the Qing Dynasty, the rise of the Republic of China (ROC), and the transformative economic reforms under Deng Xiaoping, you will understand China's intricate political and economic landscape deeply. Furthermore, the chapter ignites contemplation on China's profound global impact, encompassing its trade agreements with the United States and its pivotal role in shaping international relations.

1. Timeline

It is imperative to thoroughly analyze the country's history to understand the current situation in China. China is unambiguously considered a totalitarian regime. The disparity in income between the coastal regions and the inland cities is substantial. The coastal provinces of China undeniably enjoy relative wealth, while the country's inland areas incontrovertibly experience a gradual decline in prosperity (Refs 1, 2, 3, and 16).

1644–1912: The Qing Dynasty.

1912: The Nationalist Party was established, and China proclaimed itself a republic with Sun Yat-sen as the first president, who later resigned in favor of Yuan Shihkai.

1916–1926: Warlord period.

1917: Sun Yat-sen set up a rival government in Canton.

1917-1918: China joined the Entente Powers including France, the United Kingdom of Great Britain, Italy, Japan, and the United States in World War I.

1921: Founding of the Chinese Communist Party in Shanghai.

1926–1927: The Northern Expedition led by General Chiang Kai-shek substantially reunified China under the Nationalist government.

1940: President Roosevelt approved $25 million in military aid to China, allowing the Chinese to buy one hundred P-40 pursuit aircraft to fight against Japan. China had been at war with Japan since 1937 and continued the fight until the Japanese surrendered in 1945.

1946–1949: Civil war between the Communists and Nationalists.

1949: The Communist Party's leader, Mao Zedong, ruled China.

1949–1951: Anti-Western, pro-Soviet.

1950–59: China invaded and claimed Tibet as Chinese territory.

1952–1957: China received financial and technical assistance from the Soviet Union.

1958–1960: Mao launched the "Great Leap Forward."

1961–1965: Emphasized on agriculture; chemical fertilizers' usage.

1966–1969: Mao orchestrated the Cultural Revolution that paralyzed everyday life and disrupted the economy.

1971: China joined the United Nations.

1972: President Nixon visited Beijing to facilitate trade between China and the United States.

1976: Death of Mao and the end of the Cultural Revolution.

1976–1978: Hua Guofeng assumed the leadership of China but struggled.

1978–1989: Deng Xiaoping became China's leader and reformed the economy, also shifting from a rural economy to light manufacturing.

1979: President Jimmy Carter signed a bilateral trade agreement with China.

1979: China launched the one-child policy.

1980–1984: China established Special Economic Zones (SEZs).

1981: The National Household Responsibility System was implemented.

1981: The first treasury bonds were sold to enterprises and individuals.

1984: Economic and Technical Development Zones in 14 coastal cities.

1985: Foreign banks were established in the Special Economic Zones.

1986: The Contract System was implemented for state-owned companies.

1988: Allowed enterprises with eight or more employees to operate as private enterprises.

1989: Tiananmen Square massacre by Chinese military.

1989: After the protests in Tiananmen Square, Deng resigned from all his official positions. Deng and his chosen successors, Jiang Zemin and Hu Jintao, played a significant role in China becoming the world's second-largest economy by nominal GDP in 2010.

1990: Shanghai Stock Exchange.

1991: Shenzhen Stock Exchange.

1993: President Clinton secured Most Favored Nation (MFN) status for China (1).

1993–2003: Jiang Zemin became China's president.

1994–1996: National Poverty Reduction Plan.

1994: State-owned enterprise Shandong Huaneng Power Development listed on the New York Stock Exchange.

1996: China removed restrictions on exchanging currency for international trade.

1997: Death of Deng Xiaoping.

1997–1999: Hong Kong and Macao handover; Asian Financial Crisis.

1999: Western Development Strategy to open doors to Westerners.

2001: China was admitted to the World Trade Organization (2) and the Qualified Foreign Institutional Investor (QFII) program (3).

2003–2013: Hu Jintao became China's president.

2004: China signed a landmark trade agreement with 10 Southeast Asian countries to provide a free-trade zone.

2005: China became the world's fourth-largest economy.

2006: China's foreign currency reserves became the world's most enormous, at $1 trillion.

2006: Medium-term Plan for Scientific Development.

2010: China became the world's second-largest economy.

2013: Xi Jinping became China's president.

2013: China proposed the Bell and Road Initiative.

2014: Alibaba went public.

2015: Launched "Made in China 2025" and "Two Child Policy."

2016: China opened the Asia Infrastructure Investment Bank.

2020: There are 878 billionaires in China with a total combined net worth of $4 trillion. There is a population of 1.4 billion people, and over 50 percent are middle class.

2022: Formation of the Regional Comprehensive Economic Partnership (RCEP).

2023: Russia-Sino Joint military exercises in the Sea of Japan.

Notes:

(1) Most Favored Nation (MFN) status refers to an economic position in which a country receives terms no less favorable than those extended to any other trading partner. This includes equal tariffs, quotas, and market access. In essence, all MFN trade partners must be treated equally.

(2) The World Trade Organization (WTO) is the only global international body responsible for setting and enforcing rules for trade between nations. Founded in 1995, the WTO had 166 members as of 2024, accounting for approximately 98% of world trade. Its members agree to these rules and participate in trade negotiations. The WTO's main functions include administering trade agreements, providing a forum for trade liberalization, and resolving trade disputes. Its overall goal is to ensure that international trade flows as smoothly, predictably, and freely as possible.

(3) The Qualified Foreign Institutional Investor (QFII) program allows specified licensed international investors to participate in mainland China's stock exchanges.

2. The Fall of the Qing Dynasty

The Qing dynasty, established by the invading Manchus, ruled China from 1644 to 1912. In the 16th century, China boasted the world's most sophisticated and productive economy. The Chinese people enjoyed a high standard of living in a culturally and materially prosperous country with abundant natural resources. The Chinese royal family was held in high regard, and China wielded significant political and economic influence worldwide until the mid-1800s. However, the ruling monarchy weakened, and the central government gradually ceded power to warlords and foreign nations. In 1850, Britain surpassed China as the world's largest economy.

Empress Dowager Cixi of China (1835–1908) entered the imperial court at age 17 as a concubine of the Xianfeng Emperor. She later gave birth to his only son, Tongzhi. When Emperor Xianfeng died in 1861 at the age of 30, Tongzhi ascended the throne at just six years old, with Cixi exercising significant influence during his reign (1861–1875). After Tongzhi died without an heir, Cixi placed her four-year-old nephew on the throne as the Guangxu Emperor. This move consolidated her authority, and she ruled as the de facto leader of the Qing Empire from 1861 until her death in 1908 at the age of 73.

In 1908, 22 hours before Cixi's death, Emperor Guangxu died from a single, high dose of arsenic poisoning. This fact was revealed by forensic tests of the emperor's remains in 2008. Since he had no son, his two-year-old nephew, Puyi, was chosen as China's last emperor. In February 1912, Empress Dowager Longyu (1868-1913), the spouse of the late Emperor Guangxu, negotiated and signed Emperor Puyi's abdication decree, leading to the end of two thousand years of imperial rule in China. Following this, China officially established the Republic of China (ROC), which the Nationalists organized.

3. Taiwan, the Republic of China (ROC): A Journey Through Time and Identity

Pre–1600s: Taiwan was self-governing.

17th Century: Partly colonized by the Netherlands, briefly independent, then taken over by China for over two centuries.

1895: Japan gained control of Taiwan post-First Sino-Japanese War, making it a Japanese colony.

1945: Post-World War II, Taiwan was placed under administrative control of the Republic of China (ROC).

1949-Present: The nationalist government fled to Taiwan after the Communist Party of China (CPC) ousted it from the mainland. CPC controlled the mainland China (PRC), while nationalists controlled Taiwan (ROC). No formal peace treaty was signed.

1952: Japan formally renounced sovereignty over Taiwan in the Treaty of San Francisco.

Since the 1600s, Taiwan's history has been marked by a series of significant changes. Initially self-governing, it fell under Dutch rule in the 17th century before regaining independence, only to be annexed by China for two hundred years. Following the First Sino-Japanese War in 1895, Japan took control of Taiwan, establishing fifty years of Japanese rule. After World War II, Taiwan was returned to Chinese governance (Ref 17).

In 1946, a three-year civil war broke out in China between the Communists and the Nationalists. The Communists emerged victorious in 1949, and the Nationalist forces retreated to Taiwan, where they established the Republic of China (ROC) government under martial law. The Nationalist government became authoritarian, leading to the conviction and execution of thousands of democracy activists from 1949 to 1987. In 1987, martial law was lifted, and Taiwan transitioned to a multi-party political system. In 1987, martial law was lifted, and Taiwan adopted a multi-party political system. The Nationalist Party's dominance in Taiwanese politics continued until the 2000 election, when Chen Shui-Bian, a member of the Democratic Progressive Party (DPP), was elected president.

The political status of Taiwan has been uncertain. In 2024, twelve countries, including Vatican City, officially recognized Taiwan as an independent country. Taiwan held a seat on the United Nations Security Council for twenty-two years until 1971, when it was replaced by the People's Republic of China (PRC). In 1979, the United States passed the Taiwan Relations Act after President Carter ended diplomatic recognition of Taiwan to improve its relationship with China (PRC). The Act promises to provide Taiwan with defensive weapons and commits to the preservation of the human rights of the Taiwanese. However, China still regards Taiwan as a breakaway province and passed an anti-secession law in 2005, stating that it can use military force if Taiwan declares independence.

Despite these challenges, Taiwan has emerged as a major economic powerhouse and a leading producer of computer technology. Though China restricts Taiwan's international recognition, Taiwan has established formal diplomatic relations with 12-13 countries and unofficial diplomatic relations with almost 100 countries and regions, including key global powers such as the United States, Japan, and the EU.

In 2024, Taiwan was the United States' seventh-largest goods trading partner, outranking important markets such as India, with $136.3 billion in two-way goods trade. Taiwan was the United States' 12th-largest goods export market at $42.3 billion of goods exported in 2024, an increase of 5 percent over 2023. U.S. goods exports to Taiwan accounted for 2.1 percent of U.S. total goods exports. Taiwan was the United States' eighth-largest agricultural export market in 2024, with exports totaling $3.8 billion, a 2 percent increase over 2023 ($3.7 billion). Top U.S. agricultural exports included soybeans ($601.4 million), beef and beef products ($709.2 million), corn ($383.8 million), wheat ($325.0 million), and fresh fruit ($262.1 million) (Ref trade.gov).

The United States approved the sale of new F-16 fighter jets worth $8 billion to Taiwan in 2019, the largest and most important sale of weaponry to Taiwan in decades. Additionally, in 2020, the US Congress passed The Taiwan Allies International Protection and Enhancement Initiative Act, confirming the United States' support for a close economic, political, and security relationship with Taiwan.

The unique stalemate between Taiwan and mainland China remains, with PRC claiming Taiwan as a province; and ROC (Taiwan) claiming its independence. Taiwan's quest for international recognition has been consistently thwarted by China, which has used its influence to block Taiwan's full membership in the United Nations. Regardless, Taiwan has flourished economically and technologically. Over 80% of the island's population wish to maintain the status quo and be self-governed, compared to a rising number who advocate for complete independence, highlighting Taiwan's ongoing struggle for a definitive identity on the world stage.

4. The People's Republic of China under Mao

In 1949, Mao Zedong became the leader of the Communist Party, and along with the victory in the Chinese Civil War, allowed him to govern mainland China and establish the People's Republic of China (PRC). During Mao's rule, rural land remained collectively managed and publicly owned. State-owned enterprises (SOEs) and collective farms were the predominant business models at the time.

Between 1952 and 1957, the Soviet Union provided financial aid and technical expertise to help build factories in China, focusing on steel and energy production. However, the increased coal production resulted in severe environmental degradation that will take many generations and billions of dollars to clean up. Mao's goal was to acquire foreign technology to make China independent. Despite improvements in literacy and healthcare, the state control system prevented China from progressing in the industrial and agricultural sectors. On the other hand, the country had minimal foreign debt compared to many developing countries.

In 1958, Mao launched the "Great Leap Forward," a five-year economic plan to introduce collective farming and labor-intensive industry. Unfortunately, the new plan resulted in an economic breakdown and disrupted agriculture production. This, combined with bad weather, caused the Great Chinese Famine and led to the deaths of 20 to 30 million people. Mao Zedong died from heart disease on September 9, 1976, at the age of 82.

The Great Leap Forward

Historian Frank Dikötter, author of the influential book *Mao's Great Famine*, published an article in *History Today* summarizing what happened:

> The number of victims may have been even more significant than previously thought, and the mass murder was more clearly intentional on Mao's part and included large numbers of victims who were executed or tortured, as opposed to merely starved to death. Even the previously standard estimates of 30 million or more would still make this a substantial mass murder in history.

> What comes out of this massive and detailed dossier is a tale of horror in which Mao emerges as one of the greatest mass murderers in history, responsible for the deaths of at least 45 million people between 1958 and 1962. It is not merely the extent of the catastrophe estimated earlier but also how many people died: between two and three million victims were tortured to death or summarily killed, often for the slightest infraction. When a boy stole a handful of grain in a Hunan village, local boss Xiong Dechang forced his father to bury him

alive. The father died of grief a few days later." *The Washington Post*, August 3, 2016 (Ref 15).

5. Economic Reforms under Deng Xiaoping

In 1978, Deng Xiaoping became the leader of China and introduced reforms to the country's economy. Deng believed that capitalist principles could be applied in a socialist economy. Initially, China's reforms focused on agriculture and establishing special economic zones to attract foreign capital and technology in 14 major coastal cities. In these zones, foreign-funded enterprises received preferential tax treatment and were exempt from import licenses and customs duties.

In 1981, China permitted farmers to sell crops for profit after meeting production quotas, by implementing the "National Household Responsibility System." In 1986, the "Contract Responsibility System" was introduced, allowing enterprises to keep excessive profits above the amount stated in the contract with the government. In 1988, private operation was permitted for enterprises with eight or more employees, while state-owned enterprises became fully autonomous and responsible for their profits. In the early 1990s, China experienced significant export growth in the textile, garment, shoe, and toy industries.

Deng Xiaoping established presidential term limits in the 1980s to prevent a repeat of Chairman Mao's dictatorship. He passed away in February 1997 at the age of 92 from Parkinson's disease, respiratory illness, and old age. Under his leadership, China underwent substantial economic growth. According to the World Bank, Deng's reforms lifted over 400 million people out of poverty between 1981 and 2002 (Ref 12).

6. Hong Kong and Macau

The Opium Wars were caused by China's efforts to stop the opium trade. From the 18th century, foreign traders, mainly the British, were unlawfully sending opium from India to China. The trade expanded greatly after 1820, causing widespread addiction and severe social and economic problems in China. Consequently, China ceded territories to the British and Portuguese in treaties to end the opium wars.

In 1842, the Treaty of Nanjing marked the conclusion of the First Opium War and compelled China to transfer the territory of Hong Kong to the British Kingdom. Subsequently, the Treaty of Peking, signed in 1887, marked the end of the Second Opium War. This treaty granted Portugal the perpetual right to occupy and govern Macau on the condition that Portugal would assist in preventing opium smuggling.

The return of these two territories to China more than two decades ago was based on a political principle formulated by Deng Xiaoping called "One Country, Two Systems." Under this principle, these regions maintain their governments, financial and economic systems, and trade relations with foreign countries independently from mainland China. However, the chief executive of each region is chosen by a committee (400 members for Macau, 1,500 members for Hong Kong) approved by Beijing, comprising politicians and businesspersons. Ordinary citizens do not have a direct say in appointing the chief executive.

Hong Kong

In 1997, the British returned Hong Kong to mainland China after 156 years of colonization. Although Hong Kong maintained its own governing and economic systems separately from China, in 2020, China passed a new security law that made it easier to punish protesters. This new law undermines Hong Kong's autonomy and brings it under China's control, abandoning the "One Country, Two Systems" framework in place for the past 23 years.

The United States has been closely monitoring China's actions. To continue treating Hong Kong as a separate entity, particularly for commercial purposes, Hong Kong must maintain a high degree of autonomy from China. (Refs 4, 8, and 10).

Macau (Macao)

Macau is a small peninsula covering an area of 12.7 square miles (32.9 km^2). It is located on the south coast of China near Guangzhou. In 1557, it was leased to Portugal and officially became a Portuguese colony in 1887. After the revolution in Portugal in 1974, the country offered to withdraw from Macau. However, China postponed the transfer later to preserve international and local confidence in Hong Kong. Finally, in 1987, Portugal agreed to return Macau to China by 1999. As the last European territory in continental Asia, Macau is known for its large casinos, earning it the title of "Las Vegas of the East" (Ref 13).

7. Desire to Advance in Technology

In 2015, the government initiated a program known as "Made in China 2025" to establish China as a global leader in advanced technology by the year 2049, marking the 100th anniversary of the founding of the People's Republic of China. The program is focused on dominance in global high-tech manufacturing including intellectual property and targets sectors such as electric cars, next-generation IT, robotics, and artificial intelligence. China's commitment involves investing nearly $300 billion to enhance its manufacturing capabilities across high-tech fields, including pharmaceuticals, aerospace, and robotics.

8. Trade Agreements with the United States

1972: President Nixon visited Beijing to facilitate diplomatic and trade relationships with China.

1979: President Carter signed a bilateral trade agreement with China.

1993: President Clinton renewed China's Most Favored Nation (MFN) status and signed the trade bill into law, which paved the way for China to be a member of the World Trade Organization (WTO) in 2001 and the Qualified Foreign Institutional Investor (QFII) program. QFII enables foreign investors to participate in China's stock exchanges, contributing to economic growth.

2001: President Bush signed a proclamation granting China permanent normal trading relations with the United States as the finale to President Clinton's previous efforts.

Many US presidents had somewhat facilitated the US trade with China. However, enabling China to become a World Trade Organization (WTO) member during the Clinton administration has caused the most damage to the US economy and the American people.

According to a 2016 Netflix documentary film, "Death by China," produced by Peter Navarro, Clinton pushed China to be admitted to the WTO to enable China to ship unlimited products to the United States. Clinton promised the brightest future for Americans and hoped this would free the Chinese people from communist rule. Before joining the WTO, China committed to fair competition, intellectual property protections, and more transparent market practices. Unfortunately, unfair trade tactics continued. In China's goal to be a dominant force in global trade, US manufacturing industry has declined.

"Today, the House of Representatives has taken a historic step toward continued prosperity in America, reform in China, and peace in the world. It will open new doors of trade for America and bring new hope for change in China," Bill Clinton, US President.

Did China Influence Bill Clinton?

Here is what the press said:

> President Clinton unequivocally denied any influence of Chinese money on US policy. However, former fundraiser Johnny Chung claimed to Federal investigators that a significant portion of the nearly $100,000 he donated to the Clinton campaign originated from China's People's Liberation Army, a lieutenant colonel, and an aerospace executive. Congressional committees aggressively probed whether this substantial contribution swayed the government's policy change to facilitate China's satellite launches and potential access to sensitive technology. They also scrutinized whether the Administration's policy shift on exporting satellite technology directly aided China and other nations in advancing their nuclear missile capabilities—*The New York Times*, May 18, 1998, (Refs 5 and 7).

9. China's Economic Growth

The International Monetary Fund reports that the Chinese economy has experienced remarkable growth over the past three decades, effectively transitioning from a low-income to an upper middle-income economy. According to the Word Bank's 2024 data, China's GDP reached about $18.7 trillion, roughly 65 percent of the United States' $28.8 trillion GDP, and more than 50 times its 1990 level of $361 billion. China has undeniably emerged as a critical driver of global economic growth, single-handedly contributing 35 percent of global nominal GDP growth over the last fifteen years. However, the Chinese economy is not without challenges. The substantial impact of the COVID-19 pandemic and concerns about potential weaknesses, such as real estate investment dependency on an ineffective banking system, high domestic debt, a declining property market, and a shrinking labor force, cannot be disregarded. The economy's unbalanced reforms and inconsistent approaches to the roles of the market and the state may lead to significant future financial and property market volatility. However, these factors do not indicate an imminent financial or economic collapse.

After the global financial crisis in 2008, China heavily relied on investment to drive economic growth. The government now aims to rebalance the economy by reducing reliance on investment-heavy growth, promoting household consumption as the primary contributor to GDP growth, and fostering more growth in the services sector. In recent years, household consumption has become the main driver of development, and the services sector now contributes to more than half of annual GDP and nearly half of total employment. Although debt has increased relative to the size of the economy, it remains in line with other major economies, such as the United States and Japan (Ref 16).

CHAPTER 2

CHINESE PRESENT POLITICS AND GOVERNANCE: NAVIGATING MODERN COMPLEXITY

—◊◊◊—

Under Xi Jinping's leadership, the Communist Party of China (CPC) has transformed significantly, consolidating power and implementing strategic reforms that have reshaped China's political, economic, and social landscape. Xi's governance model combines authoritarianism and economic pragmatism, facing continuous reform challenges. Key initiatives include evolving family planning policies, the rural revitalization strategy, and the controversial social credit system. Internationally, Xi's vision has stirred varied responses, particularly from the United States, which views the CPC's actions as a central threat to global stability.

1. Consolidation of Power: Xi Jinping's Vision for China

China has undergone significant changes under President Xi Jinping's leadership. His assertive governance style and ambitious policy agenda have characterized his tenure. Xi has significantly consolidated power, implementing various reforms and initiatives to strengthen the Communist Party of China (CPC)'s control over governance. His ideological campaigns, such as "China Dream," emphasize the great renewal of the Chinese nation. Xi has also initiated the "Four Comprehensives," which focus on achieving a moderately prosperous society, deepening reform, advancing the rule of law, and strictly governing the party (including anti-corruption).

Xi is determined to assert China's interests and influence on the global stage. Domestically, he has launched ambitious initiatives to address corruption, reduce poverty, and promote economic development. He has pursued an assertive foreign policy on the international front, including initiatives such as the Belt and Road Initiative (BRI) and the establishment of the Asian Infrastructure Investment Bank (AIIB). These efforts aim to enhance China's global influence and reshape the international order to serve China's interests better.

2. Anti-Corruption Campaign: Upholding Party Discipline and Accountability

Xi Jinping's anti-corruption campaign aims to eliminate corruption and misconduct within the Communist Party of China (CPC). He has implemented disciplinary measures, internal investigations, and legal reforms to promote integrity and accountability within the party, which has helped to restore public trust in China's political system.

Since assuming office in 2013, Xi has implemented various anti-corruption measures aimed at rooting out misconduct at all levels of government. These efforts have resulted in the investigation and punishment of numerous party officials, including high-profile individuals such as Bo Xilai (former member of the Politburo of the Chinese Communist Party, found guilty and convicted of bribery and embezzlement charges), Zhou Yongkang (former Minister of Public Security convicted of a series of corruption charges, including bribery, abuse of power, and leaking state secrets), and Sun Zhengcai (former Communist Party Secretary of Chongqing, found guilty of taking bribes of more than $26.7 million).

Xi's anti-corruption campaign has significantly impacted China's governance and political environment. By tackling corruption and reinforcing party discipline, Xi has sought to solidify his authority and bolster the Communist Party's control over the government. However, concerns have been raised about the lack of transparency and due process in China's legal system, as well as the potential for political persecution and abuse of power. Critics accused Xi of using the anti-corruption campaign to silence his political opponents and restrained officials who challenged his position (Refs 1, 2, and 3).

3. Xi Jinping: The Ascent of a Powerhouse

As China's president, Xi Jinping has rapidly consolidated power through an anti-corruption campaign that has punished over a million officials and removed political rivals. In 2018, the constitution was amended to abolish term limits for the president and the vice president, potentially allowing Xi to potentially remain in office indefinitely.

In 2021, the Communist Party of China (CPC) passed a resolution elevating Xi's leadership, focusing on his achievements in reducing poverty and curbing corruption. The CPC designated him the "core leader," and his name and ideology are enshrined in the party's constitution. In October 2022, Xi secured a third term as CPC General Secretary and was reelected president for a third five-year term in March 2023 after the two-term limit on the presidency was removed from the constitution in 2018.

Despite many challenges, the anti-corruption campaign has become popular among the Chinese public. They view it as a crucial effort to cleanse the party and ensure accountability in the government. Furthermore, the campaign has bolstered Xi's reputation as a dedicated and accomplished leader capable of addressing pervasive corruption and restoring public trust in the party's leadership (Ref 7).

4. Legislative Governance: The Role of the National People's Congress

The National People's Congress (NPC) is China's highest state power organ. It makes laws, amends the constitution, and oversees the government's work. The NPC comprises nearly 3,000 deputies from across the country, representing various regions, ethnic groups, and sectors of society. The NPC meets once a year in Beijing for sessions that typically last around two weeks. During the sessions, deputies review and approve key legislation, government reports, and budgets.

The NPC has several primary functions, including enacting laws, amending the constitution, and overseeing the work of the government and its various ministries and agencies. It also holds the power to elect key state officials like the president and vice president of the People's Republic of China and the National People's Congress Standing Committee (NPCSC) members. Additionally, the NPC has the authority to interpret the constitution and review decisions made by lower-level courts.

The most significant group within the NPC is the NPCSC, comprising around 150 members. It operates between NPC annual meetings and has the authority to handle legislative matters within the guidelines established by the NPC when the full NPC is not in session. Unlike most NPC members, the NPCSC is actively involved in lawmaking and amending laws. The remaining members of the NPC are usually only active in the two weeks of the year that the full NPC meets.

NPC is formally the top legislative body. However, most decisions are made by the Communist Party of China (CPC) leadership behind closed doors. Members of the NPC are chosen based on their loyalty to the party and are expected to vote according to party directives. As a result, the NPC's role in China's governance is primarily symbolic. Unlike the US Congress, the NPC is not an actual legislature (Ref 9).

5. Governance Model: Strengths, Weaknesses, and Reform Challenges

China's one-party rule has resulted in remarkable economic growth and social progress. Still, it raises concerns about accountability, transparency, and political stability due to centralized governance and restricted civil liberties. The lack of political pluralism and competition fosters corruption and abuse of power, while limitations on civil liberties impede citizen participation in the political process. Despite its strengths in resource mobilization and long-term development strategies, the governance model faces challenges such as human rights violations, censorship, and authoritarianism. These lead to increasing demands for political reform and democratization domestically and internationally. China's growing middle class and more educated population also seek greater political participation and civil liberties, challenging the CPC's monopoly on power and authority.

6. Family Planning Policies: Navigating Demographic Challenges

China's one-child policy, implemented in 1979 to control population growth, has significantly impacted demographics, the economy, and social structure. Although it was relaxed in 2015 to allow two children, its legacy still influences family planning, gender dynamics, and intergenerational relations in China.

The one-child policy was introduced in response to concerns about overpopulation and resource scarcity. It was one of modern history's most controversial and far-reaching social policies. The policy mandated that most couples have only one child, with exceptions granted in cases of rural families, ethnic minorities, and other exceptional circumstances. The policy was enforced through rewards, penalties, and social pressure, resulting in widespread domestic and international criticism and controversy.

The implementation of the one-child policy in China resulted in several demographic consequences. This included a significant decrease in the birth rate, an aging population, and a disproportionate gender ratio due to the traditional preference for male children. These demographic challenges have considerably impacted China's economy and society. Labor shortages, rising healthcare costs, and increased pressure on social welfare systems exist. The one-child policy has also had significant social and psychological effects, primarily on women and families. They were pressured to comply with the government's mandated family planning quotas and restrictions.

China's one-child policy was eased in the early 2000s, allowing some couples to have a second child under specific conditions. It officially ended in 2015 and was replaced with a new policy that allowed all couples to have two children. The benefits of the new policy include a significant reduction in abortions of unapproved pregnancies, virtually eliminating the problem of unregistered children, and achieving a more balanced sex ratio. The universal two-child policy aims to address the challenge of an aging population and reduce the imbalance in the sex ratio at birth. While many welcomed this change, it raised concerns about government involvement in family planning decisions and its potential impact on China's demographic future (Ref 10).

7. Rural Revitalization Strategy: Bridging the Urban-Rural Divide

China has made significant progress in poverty alleviation and rural development under the leadership of President Xi Jinping and the Chinese Communist Party (CPC). The focus on poverty alleviation and community revitalization aligns with the goals set by the founding fathers of the People's Republic of China (PRC) to celebrate 100 years of the establishment of the CPC. China's plan to rejuvenate rural areas aims to address the growing disparity between urban and rural areas, leading to increased social inequality, migration, and declining rural population. The plan focuses on narrowing this gap by improving rural communities' infrastructure, public services, and income levels. China's rural revitalization strategy consists of poverty alleviation and agricultural modernization. Poverty alleviation involves providing financial aid, vocational training, and targeted infrastructure development. Agricultural modernization aims to increase productivity, enhance food security, and promote sustainable practices.

China's rural areas and agriculture play a crucial role in the country's economic welfare, making rural revitalization, food security, and poverty relief top priorities. The development of the rural economy aims to build a solid foundation for the country's overall development. The rural development process has been divided into two significant periods: the period from the founding of the PRC in 1944 until the beginning of reform in 1978 and the reform period since 1978. Policies and frameworks have been established to improve further and expedite the development process, connecting rural areas to China's industrial ecosystem.

In 2017, President Xi Jinping introduced the rural revitalization strategy to tackle poverty and hunger. Efforts include improving governance structures, living conditions, and public services in rural areas. The National Administration for Rural Revitalization (NARR) replaced the Leading Group Office of Poverty Alleviation and Development of the State Council. In 2020, the Central Committee of the Communist Party of China emphasized rural revitalization, focusing on high-quality agriculture, improved living conditions, and prosperity for rural residents. The CPC aims to shift the focus from poverty alleviation to comprehensive rural revitalization. In 2021, President Xi declared victory against poverty and announced an investment of nearly 1.6 trillion yuan in fighting poverty and bridging the urban-rural development gap. China aims to enhance rural areas and improve infrastructure, education, healthcare, and tourism while fostering entrepreneurship and supporting small and medium-sized enterprises. Simplifying rural-to-urban migration is expected to generate new economic prospects and bridge the gap between rural and urban regions (Refs 12, 13, and 14).

8. Social Credit System: Governing Behavior in the Digital Age

In 2020, China completed a critical construction phase of its Social Credit System (SoCS), a cornerstone of its data-supported governance. The system monitors and regulates individual behavior using technology and assigns social credit scores based on compliance with laws and social norms. Positive behavior is rewarded, and hostile behavior is punished. However, concerns about privacy and potential misuse of surveillance and control have been raised.

The Chinese government has implemented a social credit system to encourage legal compliance and positive societal contributions. Low credit scores may restrict access to certain services, while high scores may lead to preferential treatment. However, there is no unified social credit score, and regional differences in implementation pose challenges. Efforts are underway to define social credit, improve credit repair measures, and develop a Social Credit Law. The system remains less digitized than other tech-driven initiatives and relies on human investigations, reports, and decisions, leaving room for traditional influences.

9. American Perspectives on the Chinese Communist Party

According to a document published by the US Department of State, the Communist Party of China (CPC) is considered to be the central threat of our times. It undermines global stability in pursuit of its hegemonic ambitions. Despite efforts to defend its actions, the

People's Republic of China (PRC) is not behaving as a model world citizen. Under the leadership of President and General Secretary Xi Jinping, the CCP is expanding its power and influence at the expense of others in at least six ways (Ref 11).

Predatory Economic Practices

The PRC engages in predatory economic practices by violating international standards through massive subsidies, intellectual property theft, forced tech transfer, corrupt trade practices, and predatory lending via the Belt and Road Initiative. These practices harm other economies, undermine the rule of law, and unfairly benefit Chinese workers and firms.

Military Aggression

China's Military-Civil Fusion strategy aims to build the People's Liberation Army (PLA) into a "world-class military" by 2049 by incorporating advanced civilian technology (Ref 26). The PLA seeks to expand its global presence through the Belt and Road Initiative (BRI) and military cooperation agreements to assert dominance in the Indo-Pacific region and challenge the United States. Additionally, Beijing is rapidly increasing its secret nuclear weapons stockpile, potentially tripling its arsenal within the next ten years. This escalates tensions in the South China Sea and the Himalayas by intimidating neighboring countries, threatening maritime shipping routes, and destabilizing borders.

Undermining Global Norms and Values

China undermines global norms and values by disregarding its commitments, manipulating international organizations, and promoting its authoritarian ideology. Initiatives like the Belt and Road Initiative foster corruption and create unsustainable debt burdens.

Coercive Tactics Abroad

The Communist Party of China (CPC) uses its controlled media to spread propaganda globally, manipulates foreign news and entertainment media, and pressures foreign officials. The CPC's presence on overseas campuses undermines academic freedom, luring foreign researchers into engaging in illegal activities for China's gains. Additionally, the CPC subsidizes China-based 5G vendors like Huawei and ZTE and pressures foreign countries to select them to gain access to personal data, intellectual property, and critical infrastructure control.

Disregard for Human Rights

The Chinese Communist Party silences dissent and restricts the rights of its citizens, including forced population control, arbitrary detention, censorship, forced labor, and violations of religious freedom. It continues to commit abuses against Uyghurs, Christians, and other minorities while manipulating international organizations, governments, and companies to hide its abuses.

Environmental Abuses

China has a terrible environmental record. It is the world's largest emitter of greenhouse gases and marine debris, a significant builder of dirty coal-burning plants, and the top perpetrator of illegal fishing. China's reckless environmental practices threaten the global economy and public health.

CHAPTER 3

THE NEW COLD WAR: CHINA-RUSSIAN RELATIONS AND THEIR IMPACT ON GEOPOLITICS

—⟋⟍⟍—

The New Cold War is characterized by intense competition and shifting alliances, challenging China and Russia's traditional dominance of the West. These two powerful nations are reshaping global power dynamics and strategic calculations in a multipolar world order. China, in particular, is confronted with a significant strategic challenge in responding to Russia's war on Ukraine. Navigating a delicate path, it must maintain its strategic partnership with Russia while avoiding reputational and economic costs, emphasizing the gravity of the situation. The current goals of the United States and China do not involve destroying each other's systems but are focused on competing for global influence, particularly in the Indo-Pacific region. This competition is viewed as a battle to control the world's economic levers and influence global institutions in the 21st century.

1. The Sino-Russian Strategic Alliance: A Major Concern for the United States

A. Formidable Partnership

The alliance between China and Russia has become a formidable presence on the world stage, characterized by shared goals and interests. This partnership involves economic cooperation, military collaboration, and diplomatic alignment. China's goal to elevate the People's Liberation Army (PLA) into a 'world-class' military by 2049 emphasizes the importance of this alliance.

US Concerns Over Sino-Russian Collaboration

A report from the US State Department highlights the collaboration between China and Russia and emphasizes the strategic threat posed by their alliance. The report expresses concern about the two nations' military modernization, technology sharing, and geopolitical alignment. In line with these concerns, the US Defense Secretary has cautioned about the increasing military cooperation between China and Russia and its significant implications for global security. This alliance has the potential to alter the international balance of power and influence significantly.

A key concern in this New Cold War is the potential for direct conflict. China is rapidly advancing its capability to forcibly take over Taiwan, with US intelligence reporting that Chinese President Xi Jinping has set a deadline for the military to be prepared for war by 2027. This looming threat should not be underestimated, as it could have profound and far-reaching global implications. During a visit to China on February 4, 2022, Xi Jinping and Vladimir Putin reaffirmed their mutual support for protecting their core interests, state sovereignty, and territorial integrity in solidarity. Putin reiterated his support for the One-China principle, confirming that Taiwan is an undisputable part of China and opposing any form of Taiwanese independence. This strong alliance further solidifies their united front against external interference (Ref 8).

B. US Strategic Posture Review

In response to increasingly assertive military actions by Russia and China over the past decade, the US Congress reviewed the United States' strategic posture in 2022. This review includes assessing nuclear weapons policy, strategy, and force structure. The rapid military expansion of China, particularly in its nuclear capabilities, and Russia's diversification and expansion of its non-strategic nuclear weapons systems have significantly altered the geopolitical landscape. Russia's invasion of Ukraine in 2014, followed by the full-scale invasion in February 2022, has further complicated the global security situation.

C. Global Security Challenges

The United States is currently facing new global security challenges, including potential military conflicts and concerns about deterring two nuclear-armed adversaries. The strategy should prioritize deterring and defeating potential aggression from Russia and China in Europe and Asia. If conventional forces prove to be insufficient, the US may need to rely more heavily on nuclear weapons. It is crucial that the US not underestimate China's nuclear forces and maintain an atomic posture capable of deterring both countries simultaneously (Ref 1).

2. Space Collaboration

In 2015, Russia and China decided to actively promote the implementation of the project in the " China-Russian Space Cooperation Framework 2013- 2017." They agreed to actively carry out follow-up cooperation in earth observation and remote sensing satellite data exchange between the two countries. Both sides agreed to cooperate in exploring the moon and Mars; Russia hopes to take advantage of China Chang E IV lunar probe satellite equipped with Russian scientific instruments (Ref 12).

In 2021, a Memorandum of Understanding was signed to construct the International Lunar Research Station (ILRS). It aims to enhance scientific research exchanges and will be accessible to all interested countries and international partners. The ILRS, to be built on the lunar surface and in lunar orbit, will conduct various scientific research activities, including lunar exploration, observation, experiments, and technical verification. China and Russia will collaborate closely in its development, leveraging their expertise in space science and technology (Ref 18).

3. Strengthening Bonds Through Trade and Investment

In 2023, the two-way trade between China and Russia reached a new record of $240 billion despite the conflict in Ukraine and Western sanctions on Russia. China has emerged as a crucial market for Russia's energy exports. The dollar-denominated trade between the two countries grew by 26.3% in 2023. Notably, in 2023, half of Russia's oil and petroleum exports were sent to China. As a result of the Ukraine conflict, Russia faced substantial Western sanctions and consequent isolation from the global economy. However, China has extended economic support to Russia, mitigating the impact of its exclusion from the international financial system (Refs 3, 10, and 11).

Russia-China Gas Deal

In 2014, China and Russia signed a 30-year, $400 billion gas supply deal after lengthy negotiations. The deal coincided with the escalating Ukraine crisis in Europe, highlighting Russia's shift towards Asia amid strained relations with the West. The agreement involved Russian state-owned gas companies Gazprom and CNPC (China National Petroleum Corporation). It was signed by the leaders of both countries, Vladimir Putin and Xi Jinping, during Putin's visit to Beijing.

The deal aimed to provide 38 billion cubic meters of gas annually, with China negotiating a lower price than Russia initially wanted. Russia agreed to the deal despite potential initial losses, viewing it as a strategic response to strained relations with the West over the Ukraine crisis. The proposed route to supply gas to China from Russia was the Siberia pipeline, covering 4,000 km and requiring a $55 billion investment from Russia and at least a $20 billion investment from China.

Moreover, Russia lifted a ban on foreign ownership of strategic assets, allowing Chinese companies to participate in developing gas fields and pipelines. Additionally, Russia offered to exempt gas destined for China from taxes on resource extraction, while China agreed to cancel import duties on the gas (Refs 14 and 17).

4. The Evolving Sino-Russian Military Relationship

A. Historical Enemies to Strategic Partners

In the late 1980s, China and the Soviet Union were adversaries, devoting significant defense and military resources to counter each other along their extensive border. Fast forward to today, and the dynamic between Russia and China has transformed into a practical partnership. This relationship is based on mutual skepticism of the US-led international order. Despite their inherent differences, Russia and China recognize the need to rely on each other. Any future military cooperation between these nations is driven more by a shared aversion to the United States than by a unified strategic vision or common values. The strong bond between Vladimir Putin and Xi Jinping, along with their unwavering commitment to the Russia-China partnership, especially in the context of Russia's invasion of Ukraine, highlights the strategic importance of their alliance (Ref 4).

Military Cooperation: Strategic Exercises in the East China Sea

In July 2023, the Chinese defense ministry announced the deployment of a Chinese naval flotilla in the East China Sea near disputed islands controlled by Japan to participate in a joint "Northern/Interaction-2023" exercise with Russian forces. The exercise aims to protect important waterways and demonstrates a significant increase in military cooperation between China and Russia. This marks the first time Russian troops will engage in joint military exercises with China (Ref 13).

These exercises involve over ten vessels and more than 30 aircraft and include naval combat drills, ship escort operations, and live artillery fire. By utilizing a Russian airfield, the forces can promptly respond to potential threats in the Sea of Japan. These drills are intended to improve the operational capabilities of both forces and are focused on Japan, the US, and South Korea. These joint military exercises are part of a broader trend of increased military cooperation, which encompasses joint training, drills, and technology exchanges meant to enhance coordination and efficiency between the Chinese and Russian armed forces (Ref 9).

B. Implications for Global Security

Russia is an essential partner for China, especially as the US intensifies efforts to limit Beijing in security and advanced technology areas. Meanwhile, Russia seeks support from China due to its need for solid allies. The joint military exercises between China and Russia indicate a deepening of military cooperation, which has significant implications for regional security and global power dynamics. NATO has expressed concerns about their collaboration, emphasizing the risks it poses to Euro-Atlantic security and transatlantic relations.

C. US Strategic Posture: Growing Risks and Challenges

In its October 2023 Final Report, the Congressional Commission on the Strategic Posture of the United States emphasized the increased risk of potential conflicts with China, Russia, or both, which could lead to military confrontation. The commission expressed concerns about the possibility of these conflicts escalating into large-scale nuclear war. They emphasized that such a scenario would differ from past world wars. The commission also raised alarms about the potential threat posed by new developments in genetically engineered and novel biological agents, stating that these advancements could significantly endanger the security of the United States and its allies. Additionally, they assessed that the Biological Weapons Convention (BWC) would not be effective in preventing the development and deployment of new biological weapons.

The Commission has observed aggressive actions from China and Russia, including expanding their strategic arsenals. As a result, it has been concluded that more than the United States' current strong posture may be required to handle potential existential challenges expected between 2027 and 2035. Urgent and decisive changes are needed to address these emerging threats effectively (Ref 1).

CHAPTER 4

CHINA'S GLOBAL ASCENT: DIPLOMACY, ECONOMY, AND MILITARY STRATEGY

—⁓—

The 21st century marks China's unprecedented rise as a global powerhouse. China has transformed the geopolitical landscape through strategic economic diplomacy, sweeping infrastructure initiatives, and a formidable military presence. This chapter examines China's multifaceted strategies, including key initiatives and the Asian Infrastructure Investment Bank, as well as assertive actions in the South China Sea and the modernization of the People's Liberation Army. As China reshapes alliances, fosters global partnerships, and challenges established powers, understanding its ambitions is crucial to grasping the future of international politics and economics. Embark on your journey to explore how China is redefining the world order and asserting its influence on the global stage.

1. China's Economic Diplomacy: Strategic Influence

In recent years, China's increasing economic influence and strategic presence in the region have strengthened its ties with Southeast Asian nations, leading to enhanced economic cooperation, security collaboration, and the management of geopolitical tensions. Investments in infrastructure, manufacturing, and natural resources have spurred economic growth in Southeast Asia, creating new opportunities for trade, investment, and regional economic integration.

From 2000 to 2021, Chinese financial institutions have lent $1.34 trillion to developing countries, making China the world's largest bilateral lender (Ref 19). Key initiatives such as the Belt and Road Initiative (BRI), the Asian Infrastructure Investment Bank (AIIB), and the Regional Comprehensive Economic Partnership (RCEP) illustrate China's commitment to promoting connectivity, infrastructure development, and regional integration, thus expanding its economic and geopolitical influence.

China's strategy also emphasizes building partnerships and increasing its presence in emerging regions and developing countries. Through active engagement with nations in Asia, Africa, Latin America, and the Middle East, China provides economic assistance, development cooperation, and diplomatic support to strengthen relationships and enhance mutual trust. Initiatives like the Forum on China-Africa Cooperation (FOCAC), the China-Arab States Cooperation Forum (CASCF), and the China-Latin America and Caribbean Forum (CELAC) underscore China's dedication to fostering political dialogue, economic cooperation, and cultural exchanges with its global partners.

2. Key Initiatives and Global Partnerships

A. The Association of Southeast Asian Nations (ASEAN)

The Association of Southeast Asian Nations, also known as ASEAN, was established in Bangkok, Thailand, in 1967. The original members were Indonesia, Malaysia, the Philippines, Singapore, and Thailand. Brunei joined ASEAN in 1984, followed by Vietnam in 1995, Laos and Myanmar in 1997, and Cambodia in 1999. This brings the total number of ASEAN member countries to ten.

The ASEAN Free Trade Area (AFTA) was established at the 1992 ASEAN Summit in Singapore. Its primary goals are to develop a single market and international production base, as well as to attract foreign direct investments. AFTA partners include Australia, the People's Republic of China, India, Japan, Korea, and New Zealand (Ref 6).

B. Formation of the Regional Comprehensive Economic Partnership (RCEP)

The discussions for the Regional Comprehensive Economic Partnership (RCEP) began in 2012, when leaders from 10 ASEAN member states and six AFTA partners met during the 21st ASEAN Summit in Phnom Penh, Cambodia. The RCEP negotiation covers trade in goods, services, investment, economic and technical cooperation, intellectual property, competition, dispute settlement, e-commerce, small and medium enterprises, and other issues. The RCEP officially took effect on 1 January 2022.

The Regional Comprehensive Economic Partnership (RCEP) has the potential to create significant opportunities for businesses in East Asia. The 16 RCEP participating countries collectively account for nearly half of the world's population, contributing about 30 percent of global GDP and over a quarter of world exports. RCEP aims to lower trade barriers, improve market access, facilitate trade and investment, enhance transparency, and promote the engagement of small and medium-sized enterprises in global supply chains. The agreement also recognizes the importance of inclusivity and is committed to providing fair regional economic policies that benefit both ASEAN and its AFTA partners.

C. The Asian Infrastructure Investment Bank (AIIB): Shifting Economic Power from the United States to China

In January 2016, China launched the Asia Infrastructure Investment Bank (AIIB) for business. This action can potentially shift economic power from the United States to China. The establishment of AIIB presents a challenge to the US-dominated World Bank and International Monetary Fund (IMF), both of which were formed after World War II. The World Bank provides loans to developing countries for economic development, but these loans come with conditions known as the Washington Consensus. These conditions aim to promote private markets, protect the environment and human and workers' rights, and prevent corruption in government.

The United States and China have different approaches to handling other countries' internal affairs. The United States has expressed concerns that the Asian Infrastructure Investment Bank (AIIB) set up by China may not enforce responsible social policies for its loans. As a result, the United States chose not to join the AIIB and tried to discourage its allies from joining. However, despite these efforts, most of the United States' allies, except Japan, decided to join the AIIB. This was seen as a setback for the United States. For over seven decades, the United States has been a vital supporter of the global financial system. However, establishing the AIIB could indicate China's potential to replace the United States as the leading authority in shaping international trade and finance rules in the twenty-first century.

Members and Voting Power

The Asian Infrastructure Investment Bank (AIIB) aims to provide developing countries with an alternative to Western lending institutions like the World Bank and the International Monetary Fund. It is a multilateral development bank and an international financial institution that works to improve economic and social outcomes in Asia. The bank has 109 members worldwide, including 13 prospective members in 2024. The distribution of the 109 members by continent is as follows: 27 in Asia, 27 in Europe, 21 in Africa, 14 in the Middle East, 10 in the Pacific, 9 in South America and the Caribbean, and 1 in North America, with Canada being the sole member from North America.

The bank is headquartered in Beijing, China, and started operating after the agreement was enacted on December 25, 2015. China is the largest shareholder, with 26.5% of the current voting shares and veto power. It is followed by India (7.6%), Russia (6%), Germany (4.2%), Australia (3.5%), Korea (3.5%), France (3.2%), and Indonesia (3.2%).

Accomplishments

As of November 2022, AIIB has financed 194 projects totaling $37 billion, an increase from $29 billion in October 2021. Many of these projects contribute to the objectives of the United Nations' 2030 sustainable development goals, which include clean water and sanitation initiatives, affordable and clean energy, and sustainable cities (Refs 4, 5. and 7).

D. China's Belt and Road Initiative: Global Connectivity

Belt and Road Initiative Logistics

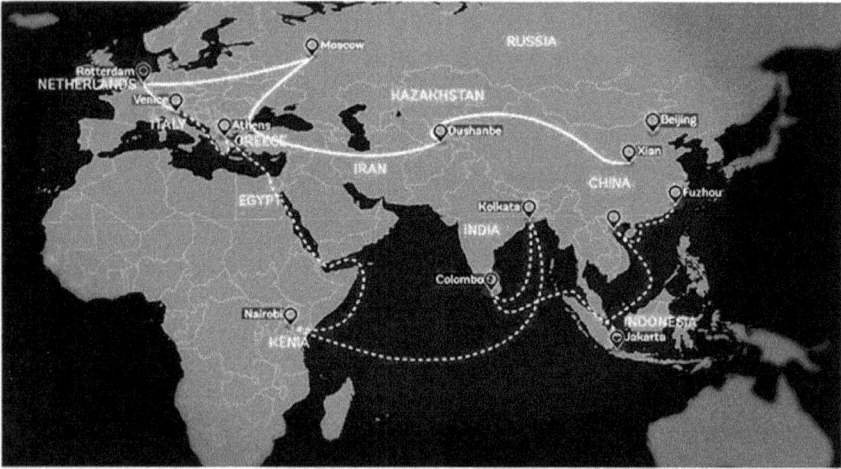

Source: World Bank, Belt and Road Initiative, March 29, 2018

In 2013, Chinese President Xi Jinping launched the Belt and Road Initiative (BRI). It is a global development strategy to enhance connectivity and cooperation across Asia, Africa, and Europe through infrastructure development, trade facilitation, and people-to-people exchanges. This initiative encompasses the Silk Road Economic Belt and the 21st Century Maritime Silk Road, focusing on land-based transportation routes and maritime connectivity. China's investments in roads, railways, ports, and energy facilities are designed to unlock growth potential across different regions. Nonetheless, economies along the BRI corridor face challenges due to infrastructure and policy gaps, hindering trade and foreign investment. Closing these gaps would necessitate costly new infrastructure. The integration of corridor economies is imperative due to trade and investment policies, infrastructure gaps, and a lack of cross-regional integration. It has been firmly estimated that reducing travel times by one day could increase BRI trade by 5.2% (Ref 1).

Debt, Development, Risks, and Benefits: The Complex Impact of the Belt and Road Initiative

The Belt and Road Initiative (BRI), which involves 150 countries, has faced criticism. According to a 2019 World Bank study, BRI entails significant debt financing estimated at $575 billion, leading to a rapid increase in public and external debts, mainly from China, in countries at higher risk of debt distress. Debt-financed investments pose risks to debt sustainability, and there are governance risks, such as corruption and procurement failures, with Chinese firms dominating BRI contracts. Additionally, the BRI carries risks typical of large infrastructure projects, including limited transparency, weak economic fundamentals, and governance issues. Furthermore, BRI transport projects present environmental and social risks, requiring urgent strategic environmental and social assessments to address these concerns.

Despite the negative impact, the BRI initiative provides substantial benefits for trade, foreign investment, and living standards in participating nations. BRI transport projects can have positive impacts, such as improving trade, attracting foreign investment, and reducing poverty. However, estimating the initiative's effects is challenging due to its complexity and uncertainty. The projects have the potential to uplift millions of people from extreme poverty and reshape economic geography, although income gains would be distributed unevenly across countries (Ref 1).

The 2nd Belt and Road Forum in April 2019 marked a significant milestone. However, there is a need for more multilateral cooperation and domestic policy reform. Despite these challenges, the BRI continues to evolve and expand, with China reaffirming its commitment through policy adjustments and enhanced cooperation mechanisms. China has emphasized the principles of openness, transparency, inclusiveness, and sustainability in BRI implementation, aiming to address concerns and build trust (Refs 1 and 2).

Members of the Belt and Road Initiative

In December 2023, 150 countries signed a Memorandum of Understanding (MOU) with China to join the Belt and Road Initiative (BRI). About half of the members are countries classified by the World Bank as low—to lower-middle-income. Nearly one-third are from the Sub-Saharan Africa region (Refs 2 and 3).

Income Group	Particpants	Percentage
High income	33	22%
Upper middle income	43	29%
Lower middle income	46	31%
Low income	28	19%
Total	150	100%

Source: www.greenfdc.org and World Bank (Refs 2 & 3)

Region	Total	Percentage
East Asia & Pacific	25	17%
Europe & Central Asia	34	23%
Latin America & Caribbean	22	15%
Middle East & North Africa	19	13%
South Asia	6	4%
Sub-Saharan Africa	44	29%
Total	150	100%

South Asia	Income Group	Date Joined
Afghanistan	Low income	5/1/2023
Bangladesh	Lower middle income	3/1/2019
Maldives	Upper middle income	8/1/2017
Nepal	Lower middle income	5/1/2017
Pakistan	Lower middle income	12/1/2013
Sri Lanka	Lower middle income	4/1/2017
Total: 6 Countries		

East Asia & Pacific	Income Group	Date Joined
Brunei Darussalam	High income	11/1/2018
Cambodia	Lower middle income	12/1/2013
China, P.R.	Upper middle income	12/1/2013
Cook Islands	Upper middle income	11/1/2018
Fiji	Upper middle income	11/1/2018
Indonesia	Lower middle income	3/1/2015
Kiribati	Lower middle income	1/1/2020
Korea, Rep.	High income	5/1/2018
Lao PDR	Lower middle income	9/1/2018
Malaysia	Upper middle income	5/1/2017
Micronesia, Fed. Sts.	Lower middle income	11/1/2018
Mongolia	Lower middle income	12/1/2013
Myanmar	Lower middle income	8/1/2016
New Zealand	High income	3/1/2017
Niue	Lower middle income	7/1/2018
Papua New Guinea	Lower middle income	7/1/2016
Philippines	Lower middle income	11/1/2017
Samoa	Upper middle income	10/1/2018
Singapore	High income	4/1/2018
Solomon Islands	Lower middle income	10/1/2019
Thailand	Upper middle income	12/1/2014
Timor-Leste	Lower middle income	4/1/2017
Tonga	Upper middle income	3/1/2018
Vanuatu	Lower middle income	11/1/2018
Vietnam	Lower middle income	11/1/2017
Total: 25 Countries		

Europe & Central Asia	Income Group	Date Joined
Albania	Upper middle income	5/1/2017
Armenia	Upper middle income	12/1/2015
Austria	High income	TBA
Azerbaijan	Upper middle income	12/1/2015
Belarus	Upper middle income	12/1/2013
Bosnia and Herzegovina	Upper middle income	5/1/2017
Bulgaria	Upper middle income	11/1/2015
Croatia	High income	5/1/2017
Cyprus	High income	4/1/2019
Czech Republic	High income	11/1/2015
Estonia	High income	11/1/2017
Georgia	Upper middle income	12/1/2016
Greece	High income	8/1/2018
Hungary	High income	6/1/2015
Kazakhstan	Upper middle income	8/1/2015
Kyrgyz Republic	Lower middle income	12/1/2013
Latvia	High income	11/1/2016
Lithuania	High income	11/1/2017
Luxembourg	High income	3/1/2019
Moldova	Upper middle income	12/1/2013
Montenegro	Upper middle income	5/1/2017
North Macedonia	Upper middle income	12/1/2013
Poland	High income	11/1/2015
Portugal	High income	12/1/2018
Romania	Upper middle income	6/1/2015
Russian Federation	Upper middle income	TBA
Serbia	Upper middle income	11/1/2015
Slovak Republic	High income	11/1/2015
Slovenia	High income	11/1/2017
Tajikistan	Lower middle income	10/1/2018
Turkey	Upper middle income	11/1/2015
Turkmenistan	Upper middle income	06/2017
Ukraine	Lower middle income	12/1/2017
Uzbekistan	Lower middle income	6/1/2015
Total: 34 Countries		

Latin America & Caribbean	Income Group	Date Joined
Antigua and Barbuda	High income	6/1/2018
Argentina	Upper middle income	2/6/2022
Barbados	High income	2/1/2019
Bolivia	Lower middle income	6/1/2018
Chile	High income	11/6/2018
Costa Rica	Upper middle income	9/1/2018
Cuba	Upper middle income	6/20/2019
Dominican Republic	Upper middle income	12/1/2019
Dominica	Upper middle income	7/13/2018
Ecuador	Upper middle income	12/1/2018
El Salvador	Upper middle income	11/1/2018
Grenada	Upper middle income	9/1/2018
Guyana	High income	7/1/2018
Honduras	Lower middle income	10/18/2023
Jamaica	Upper middle income	4/1/2019
Nicaragua	Lower middle income	1/6/2022
Panama	High income	6/1/2017
Peru	Upper middle income	5/1/2019
Suriname	Upper middle income	7/1/2018
Trinidad and Tobago	High income	5/1/2018
Uruguay	High income	2/1/2018
Venezuela, RB	Upper middle income	9/1/2018
Total: 22 Countries		

Middle East & North Africa	Income Group	Date Joined
Algeria	Lower middle income	7/10/2018
Bahrain	High income	7/1/2018
Djibouti	Lower middle income	9/1/2018
Egypt, Arab Rep.	Lower middle income	1/1/2016
Iran, Islamic Rep.	Lower middle income	11/1/2018
Iraq	Upper middle income	12/1/2015
Jordan	Lower middle income	12/2/2023
Kuwait	High income	5/1/2018
Lebanon	Lower middle income	9/1/2017
Libya	Upper middle income	7/1/2018
Malta	High income	11/1/2018
Morocco	Lower middle income	11/1/2017
Oman	High income	5/1/2018
Qatar	High income	1/1/2019
Saudi Arabia	High income	8/1/2018
Syrian Arab Republic	Low income	01/2022
Tunisia	Lower middle income	7/1/2018
United Arab Emirates	High income	7/1/2018
Yemen, Rep.	Low income	11/1/2017
Total: 19 Countries		

Sub-Saharan Africa	Income Group	Date Joined
Angola	Lower middle income	9/1/2018
Benin	Lower middle income	9/1/2018
Botswana	Upper middle income	1/7/2021
Burundi	Low income	9/1/2018
Cabo Verde	Lower middle income	9/1/2018
Cameroon	Lower middle income	8/1/2015
Central African Republic	Low income	11/1/2021
Chad	Low income	9/1/2018
Comoros	Lower middle income	12/1/2015
Congo, Dem. Rep.	Low income	1/6/2021
Congo, Rep.	Lower middle income	TBA
Côte d'Ivoire	Lower middle income	5/23/2017
Equatorial Guinea	Upper middle income	4/1/2019
Eritrea	Low income	11/25/2021
Ethiopia	Low income	9/1/2018
Gabon	Upper middle income	9/1/2018
Gambia, The	Low income	9/1/2018
Ghana	Lower middle income	9/1/2018
Guinea	Lower middle income	9/1/2018
Guinea-Bissau	Low income	11/24/2021
Kenya	Lower middle income	6/1/2017
Lesotho	Lower middle income	6/1/2019
Liberia	Low income	4/1/2019
Madagascar	Low income	3/1/2017
Malawi	Low income	3/24/2022
Mali	Low income	7/26/2019
Mauritania	Lower middle income	9/1/2018
Mozambique	Low income	9/1/2018
Namibia	Upper middle income	9/1/2018
Niger	Low income	TBA

Sub-Saharan Africa (Cont'd)	Income Group	Date Joined
Nigeria	Lower middle income	9/1/2018
Rwanda	Low income	7/1/2018
Senegal	Lower middle income	7/1/2018
Seychelles	High income	9/1/2018
Sierra Leone	Low income	8/1/2018
Somalia	Low income	8/1/2015
South Africa	Upper middle income	12/1/2015
South Sudan	Low income	9/1/2018
Sudan	Low income	9/1/2018
Tanzania	Lower middle income	9/1/2018
Togo	Low income	9/1/2018
Uganda	Low income	9/1/2018
Zambia	Lower middle income	9/1/2018
Zimbabwe	Lower middle income	9/1/2018
Total: 44 Countries		

Source: www.greenfdc.org and World Bank (Refs 2 & 3)

E. Growing Role in Africa: Investment, Trade, and Development

China's growing engagement in Africa is driven by its expanding economic and strategic interests, including a pursuit of resources, markets, and geopolitical influence. As Africa's largest trading partner and investor, China has significantly increased its presence across various sectors, including energy, infrastructure, mining, manufacturing, and agriculture. China's involvement in Africa encompasses a wide range of activities, from promoting investment and infrastructure development to facilitating trade and engaging in development cooperation.

China is increasingly involved in Africa due to its increasing need for natural resources, such as oil, minerals, and agricultural products. China's fast-paced industrial and urban development has led to a greater demand for raw materials, prompting the country to search for new supply sources and ensure access to vital resources. With its plentiful oil, gas, minerals, and agricultural land reserves, Africa is an essential supplier for China's expanding economy, providing opportunities for investment, trade, and collaboration.

China's involvement in Africa is not just about diversifying market access and increasing export opportunities but also about fostering a strong and mutually beneficial partnership. China has become a significant trading partner for numerous African nations, providing various manufactured goods, consumer products, and industrial equipment at competitive prices. Moreover, China has actively promoted investment and industrialization in Africa through initiatives like the Forum on China-Africa Cooperation (FOCAC), the China-Africa Development Fund, and the China-Africa Industrial Capacity Cooperation Fund. This partnership is a testament to the strategic importance of Africa for China's global economic and geopolitical objectives.

Furthermore, China's engagement in Africa is for immediate economic objectives and broader strategic and geopolitical motives. China views Africa as a crucial partner in furthering its Belt and Road Initiative (BRI) and advancing its global leadership goals. China is strategically enhancing connectivity, promoting economic development, and expanding its geopolitical influence within the continent and worldwide by investing in infrastructure projects, energy facilities, and transportation networks in Africa. This long-term vision is a crucial aspect of China's involvement in Africa.

China's increasing presence in Africa has sparked debates and controversies about debt sustainability, labor rights, environmental protection, and governance standards. Critics argue that China's investments may worsen debt burdens, promote corruption, and undermine local industries and livelihoods in African countries, leading to concerns about the long-term impact of China's involvement. Additionally, there are questions about the transparency and accountability of China's investments and their alignment with international norms and standards.

F. Forum on China-Africa Cooperation (FOCAC)

In 2000, the Forum on China-Africa Cooperation (FOCAC) was established to strengthen cooperation between China and African countries in the contemporary era and tackle the challenges posed by economic globalization. The aim is to negotiate on an equal footing, promote mutual understanding, reach consensus, cultivate friendship, and encourage collaboration. This group includes China, 53 African countries that have established diplomatic relations with China, and the African Union Commission (Ref 12).

Forum on China-Africa Cooperation (FOCAC) Members

1. Algeria	15. Djibouti	29. Madagascar	43. Sierra Leone
2. Angola	16. Egypt	30. Malawi	44. Somalia
3. Benin	17. Equatorial Guinea	31. Mali	45. South Africa
4. Botswana	18. Eritrea	32. Mauritania	46. South Sudan
5. Burkina Faso	19. Ethiopia	33. Mauritius	47. Sudan
6. Burundi	20. Gabon	34. Morocco	48. Tanzania
7. Cabo Verde	21. Gambia	35. Mozambique	49. Togo
8. Cameroon	22. Ghana	36. Namibia	50. Tunisia
9. Central Africa	23. Guinea	37. Niger	51. Uganda
10. Chad	24. Guinea-Bissau	38. Nigeria	52. Zambia
11. Comoros	25. Kenya	39. Rwanda	53. Zimbabwe
12. Congo (Brazzaville)	26. Lesotho	40. São Tomé and Príncipe	The Commission of
13. Congo (Kinshasa)	27. Liberia	41. Senegal	the African Union
14. Cote d'Ivoire	28. Libya	42. Seychelles	China

Source: www.focac.org, June 15, 2024

Between 2000 and 2022, Chinese lenders provided an estimated $170.08 billion in loans to African sovereign borrowers. Out of this total, $134.01 billion was provided by China's two primary development finance institutions (DFIs): The Export-Import Bank of China (CHEXIM) and the China Development Bank (CDB). Despite China becoming Africa's largest bilateral creditor due to this loan financing, Chinese lenders have steadily decreased their loan provisions since 2016. This decline is attributed to existing debt burdens and the increased borrowing cost, leaving little room for African sovereigns to take on additional debt (Ref 18).

G. China-Arab States Cooperation Forum (CASCF)

CASCF is a formal dialogue initiative between China and the Arab League that was established in 2004. It is the primary multilateral coordination mechanism between China and the Arab states.

In his keynote speech at the CASCF conference in May 2024, Xi Jinping pledged that China would collaborate with Arab nations as equal partners to model world peace and stability. He emphasized that their cooperation would showcase high-quality Belt and Road initiatives, exemplify harmonious coexistence between civilizations, and promote effective global governance (Ref 13).

H. Forum of China and Community of Latin American and Caribbean States (CELAC)

The Community of Latin American and Caribbean States (LAC) was formally established in 2011, encompassing all 33 countries in Latin America and the Caribbean. The China-CELAC Forum officially launched in Beijing in 2015. China-CELAC Forum aims to promote the development of a comprehensive cooperative partnership based on equality, mutual benefit, and joint development between China and LAC states (Ref 15).

Community of Latin American and Caribbean States (LAC)

1. Antigua and Barbuda	12. Dominican Republic	23. Nicaragua
2. Argentina	13. Dominica	24. Panama
3. Bahamas	14. Ecuador	25. Paraguay
4. Barbados	15. El Salvador	26. Peru
5. Belize	16. Grenada	27. Saint Kitts and Nevis
6. Bolivia	17. Guatemala	28. Santa Lucia
7. Brazil	18. Guyana	29. Saint Vincent & Grenadines
8. Chile	19. Haiti	30. Suriname
9. Colombia	20. Honduras	31. Trinidad and Tobago
10. Costa Rica	21. Jamaica	32. Uruguay
11. Cuba	22. Mexico	33. Venezuela

Source: Ministry of Foreign Affairs of China (Ref 15)

The United States is the most significant economic and security partner in Latin American and Caribbean States (LAC). However, China has rapidly increased its economic, diplomatic, and military engagement in the past decade, becoming the region's largest creditor and second-largest trading partner. Four key objectives drive China's efforts in the region: (1) ensuring access to the region's abundant natural resources and consumer markets; (2) gaining LAC support for its foreign policies; (3) shaping LAC perceptions and discourse about China; and (4) gaining geopolitical influence in the region (Ref 14).

3. China's Assertive Actions in the South China Sea

A. Territorial Disputes with Neighboring Countries

Tensions in the South China Sea have persisted for centuries due to territorial disputes among countries such as China, Vietnam, the Philippines, Taiwan, Malaysia, and Brunei. China's recent extensive claims, including sovereignty over land masses and their surrounding waters, have notably antagonized other claimants. China's "nine-dash line" claim encompasses a significant portion of the South China Sea, but its exact extent is contentious and challenged by neighboring countries. Vietnam, the Philippines, Malaysia, and Brunei assert competing claims in the region, drawing upon historical, geographical, and international law arguments. China's assertive actions have led to disputes and confrontations with neighboring countries claiming sovereignty over parts of the contested waters.

B. China's Use of Coercive Measures: Militarization and Its Impact on Regional Security

China's actions, from the construction of artificial islands, military installations, and naval patrols in disputed waters, have raised significant concerns about its intentions and objectives. Additionally, China's enforcement of its maritime claims through coercive measures, such as deploying coast guard vessels and naval militia, has escalated tensions and increased conflict. China's unilateral actions, including declaring air defense identification zones (ADIZs) and fishing bans, have strained relations with its neighbors. Neighboring countries and the international community are alarmed by China's territorial claims and military buildup in the disputed waters, where it asserts sovereignty over contested islands, including the Spratly Islands, Paracel Islands, and Scarborough Shoal. This militarization has heightened regional anxieties about China's intentions, particularly concerning strategic interests and access to crucial sea lanes and resources.

In November 2023, the foreign ministers of Canada, France, Germany, Italy, Japan, the United Kingdom, and the United States of America, along with the representatives of the European Union, released the following statement (Ref 20):

> We are deeply concerned about the situation of the East and South China Seas. We strongly oppose unilateral attempts to change the status quo through force or coercion. The decision made by the Arbitral Tribunal on July 12, 2016, is a significant milestone and is legally binding on the parties involved. We

believe it provides a helpful basis for peacefully resolving disputes. We emphasize the importance of peace and stability across the Taiwan Strait, which is essential for security and prosperity globally, and we call for the peaceful resolution of Cross-Strait issues. We continue to support Taiwan's meaningful participation in international organizations, including the World Health Assembly and WHO technical meetings.

C. Strategic Importance and Economic Implications

The South China Sea is a crucial shipping route. According to the United Nations Conference on Trade and Development, over 21% of global trade, totaling $3.37 trillion, passed through these waters in 2016. Additionally, the area is rich in fishing grounds that support the livelihoods of millions of people in the region, with more than half of the world's fishing vessels operating there. While the Paracels and the Spratlys are primarily uninhabited, they may contain natural resources (Ref 8).

D. Cross-Strait Tensions: China's Pressure on Taiwan

Moreover, China's assertive actions in the Taiwan Strait have contributed to regional security concerns and instability. China views Taiwan as an integral part of its territory and has pledged to reunite the island with the mainland by force if necessary. China has escalated military exercises, conducted air and naval patrols, and employed diplomatic pressure tactics to isolate Taiwan and undermine its international recognition. These actions have sparked concerns about a potential military conflict between China and Taiwan, along with the risk of escalation and intervention by external powers such as the United States and Japan.

E. Fortress Nations: Neighbors Bolster Defenses Against Rising Threats

In response to China's actions, neighboring countries, the United States, and other external powers have sought to strengthen their defense capabilities, deepen security cooperation, and enhance deterrence against potential threats. Countries such as Vietnam, the Philippines, and Malaysia have bolstered their maritime surveillance, conducted joint patrols, and improved maritime domain awareness to monitor and respond to China's activities in disputed waters.

On July 13, 2020, Secretary of State Michael Pompeo bolstered the US stance in the South China Sea and denounced Beijing's illegal claims and coercive tactics. The US sided with the Arbitral Tribunal's ruling and dismissed China's maritime claims in specific regions. The statement emphasized the support for Southeast Asian allies and partners in defending their sovereign rights to offshore resources according to international law (Ref 16).

Nations like Japan, Australia, and India have solidified their military alliances, expanded defense partnerships, and increased defense spending to counterbalance China's escalating influence and assertiveness. Moreover, regional organizations such as the Association of Southeast Asian Nations (ASEAN) have been instrumental in promoting dialogue, confidence-building measures, and multilateral cooperation to manage tensions and avert regional conflicts (Ref 9).

The Asia-Pacific region is becoming the new economic and strategic center, leading to a surge in US military presence and alliances. Japan is revamping its military and security policies. Ongoing disputes over China's territorial sovereignty, maritime rights, and external involvement in South China Sea affairs further complicate the situation. The Korean Peninsula and Northeast Asia are grappling with instability, and there are mounting concerns about terrorism, separatism, and extremism in the region, all of which are impacting China's security and stability along its periphery.

4. Modernizing the People's Liberation Army (PLA)

China's People's Liberation Army (PLA) is undergoing extensive modernization to improve its capabilities across all domains of warfare, including air, sea, land, space, and cyber operations. Key aspects of this modernization include (Ref 16):

A. Naval Prowess

Largest Navy: The People's Liberation Army Navy (PLAN) now includes over 370 ships and submarines.

Aircraft Carriers: Launched its third aircraft carrier and commissioned its third Assault Ship in 2022.

Precision Strike: Enhancing long-range precision strike capabilities for power projection and deterrence.

B. Aviation Dominance

It boasts the most significant aviation force in the Indo-Pacific, reintroducing its nuclear triad with the H-6N bomber in 2019.

C. Strategic Deterrence

China is developing new ballistic and intercontinental-range missile systems to enhance strategic deterrence.

D. Global Ambitions

China's military strategy aims to extend beyond regional dominance to global influence. The PLA is implementing significant structural reforms to enhance operational efficiency and combat readiness. This includes introducing new military doctrines emphasizing joint operations and rigorously testing its capabilities within and beyond the First Island Chain, a crucial strategic area. These efforts reflect China's intent to establish itself as a formidable global military power.

5. China's Growing Military Power Concerns the United States

China's aggressive military modernization has caused concern among its neighbors and global powers. The country's increased military budget, advanced weapons systems, and expanded power projection capabilities, such as aircraft carriers, ballistic missiles, and cyber warfare technologies, threaten regional stability and sovereignty.

The South China Sea (SCS) and East China Sea (ECS) have become critical battlegrounds for strategic competition between the United States and China. China's aggressive activities, such as constructing islands and military bases in the Spratly Islands and asserting territorial claims near the Philippines and Vietnam, have heightened tensions. Similarly, China's maneuvers around the Senkaku Islands in the ECS have raised concerns. Control over these areas would significantly bolster China's strategic and economic position, challenging US interests in the Indo-Pacific and beyond.

US Strategic Goals and Responses

In response to China's assertive posturing, the United States has outlined several strategic goals (Ref 11):

a) Ensuring the defense of allies in the Western Pacific.
b) Maintaining a robust US-led security presence.
c) Preventing any single power from dominating the region.
d) Advocating for diplomatic solutions to conflicts.
e) Ensuring open and accessible maritime movement.
f) Deterring China's military expansion and ensuring compliance with international laws in the SCS and ECS.

In its 2023 annual report to the US Congress, the Department of Defense highlighted China's comprehensive national strategy, which aims to achieve the 'great rejuvenation of the Chinese nation' by 2049. This strategy involves political, social, and military modernization to enhance national power, governance, and influence on the global stage. The report points out that this strategy is a response to the perceived efforts by the United States to impede China's rise, leading to increased strategic competition. China's active endeavors to strengthen its national power and assert a dominant position in the ongoing global competition underline the seriousness of the situation.

6. China's Bold Rationale: Unpacking the New Military Strategy

In 2015, the State Council of the People's Republic of China stated that the world was witnessing a new phase in the revolution of military affairs, with advancements in long-range, precise, intelligent, stealthy, and unmanned weapons. Outer and cyberspace have become crucial in strategic competition among major powers, impacting international politics and posing new challenges to China's military security (Ref 10).

China is undergoing significant changes regarding the distribution of global power, governance in various countries, and the strategic setup of the Asia-Pacific region. This region is increasingly essential for business and strategy, particularly with the heightened focus and increased military presence of the United States. There are emerging concerns due to disputes over land, disagreements on sea usage, and the proximity of terrorism and extremism to China. It is essential to safeguard China's interests abroad, as numerous potential threats exist. The nature of warfare is evolving rapidly, with increasingly advanced weapons capable of long-range and stealthy attacks. China has set ambitious development goals to become a prosperous society and a strong, modern, socialist country by 2049. Central to this plan is building a robust military as part of the Chinese Dream of national rejuvenation. The nation's security issues are multifaceted and require a comprehensive approach. The Chinese military aims to enhance cooperation with the Russian and US armed forces, develop military relations with neighboring countries, and participate in multilateral dialogues and cooperation mechanisms. Additionally, it is committed to participating in UN peacekeeping missions, providing disaster relief, and securing international sea lanes.

CHAPTER 5

CHINA'S GLOBAL AMBITIONS: INTELLECTUAL PROPERTY THEFT AND TALENT RECRUITMENT

The chapter explores China's assertive global agenda, exposing its contentious practices of intellectual property theft and talent recruitment. It confronts you with the harsh reality of widespread intellectual property theft, which poses a significant challenge to global innovation and economic stability. Furthermore, the chapter examines China's strategic efforts to attract top talent globally, prompting questions about the ethical implications of brain drain and the potential consequences for global economic dynamics.

1. Intellectual Property Theft

Over the past twenty years, China has gained a reputation for intellectual property theft. The United States Trade Representative office (USTR) has consistently kept China on the priority watch list for intellectual property protection and enforcement. In 2019, CNBC News reported that one in every five North America-based respondents to a survey of the CNBC Global CFO Council claimed that Chinese companies had stolen their intellectual property within the previous year. The CNBC Global CFO Council represents some of the world's largest public and private companies, collectively managing nearly $5 trillion in market value of intellectual property (IP) across various sectors (Ref 9).

The United States Trade Representative Office (USTR) has strongly emphasized its continued focus on holding China accountable for intellectual property protection and enforcement. This includes cracking down on trade secret theft, online piracy, and counterfeit goods. Notably, in fiscal year 2018, most of the value of all counterfeit pharmaceuticals seized at the US border was traced back to China, Hong Kong, India, and Vietnam. Furthermore, it is imperative to recognize that China and India are the leading sources of counterfeit medicines distributed worldwide, posing a significant threat to patient health and safety. The USTR has taken decisive action to address a range of unfair and harmful conduct from China, particularly concerning technology transfer requirements imposed as a condition to access the Chinese market (Ref 5).

The United States Commission on the Theft of American Intellectual Property reported that China remains the world's principal infringer of intellectual property. China (including Hong Kong) accounts for 87% of counterfeit goods seized upon entering the United States. Additionally, China continues to obtain American intellectual property from US companies operating in China and entities elsewhere. These activities include coercive actions by the state aimed at forcing the outright transfer of intellectual property or giving Chinese entities a better position to acquire or steal American intellectual property (Ref 6).

In 2020, the US government charged Huawei and two subsidiaries with federal racketeering (dishonest and fraudulent business dealings) and conspiracy to steal trade secrets from six American companies. Huawei's products include telecommunications equipment and consumer electronics, such as smartphones and tablets. In 2017, the US government also charged four members of China's military with hacking into Equifax, one of the nation's largest credit reporting agencies, and stealing trade secrets and personal data of about 145 million Americans. Based on this trend, it is likely that China will dominate advanced industries and put American competitors out of business, similar to its impact on steel, furniture, active pharmaceutical ingredients, and solar panels. However, the stakes are even higher this time, as many of these new technologies are critical for the military, as reported by *The New York Times* (Ref 4).

2. Global Talent Recruitment Strategies

In 2020, *The Wall Street Journal* reported that a US State Department report found that China recruits top scientific and technological experts in the United States and other advanced nations through its 600 talent-recruitment stations. According to the Australian Strategic Policy Institute, these 600 stations target the United States, Germany, Australia, the United Kingdom, Canada, and Japan. The United States has the most recruitment stations, with at least 146 (Ref 10).

The Chinese government often outsources the operation of stations to local groups, including professionals, alumni, and Chinese student associations. They pay these groups $29,000 for every person they recruit, plus $22,000 annually for general operating costs. The Chinese Talent program provides incentives that lead to intellectual property theft and create conflicts of interest when scientists maintain their positions in the US while also running labs in China. The Justice Department has filed several cases against program participants and Chinese military researchers for allegedly lying about their work with China or their status in the People's Liberation Army.

FBI agents have questioned several researchers about their work and military connections. Postgraduate researchers in biomedicine and artificial intelligence have hidden their active-duty status with the Chinese People's Liberation Army from immigration authorities. For example, federal prosecutors accused an artificial intelligence researcher at the University of California, Los Angeles (UCLA) of destroying evidence related to potential technology theft. Additionally, a scientist studying fluid dynamics at the University of Virginia was charged with stealing proprietary software codes from a US Navy-funded project developed over the past 20 years.

CHAPTER 6

GLOBAL POWER PLAY: CHINESE INVESTMENTS, REGULATIONS, AND OWNERSHIP

—⟋⟍⟍⟋—

This chapter will thoroughly explore the intricate dynamics of global power play, where Chinese investments intersect with regulatory landscapes and ownership structures. We will comprehensively analyze the complex interplay between economic interests and regulatory frameworks, highlighting actions such as blocking Chinese acquisitions and imposing stringent European regulations. By focusing on the strategic importance of Chinese investments in Europe and America, we aim to give you profound insights into the global economic shifts that are shaping geopolitical landscapes. Our examination of Chinese real estate investments and ownership will underscore the evolving contours of global economic influence. Navigating these nuanced dynamics will empower you to appreciate the intricate power dynamics that shape the global economy.

1. Regulations to Block Chinese Acquisitions

China has been eager for overseas investments for nearly two decades, particularly in the United States and Europe. Chinese global investments peaked in 2016 but began to decline in 2017 due to stricter administrative controls on overseas investments in China.

American Legislation

In 2018, Congress passed legislation that significantly expanded the government's powers to block transactions on national security grounds. This included requiring the United States Committee on Foreign Investment to review Chinese deals carefully. The stricter law was a direct response to China's increasing economic and security threat to the United States. China is making significant progress in various technologies, such as artificial intelligence, facial recognition, microchips, and computer technology, which could give the country an economic and military advantage. The gravity of these regulatory changes cannot be overstated, as they have a profound impact on the global economic landscape.

The new US law targets Chinese companies that acquire US companies collecting various data on American citizens, including their social media activity, health information, and financial transactions. The Committee on Foreign Investment has blocked several Chinese deals, including the acquisition of StayNTouch, a US company that creates cloud-based hotel management software. StayNTouch's software tracks hotel guests and alerts management when they leave their rooms for housekeeping. There are concerns that this software could potentially track military personnel or federal agents during their stays. Chinese investment in the United States decreased to $3.2 billion in 2019 from its peak of $53 billion in 2016 (Ref 10).

Holding Foreign Companies Accountable

The US Senate passed the Holding Foreign Companies Accountable Act in 2020. This act mandates that certain foreign-owned companies that issue securities traded on US stock exchanges certify that they are not owned or controlled by a foreign government. Additionally, foreign issuers of securities must disclose the percentage of shares owned by governmental entities in the country where the issuer is incorporated.

a) Do these governmental entities have a controlling financial interest?

b) Information related to any board members who are officials of the Communist Party of China.

c) Do the articles of incorporation of the issuer contain any charter of the Communist Party of?

This bill forces Chinese-owned companies to comply with the US securities law and requires some to be removed from American stock exchanges (Ref 9).

European Regulations

In 2021, the European Union took decisive action by initiating the development of a new tool to prevent companies, particularly those with foreign government backing, from acquiring European firms. Additionally, countries within the EU, such as France, Spain, and Italy, have been actively exploring similar protective measures for their strategic assets, including those in the healthcare sector (Ref 1).

Since 2018, the EU, like the United States, has made significant changes to its foreign acquisitions review due to increasing concerns about security risks from Chinese investments. While these changes have mainly focused on Foreign Direct Investment (FDI) and other types of equity investments, collaborations in research and development (R&D) have yet to be closely regulated. This lack of regulation has allowed Chinese companies to strategically increase their R&D investments and form partnerships with European companies, universities, governments, and other relevant entities. This has given Chinese entities access to potentially sensitive European assets, often needing the knowledge of their European partners. Notably, there have been documented cases where R&D activities have led to the transfer of vital technologies to China's military and enhanced the state's ability to exert control over its population. These risks underscore the urgent need for tighter regulations in this area (Ref 3).

In 2018, the German government responded to increasing concerns about Chinese companies gaining excessive access to essential technologies by implementing the 12th amendment to the German Foreign Trade Regulation. This amendment expands the government's authority to prevent foreign investors from acquiring direct or indirect stakes in German companies if the acquisition threatens Germany's security. The amendment also lowers the threshold for scrutiny from 25% to 10% - meaning that any foreign acquisition of 10% or more of a German company's shares would require thorough screening. These measures protect critical infrastructure such as energy, water, food supply, telecommunications, defense, finance, and transportation. As a result, a German state bank took a stake in high-voltage grid operator 50Hertz to prevent China's State Grid from purchasing it after no alternative private investor was found in Europe. Notably, European Union states recognized the need for a unified approach and agreed to establish a comprehensive system to coordinate the screening of foreign investments in Europe, particularly from China (Ref 7).

2. Chinese Investments and Ownership

According to the Rhodium Group, Chinese foreign direct investment (FDI) in Europe reached a 10-year low in 2019, with completed deals totaling just $11.7 billion. Chinese FDI in the EU has been declining in recent years after reaching a peak of €37 billion in 2016 due to stricter administrative controls on overseas investments in China starting in 2017.

From 2000 to 2019, Chinese investments in Europe totaled nearly €163 billion, focusing mainly on five sectors: automotive, financial and business services, consumer products and services, health and biotechnology, and information and communication technology. Approximately 55% of these investments came from Chinese state-owned enterprises. The United Kingdom received the largest share of these investments (€50.3 billion), followed by Germany (€22.7 billion), Italy (€15.9 billion), and France (€14.4 billion).

Historically, Chinese investors have sought opportunities in Europe during financial crises. However, in response to the COVID-19 crisis, the European Central Bank has allocated €750 billion in assets to support domestic enterprises. Furthermore, the European Commission has issued updated screening guidelines to ensure member states safeguard critical European assets and technology during the coronavirus crisis. Europe's revised investment screening policy has empowered regulators to intervene in foreign takeovers more effectively than in previous financial crises (Ref 3).

A. 2013-2017 Investments

Tasmanian Van Diemen's Land Company (VDL): In 2016, not long after China's leader Xi Jinping visited the remote island state of Tasmania, Lu Xianfeng (Chairman of Ningbo Xianfeng) purchased Tasmanian Van Diemen's Land Company (VDL), Australia's most extensive dairy operation for more than $200 million. Mr. Lu paid for the purchase with three loans, one from a lender in Australia and two from China's biggest state-run banks, the Industrial and Commercial Bank of China and the China Zheshang Bank.

According to the Australian Government, Department of Foreign Affairs and Trade, the United States and the United Kingdom were the most prominent investors in Australia in 2019, followed by Belgium, Japan, and Hong Kong. China was the ninth largest foreign investor, with 2% of the total foreign investments. However, Hong Kong and Chinese investments in Australia have grown significantly over the past decade (Ref 5 and www.dfat.gov.au).

Canadian Oil Company: In 2013, CNOOC acquired the Canadian oil and gas company Nexen Inc. for $15.1 billion. The Canadian government stated that the CNOOC-Nexen acquisition would be the final deal it approved, and it also placed limits on Chinese state-controlled companies from acquiring any further majority stakes in the oil sector. The United States previously blocked CNOOC's $18.5-billion bid for Unocal due to national security concerns (Ref 2).

Smithfield Foods Inc.: In 2013, WH Group Ltd. acquired Virginia-based Smithfield Foods Inc. for $4.7 billion. This acquisition, which exceeded the company's market value by 30%, led to WH Group becoming the top pork producer globally. Smithfield Foods Inc. has its US headquarters in Virginia and operates facilities in Mexico, Poland, Romania, Germany, and the United Kingdom. The Bank of China, a state-owned bank, approved a $4 billion loan to purchase Smithfield in just one day. This investment was part of a $52 billion overseas spending spree by Chinese food companies since 2005 in response to China's population's growing concerns about domestically produced food. WH Group's factory in Zhengzhou, China, produces American-style pork using imported Smithfield meat (Ref 4).

China Used Smithfield to Acquire Many More Businesses:

In 2016, Smithfield Foods acquired California-based Clougherty Packing from Hormel Foods for $145 million. The acquisition included brands such as Farmer John and Saag's Specialty Meats. Clougherty had a large selection of pork products and an extensive sales network in the southwestern United States. As part of the deal, Smithfield also acquired hog farms in Arizona, California, and Wyoming.

In 2017, Smithfield Foods acquired the remaining 66.5% of the equity in Pini Polonia, which has a slaughterhouse in Poland and facilities in

Italy and Hungary. The deal included the acquisition of Pini Polska, Hamburger Pini, and Royal Chicken.

B. 2018 Investments

A consortium led by China's Anta Sports acquired Finland's Amer for €4.6 billion.

Haier has acquired Candy, an Italian domestic appliance manufacturer, for €475 million, accelerating its expansion into the European market.

Goodix acquired the German cellular IoT intellectual property company CommSolid to support the development of its System-on-Chips (SoCs) solutions, targeted at new applications for IoT and smart devices.

C. 2019 Investments

Jiangsu Shagang Group has acquired an additional 24% stake in UK-based Global Switch for £1.8 billion. Global Switch operates and develops data centers in Europe and Asia. The investment increased the Chinese equity stake in Global Switch to 49.9%.

Shenzhen Goodix Technology Co Ltd acquired NXP Semiconductors' (Netherlands) voice and audio business for an undisclosed sum. The transaction includes NXP's engineering team and relevant intellectual properties.

Alibaba acquired Data Artisans, a Berlin-based startup, for €90 million. The startup provided distributed systems and data streaming services for enterprises.

Evergrande first began investing in Swedish clean car company NEVS via its Mini Minor subsidiary. In 2020, Mini Minor purchased the remaining 17.6% of the equity in NEVS for around $380 million, which valued NEVS at almost $2.2 billion.

CIC acquired the remaining ownership interest in National Grid's stake in the UK's Cadent gas network, the largest natural gas distribution network in the UK.

D. Other Chinese Acquisition in the United States

The American Security Institute reported that Chinese firms and investors own a controlling majority in nearly 2,400 US companies (Ref 6). These include:

1. Cirrus Wind Energy (energy)
2. Complete Genomics (health care)
3. First International Oil (energy)
4. G.E. Appliances (technology)
5. GNC (vitamins and supplements)
6. IBM—P.C. division (technology)
7. Legendary Entertainment Group (entertainment)
8. Motorola Mobility (technology)
9. Nexteer Automotive (automotive)
10. Riot Games (entertainment
11. Teledyne Continental Motors and Mattituck Services (aerospace)
12. Terex Corp. (machinery)
13. Triple H Coal (mining)
14. Zonare Medical Systems (health care)

E. Real Estate Investments in the United States

In 2019, the Wall Street Journal reported that Chinese net investment in commercial real estate in the United States dropped to the lowest level since 2012. The Chinese government has pressured investors to bring cash back to mainland China to stabilize the economy. Some Chinese developers have been facing tighter credit conditions at home; therefore, they sold some of their US properties to raise money. Chinese were net buyers of $2.63 billion of US commercial real estate in 2018 versus over $19 billion in 2016, the investment peak. Chinese residential investors have also been selling their US homes, and new-home purchases by Chinese in the US have dropped. These investors will likely continue to divest from US real estate shortly.

The Chinese began investing heavily in the US real estate market a decade ago after their government loosened restrictions on foreign investments. They spent tens of billions of dollars on trophy properties such as the landmark Waldorf Astoria in New York, skyscraper development in Chicago, and a residential project in Beverly Hills, California. This has caused real estate prices to increase in specific market segments. The Chinese are the most significant group of foreign investors in the United States (Ref 8).

CHAPTER 7

CHINA'S ECONOMIC TACTICS:
CURRENCY MANIPULATION AND SUBSIDIES

—⁓⟋⟍⁓—

The chapter explores China's intricate economic strategies, focusing on its contentious currency manipulation practices and government subsidies. Through a comprehensive analysis, it sheds light on the complexities of currency manipulation and its broad impact on global trade dynamics. Furthermore, the chapter underscores China's extensive reliance on government subsidies to bolster its domestic industries and enhance its global competitiveness, prompting concerns about fair market practices and the integrity of international trade.

1. Currency Manipulation

For over twenty years, China has been employing currency devaluation and government subsidies to gain a competitive edge in exports. This is not just a national issue but a global one that demands immediate attention and international cooperation. China manipulates its currency by devaluing the Chinese Yuan by 25% to 40% against the US Dollar, making Chinese exports significantly cheaper. Unlike most advanced economies with floating exchange rates, China fixes its currency, the yuan, to the US dollar. By keeping the yuan artificially low, China aims to make its exports more competitive globally. This leads to cheaper Chinese goods for US buyers. The United States has labeled Beijing as a currency manipulator and requested the International Monetary Fund to investigate the issue. In response to higher tariffs from the United States, the Chinese government has continued to let the yuan weaken to help exporters (Refs 1, 2, 3, and 5).

2. Chinese Government Subsidies and Global Impact

The Chinese government is illegally subsidizing the export of goods to America and is also using forced labor from prisoners who work for a small wage or free of charge. This practice makes it impossible for American manufacturers to compete with goods made in China (Ref 4).

The EU has strict laws to prevent its member states from distorting the market through state subsidies. However, legislation needs to address the issue, especially when outside countries are engaging in the same practices. Chinese government subsidies to foreign companies operating in the EU allow them to undercut their European rivals in public procurement. Recently, the EU found that two Egyptian exporters had illegally used subsidies from the Chinese government to undercut European glass-fiber fabric producers.

3. Reforming Trade: Addressing China's WTO Violations and Policies

In 2020, the European Union, the United States, and Japan stood together, announcing their agreement to enhance existing rules on industrial subsidies. They condemned the practice of forced technology transfers in China. They recognized that the current list of prohibited subsidies under the World Trade Organization's (WTO) rules is inadequate to address market and trade-distorting subsidization in certain jurisdictions. As a result, they stressed the urgent need to include new types of unconditionally prohibited subsidies in the WTO Agreement on Subsidies and Countervailing Measures.

The recent strong support for industrial policy builds on the ongoing efforts by the US Congress to address China's violation of WTO rules. This includes its use of state subsidies for exports, export restrictions, and attempts to obtain Western intellectual property, sometimes through illegal means. A significant development is an increasing interest in implementing an annual review of China's permanent normal trade relations (PNTR) status or even revoking it altogether to pressure China into making necessary reforms.

4. Enforcing Fair Trade: Protecting US Workers and Businesses

In May 2024, to encourage China to halt these practices, the United States took a significant step by raising tariffs on crucial sectors such as steel, aluminum, semiconductors, electric vehicles, batteries, critical minerals, solar cells, ship-to-shore cranes, and medical products. The most substantial increase was the 100% tariff imposed on electric vehicles (Ref 9).

Treasury Secretary Janet L. Yellen justified the tariffs, citing China's excess industrial capacity posing a threat to the United States and its allies. China, in response, criticized the decision, labeling it as political manipulation and threatening retaliatory measures (Ref 10).

Steel and Aluminum

The tariff rate on specific steel and aluminum products (under Section 301) increased from 0–7.5% to 25% in 2024. The US has announced a $6 billion investment in 33 clean manufacturing projects, including steel and aluminum. This includes support for the first new primary aluminum smelter in four decades. These investments will make the United States one of the first nations to produce clean steel using clean hydrogen, enhancing the competitiveness of the US steel industry.

Additionally, the announced actions aim to protect the US steel and aluminum industries from China's unfair trade practices.

Semiconductors

The tariff rate on semiconductors rose from 25% to 50%. China's semiconductor policies have increased market share and capacity expansion, posing risks for market-driven firms. The pandemic caused disruptions to the supply chain, underscoring the dangers of overreliance on a few markets.

In 2022, President Biden introduced the CHIPS and Science Act, which invests nearly $53 billion in American semiconductor manufacturing to counter decades of disinvestment and offshoring. This includes $39 billion in direct incentives for semiconductor manufacturing and a 25% investment tax credit for semiconductor companies. Raising the tariff rate on semiconductors is crucial for sustaining these investments.

Electric Vehicles (EVs)

The tariff rate on electric vehicles surged from 25% to 100% in 2024. The 70% increase in China's electric vehicle exports from 2022 to 2023, driven by subsidies and non-market practices, poses a risk of overcapacity and threatens investments elsewhere. To protect American manufacturers, a 100% tariff on EVs is proposed. This aligns with promoting American-made vehicles and supporting the EV market.

Batteries, Battery Components and Parts, and Critical Minerals

The tariff rates on various battery components will increase to 25% in the coming years. China's control of specific segments of the EV battery supply chain poses risks to national security and clean energy goals. The US government has invested nearly $20 billion in grants and loans to expand domestic production capacity and has established manufacturing tax credits to incentivize investment in US battery production.

Solar Cells

The tariff rate on solar cells, whether or not assembled into modules, increased from 25% to 50% in 2024. China's unfair trade practices give it control of up to 80 to 90% of certain parts of the global solar supply chain. The United States has made significant investments in the solar supply chain and offers tax credits, grants, and loan programs to support solar energy projects. Solar manufacturers have announced nearly $17 billion in planned investment, resulting in an 8-fold increase in US manufacturing capacity by 2030.

Ship-to-Shore Cranes

The tariff rate on ship-to-shore cranes increased from 0% to 25% in 2024. This increase is being implemented to protect US manufacturers from China's unfair trade practices. Port cranes are essential for continuously moving goods to and within the United States. This action aims to bring port crane manufacturing capabilities back to the United States, thus supporting US supply chain security.

Medical Products

Beginning in 2024, the tariff rates on syringes and needles increased from 0% to 50%. Furthermore, specific personal protective equipment (PPE), including certain respirators and face masks, tariff rates increased from 0–7.5% to 25% in 2024. The tariffs on rubber medical and surgical gloves will also go up from 7.5% to 25% in 2026.

The government and private sector have invested in domestic manufacturing to ensure access to vital medical supplies for American healthcare workers and patients. However, American businesses need help competing with low-priced Chinese-made supplies of poor quality, which may pose safety risks.

5. The US Cracks Down on Duty Evasion Tactics

The US Department of Commerce has discovered that certain Chinese producers send solar products to Southeast Asian countries (Cambodia, Malaysia, Thailand, and Vietnam) for minor processing to avoid paying duties. However, solar cells manufactured in Southeast Asian countries from Chinese wafers and assembled into modules are not subject to the final circumvention findings. In response to several companies attempting to bypass US duties, Commerce has issued "country-wide" circumvention findings for solar cells and modules from China involving Southeast Asian countries. Importation is not prohibited, but companies must certify compliance with the antidumping and countervailing duties orders to avoid circumvention findings (Ref 11).

CHAPTER 8

RECLAIMING US INDUSTRY: FROM CHINESE DEPENDENCY TO DOMESTIC RESURGENCE

—⟥⟨⟨⟩⟨⟩—

This chapter explores America's industrial landscape, documenting the shift from relying on Chinese manufacturing to a renewed focus on domestic production. It discusses the substantial impact of losing manufacturing to China on critical industries such as steel and textiles. The chapter also delves into the challenges and opportunities in reshaping the industrial paradigm, presenting compelling stories of businesses facing obstacles in China and relocating. Additionally, it highlights the emergence of new industrial clusters, signaling a potential reversal of trends and offering hope for revitalizing America's industrial strength in a rapidly changing global economy.

1. Loss of Manufacturing Base to China

During the 2000s, multinational corporations shifted their factories and intellectual property from the United States to China to maximize profits by exploiting cheap labor and minimal environmental regulations. As a result, 57,000 American manufacturing facilities were relocated to China, leading to the loss of 5.5 million jobs in the United States (Ref 16).

By 2018, the United States had reached a peak trade deficit of $418 billion with China. This deficit has nearly quintupled since China accessed the World Trade Organization (WTO) in 2001. China's WTO membership has provided access to 164 trading members at a reduced rate and predictable trade barriers.

2. Impact on Steel, Textile, and Other Industries

The United States has lost its entire steel industry to China because the Chinese government subsidizes Chinese steel products. This has become a point of contention in trade relations between the two countries. In 2019, President Trump imposed a 25% tariff on all steel imports, citing national security concerns. Steel imports, mainly from China, have led to the closure of half of the steelmaking furnaces in the US since 2001 and have decreased steel-industry employment by 35% (Ref 18).

In the 1990s, the American textile industry moved to countries like China, India, and Mexico to exploit cheap labor. However, in 2010, Parkdale Mills, the largest buyer of raw cotton in the US, reopened its textile mills there. Some American manufacturers found several benefits to domestic production over overseas outsourcing, including lower transportation costs, quicker turnaround times, and competitive labor costs due to automation. Managing local workers was also more accessible than dealing with cultural differences overseas (Ref 14).

A 2013 survey conducted by the *New York Times* revealed that companies often receive a boost from consumers when promoting American-made products. The survey found that 68% of respondents preferred products made in the United States, even if they cost more. Retailers like Walmart and Abercrombie & Fitch responded to consumer preferences by creating sections for American-made products (Ref 14).

Unfortunately, two decades of shifting manufacturing overseas has led to the decline of the textile industry in the United States. Today, companies aiming to produce goods locally often need help finding qualified workers for specialized jobs. Nonetheless, today's textile factories in the United States employ fewer workers than 30 years ago, as machines have replaced humans (Ref 14).

Walmart: Made-in China

Walmart is the largest retailer in the United States and the biggest importer of products from China. Walmart imports 91% of its merchandise from China (Ref 16). According to an estimate by the Economic Policy Institute, from 2001 to 2013, Walmart's imports from China eliminated over 400,000 jobs or 13% of the 3.2 million jobs eliminated in the United States during that time. In 2013, under pressure, Walmart announced that it would increase its sourcing of American-made products by $50 billion over the next ten years. This only represents a fraction of its $520 billion annual sales worldwide in 2019 (Ref 17).

3. Business Hostility in China

Business Hostility

In 2016, the European Union Chamber of Commerce in China surveyed European companies and reported that 56% of firms said doing business in China has become more complex. Complaints included the recent tightening of internet controls and inconsistent enforcement of regulations. It is more challenging for European firms to make deals in China than their Chinese rivals. In a survey by the American Chamber of Commerce in China, 77% of firms who responded said they felt less welcome in the country than before (Ref 15).

Fellowes Nightmare

Some companies learned the hard way when manufacturing in China. For Fellowes Inc., doing business in China has become a nightmare of intellectual property theft and legal battles in China's courts. Fellowes started making inexpensive shredders in China in 1998, outsourcing production to two firms owned by a family named Zhou. By 2009, the joint venture had about 120 suppliers and 1,600 employees, more than half its worldwide workforce (Ref 9).

However, in 2009, Fellowes refused to yield to its Chinese joint-venture partner's demands to surrender its assets and compromise its rights under the joint-venture contract. Fellowes' joint-venture partner then illegally blocked shipments from the joint-venture operation and shut down the joint-venture manufacturing unit overnight. Fellowes lost over $100 million and had to do damage control after that (Ref 9).

4. Global Companies' Exodus

A. Japan Helps Manufacturers Exit China

As the coronavirus pandemic highlights the risk of having supply chains concentrated in China, Japan is helping manufacturers move their operations from China to elsewhere. In 2020, the Japanese government allocated 220 billion yen ($1.5 billion) for companies to shift production back to Japan. Another 23.5 billion yen ($228 million) program focused on manufacturer relocations to Southeast Asia. The subsidies apply to producing goods that are either important to public health or are mainly manufactured in a few specific countries (Ref 7).

Furthermore, hiring a labor force in China is no longer a cost incentive for multinational corporations. In 2019, the Japan External Trade Organization surveyed the manufacturing costs for Japanese companies in Japan vs. China and Vietnam. The results indicated that the costs in China were 20% less than in Japan, and Vietnam was 26% lower than in Japan (Ref 7).

B. The United States Helps Companies Exit China

In 2020, US lawmakers and officials began constructing proposals to push American companies to move operations or key suppliers out of China. The incentives include tax breaks, new rules, and subsidies (Refs 11 and 13).

Most US companies that manufacture in China do not have an assembly line. For example, Apple has long used Foxconn, a Taiwanese multinational corporation with assembly plants in mainland China. Other US companies contract Chinese firms to do the work. Bringing the supply chain back to the United States would require hefty capital expenditures to build all the new factories or additions to existing ones (Ref 13).

C. Global Companies' Exodus

The exodus of global companies from China began in the early 2010s, with multinational corporation shifting their productions to Vietnam, Bangladesh, South Korea, India, and Taiwan due to escalating labor and environmental costs. However, the recent 25% tariffs imposed by the United States on Chinese goods, coupled with the disruption effects of the COVID, have significantly accelerated this trend. Moreover, the United and Japan have further incentivized this shift by offering tax benefits and subsidies for companies returning home (Ref 6)

In 2019, *Nikkei Asian Review* reported that over 50 global companies, including Chinese manufacturers, have either relocated or are contemplating a move out of China. Some companies are choosing to relocate parts of their production lines to Southeast Asian countries or other regions while maintaining their manufacturing operations in China for the Chinese and non-US markets. This has led to the emergence of a new global manufacturing landscape, with production leaving China and being distributed among developing countries.

Notably, a small portion of this production is being redirected to the United States, driven by the increasing role of automation in manufacturing (Refs 4 and 6).

Samsung Electronics and Apple's assembly partners are among 22 companies that have pledged 110 billion rupees ($1.5 billion) of investments to set up mobile phone manufacturing units in India. Furthermore, American Hewlett-Parker and Dell have contemplated moving 30% of their notebook production from China to Southeast Asia. Japan's Nintendo has announced that some of its game production will shift from China to Vietnam (Refs 3, 5, and 6).

Apple's Exodus

Apple has requested that its significant suppliers consider relocating 15% to 30% of iPhone production away from China. The company plans to manufacture its wireless earbuds in Vietnam. In 2020, it was reported that an Apple vendor was exploring the possibility of moving six production lines from China to India, involving $5 billion worth of iPhones. The new production facility will not only serve the Indian market but also expand operations to include tablets and laptops. In 2024, Apple doubled its iPhone production in India, with approximately 1 in 7 of its devices being made there. This move reflects Apple's efforts to diversify beyond China and reduce dependence on it amid geopolitical tensions. The Indian government, under Prime Minister Narendra Modi's administration, has provided incentives to attract high-end manufacturing, resulting in the creation of 150,000 direct jobs at Apple's suppliers. Additionally, *Bloomberg* reported that the Indian government has offered land to 1,000 American manufacturers to relocate from China to India (Refs 3, 5, 12, and 22).

D. List of Companies Moving out of China

These are the multinational corporations that are in the process of moving out of China or have already diversified their supply chains:

Relocation to the United States: Mitsuba, Iris Ohyama, Insulet Corporation, Element Electronics, Gentex, Apple, Amgen, and General Electric

Relocation to Japan: Komatsu, Toshiba Machine, Keihin, Sumitomo Heavy Industries, G-Tekt, and Mitsubishi Electric

Relocation to Thailand: Casio Computer, Ricoh, Citizen Watch, and Panasonic

Relocation to Vietnam: Iris Ohyama, Apple, Asisc, Kyocera, Sharp, Nintendo, Brook Sports, Google, TCL, and GoerTek

Relocation to Mexico: Nidec, Funai Electric, and Gopro

Relocation to India: Sketchers USA, Apple, Samsung, and Pegatron

Relocation to Taiwan: Asustek Computer, HP, and Dell

Relocation to South Korea and France: Iris Ohyama

(Refs 2, 5, 6, and 10)

E. Going Home to the United States

Many American companies are moving their manufacturing back to the United States. American companies go to Asia for lower costs, but their working capitals are tied up because of large shipments of goods that take weeks to cross the oceans. In addition, quality problems and communication are significant issues (Ref 1).

In 2018, 16 companies announced they planned to return, add, or retain approximately 73,000 manufacturing jobs. The 2022 CHIPS and Science Act also gave companies incentives to expand production in the United States. The main reasons for moving back to the United States are rising labor costs in China, lack of skilled workforce, company's supply chain consolidation, transportation costs, risk of manufacturing error, and significant tax incentives and monetary aid by the United States and local governments in the United States (Ref 2).

Apple: 22,200 jobs in Texas, computers, office equipment, moving from China

Amgen: 1,600 jobs in Rhode Island, pharmaceuticals, moving from China

Boeing: 7,725 jobs in Missouri, Montana, and South Carolina, aerospace and defense (New expansion and moving from overseas)

Caterpillar: 2,100 jobs in Georgia, Illinois, Indiana, and Texas, construction and farm machinery, moving from Mexico

Element Electronics: 1,500 jobs in South Carolina, consumer electronics, moving from China

Ford: 4,200 jobs in Indiana, Illinois, Ohio, Michigan, and New York, motor vehicles and parts, moving from Mexico

General Electric: 2,656 jobs in Alabama, Arkansas, Illinois, Kentucky, North Carolina, New York, and Ohio, industrial machinery, moving from China and Mexico

General Motors: 12,988 jobs in Michigan, New York, Tennessee, and Texas, motor vehicles and parts, moving from Mexico and new expansion

Gentex: 1,600 jobs in Michigan, motor vehicle parts, moving from China

Insulet Corp: 1,500 jobs in Massachusetts biotechnology, moving from China

Merck & Co: 1,633 jobs in New Jersey, pharmaceuticals, moving from the Netherlands

Polaris Industries: 2,000 jobs in Alabama, transportation equipment, moving from Mexico

Whirlpool: 2,165 jobs in Ohio, electronics and electrical equipment, moving from overseas facilities

F. Expansion in the United States

Dow Chemical: 2,900 jobs in Louisiana, Michigan, and Texas, chemicals

GlobalFoundries: 1500 semiconductor manufacturing jobs and 9,000 construction jobs in New York and Vermont

Intel: 4,000 jobs in Arizona, California, and Oregon, semiconductors and other electronic components

Micron: 70,000 jobs, including 20,000 direct construction and semiconductor manufacturing jobs in Clay, New York, and Boise, Idaho

Samsung Electronics: 17,000 construction jobs and more than 4,500 manufacturing jobs in Central Texas

SK Hynix: 2,100 new high-skilled jobs in semiconductors in West Lafayette, Indiana

SolarCity: 1,900 jobs in New York, energy production and storage

Taiwan Semiconductor Manufacturing Company: 6,000 semiconductor jobs in Phoenix, Arizona

Texas Instruments: 3,000 jobs in Sherman, Texas

5. Creation of New Industrial Clusters and Reversal of Trends

The development of new industrial clusters will not occur quickly. China provides comprehensive infrastructure, such as large ports and highways, skilled labor, and advanced logistics. Moreover, suppliers are near each other, producing more cost-effective and efficient production. Moving away from China will lead to a more fragmented operation, resulting in higher costs and longer delivery times.

Countries like Vietnam show promise but do not measure up to China. Some favorable aspects include labor costs being 6% lower than in China, a six-day workweek, tax incentives, and logistic advantages due to sharing a land border with China. However, Vietnam has more stringent environmental regulations than China, and its roads and ports are congested. In 2018, textiles and footwear accounted for 18% of Vietnam's total exports, while electronics and electrical equipment were 40%. Several popular clothing and sportswear brands, such as Nike and Adidas, already have a significant manufacturing presence in Vietnam. India has a large workforce but lacks skill levels, has relatively restrictive government rules, and is poorly integrated with major global supply chains (Refs 3, 4, and 7).

6. Expansion in China

Tesla in China

While multinational corporations are exiting China, Tesla opened its first plant near Shanghai, China, in 2019. Before 2018, Chinese government policy forced foreign automakers to work with a joint venture partner in China and share half the profits. However, in 2018, China began rolling back these restrictions, and Tesla seized the opportunity to build a wholly-owned factory. Tesla invested $5 billion, China's most significant single foreign-owned factory at that time. China is the world's biggest market for electric cars and the second-largest market for Tesla, behind the United States.

In addition, the Chinese government provided Tesla with many attractive incentives. First, Chinese state-controlled banks financed a substantial part of the facility. Second, Tesla cars were exempt from 10% sales tax. Finally, the Chinese government gave Tesla a subsidy of 24,750 yuan ($3,560) per vehicle. These subsidies have helped Tesla cut sticker prices by 9%.

Tesla has introduced the Model 3 luxury sedan and the Model Y crossover, and it plans to develop a new model specifically for the Chinese market in the future. The factory currently produces 150,000 vehicles annually in the first phase and plans to increase production to 500,000 cars annually in the next phase. Initially, about 30% of the parts were locally sourced. However, Tesla aims to use 100% local parts by 2021 to reduce manufacturing costs and price its cars more competitively against models from Chinese company Xpeng Motor (Refs 19 and 20).

Beyond Meat in China

In 2020, California-based Beyond Meat Inc. signed an agreement with the Jiaxing Economic and Technological Development Zone (JXEDZ) to build two state-of-the-art production facilities in China. These facilities manufacture plant-based meat products with flavors including beef, pork, and chicken under the Beyond Meat brand. Jiaxing, a northern Chinese city, is connected by water but has faced issues such as over 16,000 hog carcasses floating in the Huangpu River. Beyond Meat, Inc. is the first plant-based meat multinational corporation to establish its primary production facility in China, with full-scale production commencing in early 2021. China is expected to be one of the most important markets in the world for Beyond Meat.

Beyond Meat also operates two production facilities in Columbia, Missouri, and El Segundo, California. Additionally, the company co-manufactures its products with Zandbergen in Zoeterwoude, the Netherlands. It is currently unclear how many individual ingredients used to make its products come from China and whether the Chinese production facilities will supply products to the American market. Given China's questionable reputation for food safety, the company must persuade American consumers to buy its made-in-China meatless products.

In 2021, Beyond Meat, Inc. announced a three-year global strategic agreement with McDonald's Corporation. As part of the agreement, Beyond Meat is McDonald's preferred supplier for the McPlant. Beyond Meat also formed a global strategic partnership with Yum! Brands to co-create and offer innovative plant-based protein menu items found only at KFC, Pizza Hut, and Taco Bell (Ref 21).

.

CHAPTER 9

CHIP WAR: THE GLOBAL RACE FOR TECHNOLOGICAL SOVEREIGNTY

———〰———

The Chinese government is aggressively pursuing independence from foreign chip technology and has been significantly ramping up its efforts to acquire semiconductor equipment from other countries. In response, the US government has swiftly introduced bills to bolster the country's economic and technological competitiveness with China. Furthermore, the US has revoked export licenses for chip supply to Chinese companies, compelling China to pour billions into achieving self-sufficiency in semiconductors.

1. Snapshot of China's Semiconductor Market

China's semiconductor market is proliferating due to significant investments and a strategic focus on technological self-reliance. According to Statista, China's revenue in the semiconductor market is projected to reach $198.90 billion in 2024. Integrated circuits dominate the market, with a projected market volume of $160.10 billion in 2024. The revenue is expected to show an annual growth rate (2024-2027) of 6.16%, resulting in a market volume of $238.00 billion by 2027. Compared to the global market, most of the revenue will be generated in China (Ref 9).

2. China's Obstacles in Its Efforts to Achieve Semiconductor Independence

China is encountering obstacles in achieving semiconductor independence due to outdated technology and financial constraints related to COVID-19. Despite being the world's largest consumer of semiconductors, accounting for over 50% of global consumption, China ranks only as the fifth-largest manufacturer, trailing behind Taiwan, South Korea, Japan, and the United States. China has articulated its aspiration to become an artificial intelligence superpower shortly, leading to tensions with the US. Consequently, the US has placed Chinese companies such as Semiconductor Manufacturing International Co (SMIC) on a trade blacklist, citing security concerns. This blacklist prohibits major US chip makers, such as Nvidia and AMD, from selling and exporting chips to China. The US justifies this action by expressing apprehensions that China could potentially utilize advanced chips for military purposes. In response, China has imposed a graphite export ban on the US. Additionally, China is working to increase its domestic chip production but faces significant challenges.

China's semiconductor market is snowballing due to significant investments and a strategic focus on technological self-reliance. Political issues, corruption, and lack of oversight slowed down manufacturing. The country is also facing obstacles with intellectual property due to patented technologies protected by international companies. The Chinese government has invested one trillion yuan ($140 billion) in the semiconductor industry through state capital, such as the Integrated Circuit Investment Fund, and has given it high political priority. Despite these efforts, China has yet to be able to advance significantly in the semiconductor value chain. While there has been progress in independent chip design for various products, domestic production of semiconductors still needs to be a reality (Ref 10).

Challenges Ahead

One of the companies facing sanctions, Huawei, has recently launched a new smartphone called the Mate 60, which features a highly advanced 7-nanometer process chip. This has raised concerns about China's ability to produce sophisticated chips despite the sanctions. Chinese chipmakers are encountering challenges due to limited access to advanced foreign chip-making technology. Older technology is leading to increased costs for Chinese chipmakers like SMIC, resulting in them having to charge 40% to 50% more than their competitors. This particularly impacts 7-nanometer and 5-nanometer production, and costs are expected to rise with each new chip generation. Furthermore, using older chip technology results in lower yield, leading to fewer usable and sellable chips than more advanced technology.

China's progress in the semiconductor industry is constrained by its dependence on foreign providers, particularly the Dutch Advanced Semiconductor Materials Lithography (ASML) and the Taiwan Semiconductor Manufacturing Company (TSMC). TSMC holds a near monopoly in advanced chip manufacturing. At the same time, ASML dominates the market for photolithography machines. Huawei is now prohibited from using the extreme ultraviolet lithography (EUV) machines necessary to advance beyond 5 nanometers. The US has pressured the Netherlands to restrict China's access to chip technology. China has made strides in semiconductor production but lacks access to EUV technology, creating an innovation barrier. Lithography is crucial in chip-making, and companies like Shanghai Micro Electronics Equipment (SMEE) are developing China's own EUV machines. Shanghai Micro Electronics Equipment (SMEE) successfully released China's first 28-nanometer lithography machine at the end of 2023.

What the Future Holds

According to the Centre for International Governance Innovation, an independent, nonpartisan think tank and research center, China's chip industry has the potential to develop advanced chip-making capabilities and lead the trillion-dollar industry by 2030. Can China successfully mass-produce advanced chips, and what will the geopolitical implications be if it achieves this goal?

China could become a significant player in the computer chip market because of its skilled chip engineers and high demand for electronics. However, experts are unsure if Huawei and SMIC can compete with industry leaders TSMC and ASML without access to advanced technology. Still, China's tech industry has strengths and time to improve (Ref 15). In March 2024, *Bloomberg* reported that China is raising over $27 billion for its largest chip fund. This is to accelerate the development of cutting-edge technologies to counter a US campaign to thwart its rise (Ref 18).

3. The Rise of Huawei: From Telecom Leader to Supply Chain Integrator

Founded in 1987 by Ren Zhengfei, a former People's Liberation Army (PLA) officer, Huawei Technologies Co. Ltd. is a leading global information and communications technology infrastructure and smart devices provider. The company, located in Shenzhen, China, designs, develops, manufactures, and sells telecommunications equipment, consumer electronics, smart devices, and various rooftop solar products. Huawei's transition from a telecommunications giant to a significant semiconductor supply chain player is a testament to China's strategic moves in the tech industry, showcasing the country's long-term vision and adaptability.

In the 2000s, China aimed to catch up with the West in fundamental technologies, with Huawei playing a leading role. Huawei benefited from import substitution in building a domestic information and communication technology industry. Founder Ren Zhengfei's strong ties to the local government enabled Huawei to secure government contracts. The company focused on reducing dependence on foreign core technologies and developing self-reliant research and development (R&D). In 2023, the company invested ¥164.7 billion ($22.8 billion) in R&D, which accounted for 23.4% of its annual revenue. The company has invested ¥1.11 trillion ($154 billion) in R&D over the past decade. By the end of 2023, Huawei had over 140,000 active patents.

After the Tiananmen Square Incident in 1989, China realized the strategic importance of developing its core information technologies. This led to the government implementing policies to support Chinese companies, including Huawei. In the 1990s, Ren Zhengfei stressed the importance of telecommunications equipment to China's military. This period also marked the beginning of Huawei's ties to Xi Jinping, who envisioned that Huawei could contribute to the construction of Fuzhou Software Park, which commenced in March 1999. Today, the software park houses 510 enterprises, including 32 listed in the Shanghai Shenzhen Stock Exchange.

In the 2000s, Huawei worked to control the entire telecommunications value chain. During the 4G era, the Chinese government backed its standard, TD-LTE, and provided licenses only to ensure that Chinese equipment manufacturers dominated the market. Huawei leveraged its dominance in the Chinese market to become a significant global player. Since 2009, Huawei has received over 5 billion yuan ($687 million) in unconditional government grants for its contributions to new high-tech industries in China. Additionally, the company has consistently received funding from local and central government sources and has benefited from public procurement and domestic protectionism.

Since 2019, Huawei has encountered trade restrictions imposed by the US; however, the company has embarked on a resurgence. This revival can be attributed to the release of the Mate 60 Pro smartphone, featuring the domestically manufactured 5G-enabled Kirin 9000S chip developed by HiSilicon. Critics contend that Huawei's resurgence is significantly linked to Qualcomm's authorization to use 5G technology until 2025. In 2024, Huawei surprised the industry by unveiling a new phone powered by a sophisticated chip from Chinese chipmaker SMIC. This resulted in a notable 64% increase in Huawei smartphone sales during the initial six weeks of 2024 (Refs 12 and 17).

4. Nvidia's Dilemma in China's Chip Market Landscape

As a leading player in the global semiconductor industry, Nvidia faces unique challenges and opportunities in China. In an interview with the *Financial Times*, Nvidia's CEO, Huang, stated that China accounts for about one-third of the US tech industry's market and is irreplaceable as a source of components and an end product market.

Most of the world's advanced chips, including Nvidia's, are manufactured in Taiwan, which China claims as part of its territory. President Joe Biden has indicated that the US would intervene if China took unprovoked military action against Taiwan. Such a conflict could severely disrupt the global production of items ranging from cars to computers. In its 2023 annual report, Nvidia noted that China and Taiwan represented a significant portion of its sales. Due to US chip export controls, Nvidia cannot sell advanced chips in China, prompting local Chinese companies to develop their chips to compete with Nvidia's products.

Nvidia is leading the global race in developing AI tools and is the primary source of chips for training "large language models" like OpenAI's ChatGPT. With a valuation of $700 billion in 2023, Nvidia surpasses its US rivals Intel and Qualcomm, each worth close to $120 billion. Despite a rally in chip stocks, Nvidia remains more significant than its closest competitor, Taiwanese chipmaker TSMC, valued at about $450 billion (Ref 5).

5. US Chipmakers Navigate China's Market Amidst Increasing Restrictions

The geopolitical tensions have put US semiconductor companies in a tough spot. Despite the growing restrictions on selling advanced chips to China, American chipmakers are determined to continue serving the enormous Chinese market. China remains a crucial market for most US chipmakers, even though the US government is trying to limit chip sales to the country. Data from S&P Global shows that US chip giants Intel, Broadcom, Qualcomm, and Marvell Technology generate more revenue from China than the US. In October 2022, the US implemented a series of stricter export controls to restrict China's access to advanced chip technology, particularly those used in AI applications.

BIS Imposed $300 Million Penalty Against Seagate Technology for Shipment to Huawei

In April 2023, the US Department of Commerce's Bureau of Industry and Security (BIS) imposed a $300 million civil penalty against Seagate Technology LLC for violating US export controls. This was due to their sales of hard disk drives to Huawei Technologies Co. Ltd. violating the Foreign Direct Product rule. This represents the most significant independent administrative penalty in BIS history. Despite restrictions on certain foreign-made items associated with Huawei, Seagate persisted in conducting business with Huawei and became their exclusive supplier of hard disk drives. Following this, Seagate signed a three-year Strategic Cooperation Agreement with Huawei.

In its investigation, BIS found that Seagate violated the Export Administration Regulations by exporting over 7.4 million hard disk drives to Huawei without BIS authorization. Even after Huawei was added to the Entity List for actions against US national security, Seagate continued to ship hard disk drives to Huawei. This settlement underscores the importance of companies strictly complying with BIS export rules (Ref 41).

6. Tech Trade Tensions: US Revokes Intel and Qualcomm Licenses

In May 2024, the US Department of Commerce revoked export licenses previously granted to Intel and Qualcomm to sell computer chips to Huawei, a Chinese-based company (Ref 17). This action is a part of the US government's effort to restrict US technology exports to Huawei due to its alleged ties to the Chinese military. The specific licenses that were revoked were not disclosed by the US Department of Commerce. This decision comes amidst heightened pressure on Huawei by federal agencies to strengthen new American companies' ability to compete with Huawei. China has condemned these measures, asserting that the United States is unjustly exploiting export controls under the guise of national security to suppress Chinese companies.

Huawei, China's leading tech company, provides internet and phone networks globally, including in rural areas of the United States. There are concerns about the security of Huawei's equipment, with US officials fearing susceptibility to Chinese intelligence infiltration. Huawei denies involvement in spying for the Chinese government. In

2023, despite US efforts, Huawei remained the world's top company in patent applications and infrastructure sales.

During the Trump administration, the US government imposed export controls on Huawei, forcing it to divest parts of its business and rely on domestically produced chips. However, US companies could still sell less sensitive products to Huawei (Ref 11). In 2019, Huawei was added to a US trade restriction list (Entity List) due to concerns about potential espionage and China's military advancements. Being on this list means that Huawei's suppliers must obtain a specialized and difficult-to-acquire license before shipping any products. Despite this restriction, Huawei's suppliers have been granted licenses valued at billions of dollars to supply Huawei with goods and technology.

In May 2024, the National Telecommunications and Information Administration (NTIA) of the Department of Commerce announced $420 million in funding for US companies to build radio equipment in the US and internationally to compete with Huawei's products (Ref 40). This funding is part of the $1.5 billion Wireless Innovation Fund provided by the CHIPS and Science Act 2022. Additionally, the US Federal Communications Commission (FCC) is scheduled to vote on prohibiting Huawei from certifying wireless equipment for the US market (Ref 40). In addition to the trade tension, President Biden signed a law in April 2024 that could ban TikTok in the US unless its Chinese parent company sells it within a year. This has led TikTok to file a lawsuit, but the US Supreme Court rejected it in January 2025 (Ref 13).

7. Strategies to Counter China's Military Modernization

To curtail the People's Liberation Army (PLA), the United States can enhance its military capabilities and hinder China's military modernization by imposing restrictions on its access to US technology and resources. In 2019, Congress expanded the authority of the Committee on Foreign Investment in the United States (CFIUS) to prevent potential access to US technology (Ref 2).

Meanwhile, other countries like Japan, India, and Europe are making significant investments in the semiconductor industry. The European Chips Act, for instance, aims to mobilize public and private investments of over $47 billion. This substantial funding is a proactive step to prepare for potential supply chain disruptions. Similarly, Japan and India have allocated substantial funds for state-backed investments in the semiconductor industry (Refs 1 and 3).

The United States and the European Union, as leading superpowers, have allocated nearly $81 billion to boost the production of the next generation of semiconductors. This is intensifying the global competition with China for chip dominance. The significant investment is just the beginning of a massive $380 billion commitment by governments worldwide to support companies like Intel Corp. and Taiwan Semiconductor Manufacturing Co. in expanding the production of more powerful microprocessors. This surge in funding has intensified the competition between the US and China in cutting-edge technology, marking a crucial turning point that will profoundly shape the future of the global economy (Ref 3).

8. Netherlands and Japan Joined US Semiconductor Export Controls

In 2023, the US, the Netherlands, and Japan reached a significant agreement on export controls, with far-reaching implications for the semiconductor industry. The Netherlands' and Japan's export control systems differ significantly from the US. In the European Union, export controls are connected to the Wassenaar Arrangement, which governs international weapons transfers and dual-use items. The US Commerce Control List (CCL) aligns with the Wassenaar list, but the

US also has broader unilateral authorities under the 2018 Export Control Reform Act (ECRA).

The EU's approach to export control regulations is unique, making it more challenging, though not impossible, for EU member countries to impose controls on items not included on those lists. Under the European Union's dual-use export control regulations, EU member states can implement national security policies, including investment screening and export controls. This unique approach allows member states to restrict export control beyond the Wassenaar-controlled items list.

The Dutch government has set three main goals:

a) To stop Dutch products from being used for military purposes or to make weapons of mass destruction.
b) To avoid becoming too dependent on other countries for essential supplies.
c) To keep the lead in technology.

The Dutch government's reasons for these controls are in line with EU rules, including concerns about human rights and public safety. The Netherlands has informed the European Commission about these extra controls, demonstrating their alignment with EU regulations and their desire for these new rules to become part of the EU's export control laws.

Japan began implementing controls on 23 advanced semiconductor manufacturing equipment types. These controls directly affect major Japanese companies such as Nikon, Tokyo Electron, Screen Holdings, and Advantest. The restrictions in Japan align with those in the US and apply regardless of the destination to avoid singling out China. This creates a broader regime than the United States regarding geographic export license requirements. In Japan, national control measures are mainly connected to the Wassenaar Arrangement. Japan justifies these export controls to facilitate foreign transactions and maintain domestic and international peace and security.

In March 2024, the US government urged its allies, including the Netherlands, Germany, South Korea, and Japan, to tighten restrictions on China's access to semiconductor technology. This effort has been met with resistance in some countries. The US explicitly urges the Netherlands to prevent ASML Holding NV from servicing and repairing sensitive chip-making equipment that Chinese clients purchased before and to impose sales limits on such devices (Ref 16).

China responded to allied controls by initiating a cybersecurity review of US memory chip producer Micron. Additionally, China has requested WTO dispute consultations with the US regarding export controls and urged closer monitoring of the trilateral arrangement during an April 2023 WTO meeting. Chinese officials strongly oppose export controls and have accused the United States of seeking technology leadership. In response, China banned the export of certain rare-earth elements to the US in December 2024 (Refs 19 and 20).

9. DOD's Plan to Secure a Rare Earth Supply

In response to China's threat to impose new export restrictions on rare-earth elements, the US Defense Department (DOD) has advanced its goal of developing domestic supply chains. This is to ensure continued access to the rare-earth materials needed to manufacture the permanent magnets used in critical US military weapons systems. There are 17 elements on the periodic table known as rare earth elements. While the Department of Defense (DOD) requires nearly all of them in some capacity, three are used to make the permanent magnets critical to many defense systems. Continued US reliance on foreign sources for rare earth products risks national security. The US and most of the world depend on China for many rare earth elements. The goal is to establish a sustainable, rare-earth-element supply chain that supports all US defense requirements by 2027.

Funding

The Department of Defense (DOD) has allocated over $439 million since 2020 to establish domestic rare earth element supply chains, including refining and processing rare earth elements in the US. This initiative aims to create a complete supply chain within the country, as only one rare earth mine in the US currently supplies the commercial market (Ref 42).

The Use of Rare Earth Elements

Rare earth permanent magnets play a critical and irreplaceable role in defense systems, including the F-35 Lightning II aircraft, Virginia and Columbia class submarines, Tomahawk missiles, various radar systems, Predator unmanned aerial vehicles, and the Joint Direct Attack Munition series of smart bombs. Their unique properties make them indispensable in these systems. Moreover, they are equally vital in commercial applications in the United States, where they are used to generate electricity for electronic systems in aircraft and to focus microwave energy in radar systems, underscoring their widespread impact.

Rare earth elements have various applications beyond their use in magnets. For example, vehicle-mounted laser-range finders, like those on Abrams M1A1/2 tanks, utilize rare earth elements. Additionally, rare earth elements are used in fiber optic communication systems, cerium-polished optical lenses, and sonic transducers in submarine sonar systems.

Extraction of Rare Earth Elements

The process involves extracting rare earth elements from mineral rock and chemically treating them to produce high-purity rare earth oxides or salts. These are then transformed into metals and combined with alloying elements to produce rare earth alloys. These alloys are used to create rare earth magnets through sintering, cutting, and coating according to specifications.

DOD Investment Awardees

The Defense Department (DOD) is taking proactive steps to secure crucial sources of rare earth materials and magnets within the United States. These awards from the DOD are anticipated to contribute significantly to the growth of the domestic magnet production market, catering to defense and commercial sectors, highlighting the urgency and importance of the situation.

MP Materials

MP Materials, located in Nevada, is responsible for increasing the United States' rare earth element separation, processing, and magnet manufacturing capacity. The company operates the sole existing rare earth mine and oxide production facility in the US. With a $45 million financial assistance package from the US government, the company aims to expand its production capacity by 2025.

Lynas USA, LLC

To enhance resilience in the crucial early stages of the supply chain, Lynas USA, LLC has been granted $288 million. This funding is for a second domestic, commercial-scale oxide production capability by 2026.

Noveon Magnetics

Noveon Magnetics has established a rare earth magnet manufacturing facility in San Marcos, Texas, with a $28.8 million award from the US government. The company produces qualified magnets for defense and commercial applications using extracted or recycled materials.

TDA Magnetics

An award of $2.3 million from the US government has also helped TDA Magnetics with capacity building to source, produce, and sell qualified magnets into DOD supply chains.

E-VAC Magnetics

With a $94.1 million government award, E-VAC Magnetics will establish a commercial-scale rare earth magnet manufacturing capability by 2025. As part of this project, E-VAC will also develop domestic capacity to produce rare earth metals and alloys, a critical supply chain node linking early-stage rare earth processing to magnet production.

10. Executive Orders

A. To Ensure Robust Reviews of National Security Risks

In September 2022, President Biden signed an executive order directing the Committee on Foreign Investment in the United States to thoroughly review national security risks in critical sectors such as technology, clean energy, and agriculture. (Ref 6).

The Executive Order directs the Committee to consider five specific sets of factors:

a) A given transaction's effect on the resilience of critical US supply chains may have national security implications, including those outside the defense industrial base.

b) A given transaction's effect on US technological leadership in areas affecting US national security, including but not limited to microelectronics, artificial intelligence, biotechnology and bio-manufacturing, quantum computing, advanced clean energy, and climate adaptation technologies.

c) Industry investment trends, which may significantly affect a given transaction's impact on US national security, should be closely monitored and analyzed.

d) Cybersecurity risks that threaten to impair national security.

e) Risks to US persons' sensitive data.

B. Addressing United States Investments in Certain National Security Technologies and Products

In August 2023, President Biden declared a national emergency due to the threat posed by certain countries seeking to develop sensitive technologies critical for military and intelligence purposes. The order directs the Secretary of the Treasury to establish a program to regulate outbound investments into entities involved in advanced technologies. The identified categories include semiconductors, quantum information technologies, and artificial intelligence. The executive order mainly addresses the People's Republic of China (including Hong Kong and Macau).

a) Individuals (or corporations) are not allowed to engage in specific transactions with China or with certain other entities owned by individuals from China who are involved in activities related to technologies and products.

b) Individuals (or corporations) must inform the US Treasury about specific transactions involving certain entities in China and other entities owned by individuals from China engaging in activities related to other specified technologies and products.

The Executive Order outlines three categories of national security technologies and products. These categories were chosen because they play critical roles in progressing advanced military, intelligence, surveillance, and cyber-enabled capabilities.

1) Semiconductors and microelectronics;
2) Quantum information technologies; and
3) Certain artificial intelligence systems.

The executive order directs the Secretary to outline a more specific definition of sensitive technologies and products that are covered by the prohibition and notification requirement. Moreover, the Secretary has the authority to investigate any violations of the executive order and its related regulations and to impose penalties for such violations as necessary (Ref 8).

11. CHIPS and Science Act: Enhancing US Innovation and Competitiveness

In August 2022, President Biden signed the CHIPS and Science Act into law, which focuses on boosting American semiconductor research, development, and production. The act aims to strengthen American manufacturing, supply chains, and national security while positioning the United States as a leader in technology sectors such as nanotechnology, clean energy, quantum computing, and artificial intelligence. It encourages private-sector semiconductor investment nationwide and aims to foster economic growth across the United States.

Semiconductors, initially developed in the United States, are now used to power a wide range of technology, such as cell phones, electric vehicles, refrigerators, satellites, defense systems, and more. Despite their widespread use, the United States currently only produces approximately 10 percent of the global supply of chips and lacks production of the most advanced ones. However, the CHIPS and Science Act is paving the way for change. Several major companies have committed to expanding their semiconductor manufacturing capabilities and are reaping the benefits of the CHIPS and Science Act.

The CHIPS and Science Act allocates $52.7 billion to strengthen US semiconductor leadership. This includes $39 billion in manufacturing incentives, $13.2 billion in R&D and workforce development, and a 25 percent investment tax credit. Recipients must demonstrate significant work and community investments to ensure equitable economic growth. They are prohibited from building certain facilities in China and other countries of concern or using funds for stock buybacks and dividends (Ref 7).

Progress Report

By January 2025, the US Commerce Department has awarded over $33 billion of the over $36 billion in proposed incentives funding allocated to date. These announcements across 21 states are expected to create over 125,000 jobs. Since the beginning of the Biden-Harris Administration, semiconductor and electronics companies have announced nearly $450 billion in private investments, catalyzed in large part by public investment (Ref 48).

12. A Partial List of Companies that benefit from the CHIPS and Science Act

Intel

In March 2021, Intel Corp announced a $20 billion investment to build two new factories in Arizona, creating 3,000 permanent jobs. Intel's new strategy aims to shift technological power back to the US and Europe due to concerns about chip-making concentration in Taiwan amid tensions with China. Intel is one of the few semiconductor companies that designs and manufactures its chips. The new factories will focus on cutting-edge computing chip manufacturing. Intel also announced a new collaboration with IBM and plans to use Taiwan Semiconductor Manufacturing Company and Samsung as suppliers to make some chips more cost-effective (Ref 21).

In March 2024, the US Department of Commerce proposed up to $8.5 billion in direct funding to advance Intel's commercial semiconductor projects in Arizona, New Mexico, Ohio, and Oregon. Intel also expects to benefit from a US Treasury Department Investment Tax Credit (ITC) of up to 25% on more than $100 billion in qualified investments and eligibility for federal loans up to $11 billion. The proposed funding supports Intel's plan to invest over $100 billion in the US over the next five years. Intel's investments are expected to result in more than 10,000 company jobs and nearly 20,000 construction jobs across Intel's facilities in Arizona, Ohio, New Mexico, and Oregon (Ref 26).

Micron Technology

In 2021, Micron Technology, Inc., the only US-based chip memory manufacturer and one of the world's largest semiconductor manufacturers, announced its intention to invest more than $150 billion globally over the next decade in leading-edge memory manufacturing and research and development (R&D). Micron has a global manufacturing and R&D network that spans 13 countries. The company has accumulated over 47,000 patents in 40 years and invests billions of dollars annually in research and development (R&D). The majority of this investment takes place in the US, where Micron operates one of the world's most advanced R&D centers at its headquarters in Boise, ID.

In April 2024, the Department of Commerce reached a preliminary agreement with Micron to provide up to $6.14 billion in direct funding. This investment will support the construction of two manufacturing plants in Clay, New York, and one in Boise, Idaho. Micron's total investment will be the most significant private investment in the history of New York and Idaho. It will create 20,000 direct construction and manufacturing jobs (Ref 27).

Samsung Electronics

In April 2024, the US Department of Commerce announced a preliminary agreement to provide up to $6.4 billion in funding to Samsung Electronics. Samsung plans to invest over $40 billion in semiconductor factories in the US and claim a 25% tax credit. This investment is expected to create over 17,000 construction jobs and more than 4,500 manufacturing jobs in Central Texas within the next five years. Samsung plans to build two new leading-edge logic fabs, an R&D fab, and an advanced packaging facility in Taylor. The company will also expand its existing Austin facility (Ref 30).

Taiwan Semiconductor Manufacturing Company

Established in 1987, the Taiwan Semiconductor Manufacturing Company (TSMC) has facilities located across Asia, Europe, and North America. TSMC's semiconductors power over 12,000 electronic products from 500 companies, including home appliances, smartphones, PCs, electric vehicles, autonomous vehicles, cloud data centers, airlines, space stations, and artificial intelligence applications.

In May 2020, TSMC announced a $12 billion investment in Phoenix, Arizona, for an advanced semiconductor manufacturing facility. In December 2022, the company committed to a second fab, increasing the investment to $40 billion. In April 2024, the US Department of Commerce announced up to $6.6 billion in direct funding to TSMC. TSMC also plans to build a third fab in Arizona, bringing its total US investment to over $65 billion, creating about 6,000 jobs (Ref 34).

GlobalFoundries

GlobalFoundries (GF) is a multinational semiconductor contract manufacturing and design company headquartered in Malta, New York. GF plans to invest over $12 billion across its US sites in the next 10 years through public-private partnerships. GF is a critical supplier of AMD's high-performance computing products.

In February 2024, the Department of Commerce announced $1.5 billion in direct funding for GlobalFoundries (GF) to help the company expand its manufacturing capacity to meet the increasing demand for semiconductor chips in the US auto industry. A new fabrication plant is being constructed on the Malta campus to triple its capacity and increase wafer production to 1 million per year. Additionally, GF is upgrading its facility in Burlington, Vermont, to produce next-generation gallium nitride (GaN) semiconductors for various critical technologies. The project will create 1500 manufacturing jobs and approximately 9,000 construction jobs (Ref 29).

Microchip Technology Incorporated

Microchip Technology Incorporated provides innovative, secure embedded control solutions and development tools for various markets. Headquartered in Chandler, Arizona, the company serves approximately 125,000 customers across the industrial, automotive, consumer, aerospace and defense, communications, and computing markets.

In January 2024, the US Department of Commerce and Microchip Technology Inc. reached a non-binding agreement to provide approximately $162 million in federal incentives. This aims to support the on-shoring of the company's semiconductor supply chain, increase US production of microcontroller units (MCUs), and create over 700 direct construction and manufacturing jobs (Ref 31).

BAE Systems

In December 2023, the US Department of Commerce announced a $35 million investment in BAE Systems. The investment aims to support the modernization of the company's Microelectronics Center in Nashua, New Hampshire. The project aims to replace aging tools and quadruple the chip production necessary for critical defense programs, including the F-35 fighter jet program. Microelectronics are at the heart of the technology for next-generation aircraft, satellites, military-grade GPS, and secure communications (Ref 35).

Polar Semiconductor

Polar Semiconductor (Polar) is the only US-based manufacturer specializing in sensor, power, and high-voltage semiconductors. The company's technology plays a critical role in high-voltage applications across the aerospace, automotive, and defense sectors. In May 2024, Polar announced a historic $525 million investment in Minnesota. The US Department of Commerce reached a preliminary agreement to provide Polar with up to $120 million in federal incentives. Polar also received $75 million from Minnesota and plans to claim a 25% tax credit. The funding would help Polar expand its manufacturing facility in Bloomington, Minnesota, doubling its US production capacity of sensor and power chips within two years. The investment will create over 160 jobs (Refs 37 and 38).

Absolics

In May 2024, the US Department of Commerce announced a non-binding agreement with Absolics, an affiliate of the South Korea SK group, to provide $75 million in direct funding. Absolics will spend more than $300 million on the first phase. The investment will aid the construction of a 120,000-square-foot facility in Covington, Georgia, to develop substrate technology for use in advanced semiconductor packaging. Absolics glass substrates are being utilized as a crucial advanced packaging technology to enhance the performance of cutting-edge chips for AI, high-performance computing, and data centers. The investment will create over 1,000 construction jobs and 200 manufacturing and R&D jobs in Covington (Refs 39 and 43).

Hewlett Packard (HP)

In August 2024, the US Department of Commerce and Hewlett Packard (HP) Inc. signed a non-binding agreement to provide up to $50 million in proposed direct funding under the CHIPS and Science Act. The proposed funding would support the expansion and modernization of HP's existing facility in Corvallis, Oregon. This facility is part of the company's "lab-to-fab" ecosystem in the region, which includes research and development (R&D) activities and commercial manufacturing operations. The proposed project will capitalize on the company's 47-year presence in Corvallis and its commitment to the local workforce. Specifically, the project is expected to generate nearly 150 construction jobs and over 100 manufacturing jobs (Ref 45).

Texas Instruments (TI)

Texas Instruments (TI) was established in Dallas in 1930 and has additional locations in Richardson, Sherman, and Houston. Ranked 210th on the list of Fortune 500 companies, TI is one of the largest employers and the only semiconductor company headquartered in

Texas. TI is a global leader in analog and embedded processing semiconductors. The company has been a significant player in the U.S. economy for almost a century. TI's invention of the integrated circuit has laid the technological foundation for the modern electronics and semiconductor industries. Today, TI specializes in current-generation and mature-node chips, also known as "foundational" chips. These chips are the building blocks for nearly all electronic systems, including power management integrated circuits, microcontrollers, amplifiers, sensors, and more.

In November 2021, Texas Instruments announced a $30 billion investment to construct up to four new 300-millimeter semiconductor wafer fabrication plants in Sherman, Texas, increasing its manufacturing capacity. These plants will be capable of producing over 100 million chips daily, which will be used in various electronic devices. Production from the first fab is expected to begin in 2025. The company will create up to 3,000 jobs (Ref 36).

In August 2024, the Department of Commerce and Texas Instruments (TI) signed a non-binding preliminary memorandum of terms (PMT) to provide up to $1.6 billion. The proposed funding would support TI's investment of more than $18 billion within 10 years to construct three new state-of-the-art facilities, including two in Texas and one in Utah (Ref 44).

SK Hynix

In August 2024, the US Department of Commerce and SK Hynix signed a non-binding preliminary memorandum of terms (PMT) to provide up to $450 million in proposed federal incentives under the CHIPS and Science Act. The incentives aim to establish a high-bandwidth memory (HBM) advanced packaging fabrication and research and development (R&D) facility.

In April 2024, SK Hynix, Inc., a South Korean company that supplies chips to Nvidia, announced its plan to invest more than $3.87 billion to establish a 430,000-square-foot facility on 90 acres at the Purdue Research Park in West Lafayette, Indiana. The new facility will mass produce next-generation High Bandwidth Memory (HBM), the highest-performing Dynamic Random Access Memory (DRAM) chips. These chips are critical components of Graphic Processing Units (GPUs) that train Artificial Intelligence (AI) systems. The facility will also develop chips for future generations.

The Indiana Economic Development Corporation (IEDC) has committed to invest $3 million in incentive-based training grants, $3 million in Manufacturing Readiness Grants, and $80 million in conditional structured performance payments. Additionally, the IEDC has offered up to $554.7 million of Innovation Development District tax rebates. The IEDC has also pledged up to $45 million through the Industrial Development Grant Fund to support infrastructure improvements around the new plant. The project will create 2,100 new high-skilled jobs in Indiana (Refs 32 and 33).

Hemlock Semiconductor

In January 2025, the US Department of Commerce announced up to $325 million in CHIPS Act funding for Hemlock Semiconductor, the only U.S.-owned producer of hyper-pure polysilicon essential for advanced semiconductors. The award supports construction of a new facility in Hemlock, Michigan, expected to create about 180 manufacturing jobs and more than 1,000 construction jobs. Funds will be distributed as project milestones are met. Officials said the investment strengthens U.S. supply chain security, supports leading-edge chip production, and reinforces Michigan's manufacturing role. The award follows prior agreements and federal due diligence (Ref 48).

13. US Policy Key Takeaway

The United States has placed several measures to prevent China from acquiring advanced AI computing and supercomputing facilities. This includes blocking China from purchasing the best American-made AI chips and the best chip design software to design high-end chips. Additionally, US chip manufacturing facilities worldwide have been prohibited from accepting Chinese chip design firms building high-end chips as customers. Finally, the US has also restricted China from purchasing the necessary equipment for its advanced chip manufacturing facilities, much of which is American-made and irreplaceable.

CHAPTER 10

TRADE WARS AND FOOD FLOWS: TWO DECADES OF GLOBAL ECONOMIC DYNAMICS

———〰———

This chapter delves deeply into the intricate dynamics of global power play, where Chinese investments intersect with regulatory landscapes and ownership structures. It decisively illuminates the complex interplay between economic interests and regulatory frameworks by analyzing the blocking of Chinese acquisitions and the imposition of stringent European regulations. With a sharp spotlight on Chinese investments in Europe and America, you gain assertive insight into the strategic maneuvers shaping geopolitical landscapes. The exploration of Chinese real estate investments and ownership boldly underscores the evolving contours of global economic influence. Navigating these complex dynamics gives you a profound appreciation for the intricate power structures that shape the global economy.

1. US-China Trade Relations

The 2024 congressional report (Ref 13) strongly emphasized the trade relationship with China and raised serious concerns about the country. China is the second-largest global economy and has been a top US and international trading partner since joining the World Trade Organization in 2001. It holds enormous importance as an export market for US aircraft, agriculture, semiconductor equipment and chips, gas turbines, and medical devices. It is a crucial source of some US consumer goods and intermediates (e.g., active pharmaceutical ingredients and auto parts).

China's system integrates state and corporate interests, enabling the government to manipulate trade tools such as anti-dumping, antitrust, technical standards, and procurement, engage in economic coercion, and perpetrate China's intellectual property (IP) theft to favor its firms and economic development goals. Chinese government policies have often mandated firms to transfer technology and capabilities to operate in strategic sectors. US companies have faced a lack of reciprocity, trade barriers, and expanding Chinese state involvement in commercial activity, as well as stringent economic security and data rules. In February 2024, the American Chamber of Commerce stated that 57% of its firms lack confidence in the Chinese market opening.

The US government has expanded its focus on strategic competition with China to address practices that challenge US economic leadership. Congress is currently deliberating on using US authorities to confront these issues. In 2023, a Select Committee on the Strategic Competition between the United States and the Chinese Communist Party was established, representing a solid bipartisan effort to develop options for dealing with the China challenge.

Trade

In 2023, the United States traded $575 billion worth of goods with China, making China its fourth-largest trading partner. The US sold $147.8 billion of goods to China while importing $427.2 billion. Compared to 2022, the total trade decreased by 17%, with US exports falling by 5.1% and imports falling by 20.4%. This was due to China's economic slowdown and shifts in the global supply chain. The top exports from the United States to China include travel services, technology and intellectual property (IP) licensing, and transportation.

Investment

In December 2023, US investors held $322 billion in long-term securities in mainland China and Hong Kong, a 13.4% decrease from 2022. During the same period, mainland China and Hong Kong's holdings of US securities increased to $1.87 trillion. They became the second-largest foreign holder of US Treasuries, with $1.05 trillion, following Japan. It is important to note that this figure does not include offshore holdings.

Unfair Terms of Trade

The Chinese government wields significant control over the purchasing, financing, and pricing of important US exports to China, such as aircraft, semiconductors, medical equipment, agriculture, and energy. It actively aims to strengthen this control and reduce dependence on US imports by diversifying trade and implementing industrial policies that take advantage of US commercial ties to enhance China's capabilities. While some US companies may initially benefit from China's demand for foreign products, services, and expertise, Chinese government policies are designed to replace foreign companies once domestic capabilities are developed. Additionally, the government offers funding to specific Chinese companies and supports the acquisition of foreign firms through preferential lending and state-funded venture capital (Ref 13).

Aerospace: To meet China's terms, some US firms have partnered with and transferred advanced US technology to Chinese state-owned firms to jointly develop a Chinese aircraft (C-919).

Semiconductors: The Chinese government funds imports of US equipment to support China's semiconductor industry.

Electric vehicles (EV): Some Chinese government policies require firms to localize supply chains for EV batteries.

Medical devices and pharmaceuticals: China procurement rules set fixed prices, increasing cost pressures and encouraging firms in these sectors to produce in China.

Biotechnology: Some Chinese state firms have acquired foreign firms to enhance China's global position.

Critical mineral: China's dominant global extraction and processing role supports Chinese manufacturing.

Energy: China has increased its purchases of US liquefied natural gas, which is connected to its investments in US export terminals.

Capital markets: China seeks US financial investment in some strategic sectors in which it restricts US competition.

2. Two Decades of US Trade Deficit with China

Since China joined the World Trade Organization in 2001, the United States and the European Union have had rising trade deficits with China. In 2019, China was the Largest Exporter in the world. In 2019, China's GDP was about $14.1 trillion, and its population was 1.4 billion.

US TRADE DEFICIT WITH CHINA

USD BILLION

Year	Value
2000	84
2001	83
2002	103
2003	124
2004	162
2005	202
2006	234
2007	256
2008	268
2009	227
2010	273
2011	295
2012	315
2013	317
2014	345
2015	367
2016	347
2017	375
2018	418
2019	344
2020	310
2021	355
2022	367
2023	279

YEAR

Source: US Census

US TRADE WITH CHINA

US Exports to China   US Imports from China

USD BILLION

China Joined WTO in 2001

Trade deficit in 2018 $418 bn

YEAR

Source: US Census

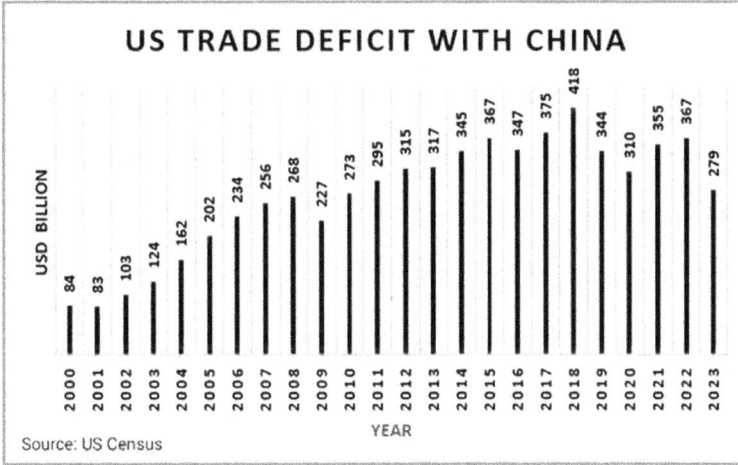

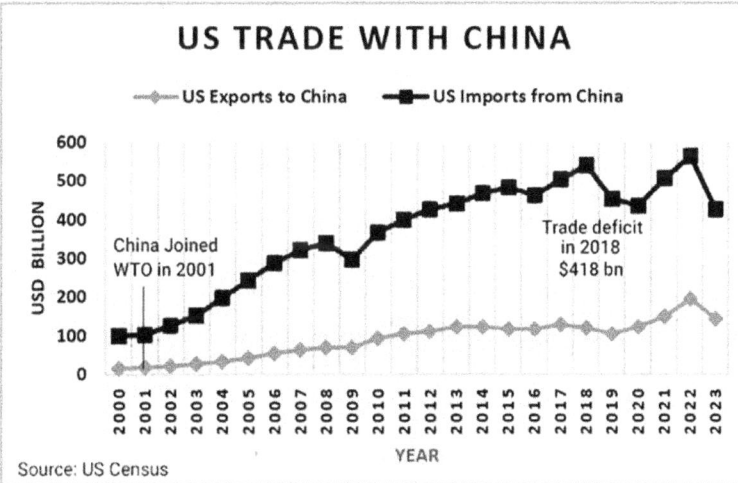

Since joining the World Trade Organization in 2001, the US trade deficit with China increased fivefold by 2018, reaching a peak of $418 billion.

3. Global Food Trade Dynamics and Impact on Agriculture

China: Largest Food Exporter Worldwide

In 2019, China was the world's biggest exporter of frozen fish ($2.9 billion), garlic ($2 billion), tea ($2 billion), apple ($1.2 billion), grape ($987.2 million), fresh ginger ($541.2 million), honey ($235.3 million), and cinnamon ($162.1 million). In terms of total global export market share, China's garlic (71.3%), whole ginger (61.4%), and tea (31.8%) were dominant.

China Ranking in Global Export Top Commodities in 2019

Rank	Product	China Exports	% Global Share
1	Frozen Fish	$2.9 billion	11.6
1	Garlic	$2 billion	71.3
1	Tea	$2 billion	31.8
1	Apple	$1.2 billion	17.8
6	Rice	$1.1 billion	4.8
1	Grape	$987.2 million	11.7
2	Onion	$604.4 million	15.2
1	Ginger (whole)	$541.2 million	61.4
7	Frozen Shrimp (seawater)	$507.3 million	2.9
6	Fresh Chicken	$253 million	3.8
1	Honey	$235.3 million	11.8
1	Cinnamon	162.1 million	23.4
8	Lemon/Lime	$153.2 million	4.6
5	Dried Legume Flour	$117.6 million	4.7
9	Wheat & Meslin Flour	$117.6 million	2.8
7	Frozen Shrimp (freshwater)	$69.1 million	4.2
6	Cucumber	$63 million	2.5
1	Ginger (crushed or ground)	$30.5 million	37.2
10	Tomato	$2.2 million	2.2

Source: www.worldstopexports.com

US Food Imports from China

In 2023, the top food commodities that the United States imported from China were fish and shellfish ($1.5 billion), fruits and juices ($597 million), sauces and processed foods ($536 million), vegetables ($529 million), spices ($166 million), and tea ($99 million). China consistently ranks as one of the top 10 food exporters to the United States, the second-largest tea exporter, and the third-largest exporter of spices. Tilapia and cod, apple juice, mandarin oranges, candy, processed mushrooms, dried garlic, sausage casings, and dry berries were popular imports from China.

Imports of Food Products from China
(In Millions of Dollars)

Products	#	2023	2022	2021	2020	2019
Fish and shellfish	7	1,512.1	1,884.3	1,665.0	1,627.6	1,896.8
Fruits & juices	9	596.9	804.3	608.1	691.8	571.2
Sauces & processed foods	5	536.4	609.9	508.7	470.7	391.7
Vegetables	4	528.8	575.2	503.9	504.7	448.2
Other edible products	2	397.1	472.0	426.6	398.5	361.6
Spices	3	165.8	153.3	152.6	152.2	167.8
Confections	6	134.0	128.2	98.0	77.2	109.5
Tea and mate	2	99.3	115.9	111.6	107.5	125.2
Nuts	5	71.5	100.2	82.5	86.2	106.0
Fowl and other meats	4	8.9	7.2	7.7	7.6	9.1
Bird eggs	4	8.1	6.8	6.0	7.5	6.9

Source: USDA, April 10, 2024

China Is the Largest Agricultural Importer

China is projected to have one of the fastest economic growth rates in the world. The country expects to add 189 million middle-class households in the coming decade, which means rising demand for meat, dairy, and other food and beverages.

China is now the world's largest agricultural importer, surpassing the European Union (EU) and the United States, with $133.1 billion in imports in 2019. As incomes rose, the average Chinese diet changed to include more meat, dairy, and processed foods, while grain consumption declined. Over 80% of China's imports from the EU are consumer-oriented products, led by dairy and pork. Other top suppliers include Australia and New Zealand, both free trade agreement partners with China.

Between 2000 and 2019, per capita consumption of poultry meat increased by 32%, soybean oil consumption more than quadrupled, and fluid milk intake more than tripled. However, domestic feed supplies have been unable to keep up with soaring demand, and imports of soybeans and other feed ingredients have expanded rapidly. Imports of consumer-oriented products continued expanding, led by meat, dairy, and horticultural products.

Pork: More recently, African Swine Fever has disrupted China's pork supply, leading to price increases in all types of animal proteins. China is the world's largest pork market, with imports totaling $6.4 billion in 2019. The EU and the United States are the top suppliers, with a market share of 63% and 16% in trade value, respectively. Brazil quickly rose as the third largest pork supplier, with a 9% market share.

Beef: Beef and beef product imports have grown exponentially since 2012, with an annual trend of 48%. China became the largest beef market in 2019, with imports at $8.4 billion. The top suppliers are Brazil, Australia, and Argentina, with market shares of 25%, 21%, and 21%, respectively.

Dairy: The EU and New Zealand are China's top dairy suppliers. The EU dominates China's infant formula market, with an overall dairy market share of 45%. New Zealand has expanded sales under its free trade agreement with China and now enjoys a 40% market share.

Fresh Fruits: China is the world's third-largest fresh fruit importer, with imports valued at $8.6 billion in 2019. Durians, cherries, and bananas account for nearly half of all fresh fruit imports. Thailand, Chile, and Vietnam are the largest suppliers.

Nuts: China's tree nut imports have grown by 26% annually since 2001, reaching $2.8 billion in 2019. The United States is the largest nut supplier, with a market share of 30%, followed by Australia (14%) and Vietnam (12%). US tree nut exports to China have expanded by over 300% since 2010, with pistachios and almonds leading the growth.

Soybean: The United States used to be China's most significant agricultural supplier, but Brazil and the EU overtook it. About 85% of Brazil's exports to China consist of soybeans. Feed ingredients destined for the livestock and poultry industries are the major US exports to China. On average, soybeans have accounted for over 50% of US agricultural shipments there since 2001. In 2013, Brazil surpassed the United States as the largest soybean supplier to China.

Processed Food: US processed food exports nearly quadrupled as Chinese consumers have grown in appetite for frozen dinners, pastry products, and soup (Ref 4).

American Meat Producers Export to China: In 2019, Tyson Foods, the largest US meat producer, was approved to export American poultry to China. China banned US poultry and eggs in 2015 over a US avian flu outbreak, closing a market that bought $500 million worth of American poultry products. US meat companies have faced a disadvantage in pork exports to China because China imposed tariffs of up to 72% on American pork as part of the countries' trade war. Tyson expects China to import more US pork and poultry to compensate for African swine fever's toll. China is an essential market for chicken parts that many US consumers do not eat, such as chicken feet and organs (Ref 6).

China Banned Ractopamine Growth Hormone: Due to safety concerns, about 160 nations, including all countries in the European Union, Russia, and China, have banned or restricted the use of ractopamine drugs during pig production. However, the US pork industry had been feeding it to an estimated 60% to 80% of American pigs to boost growth rates rapidly. Ractopamine is a feed ingredient used to promote leanness in pork and beef. The use of ractopamine was controversial as studies pointed to harmful health effects. In 2009, the European Food Safety Authority investigated ractopamine and concluded that there was not enough data to show that it is safe for human consumption. Therefore, the EU bans the drug. The US Food and Drug Administration (FDA) approved Ractopamine for use on pigs after just one human health study. The FDA required drug manufacturers to add this warning label: "Ractopamine may increase the number of injured and fatigued pigs. Not for use in breeding swine."

In 2020, Hormel Foods Corp. announced that it has joined other US pork producers in eliminating ractopamine in its supply chain. Many companies, including JBS USA and Tyson, have followed Hormel to remove ractopamine to export to China since the Chinese government banned the drug. China continues to buy pork from the US since the African Swine Fever decimated the Chinese pork supply. Smithfield Foods started phasing out ractopamine in 2013 after being acquired by the Chinese (Ref 7).

4. China Is Among the World's Largest Traders

According to data from Eurostat (Statistical Office of the European Union), in 2022, China (€3,413 billion, 17.6%) was the largest exporter in the world, followed by the EU (€2,572 billion, 13.2%), the United States (€1,960 billion, 10.1%), and Japan (€709 billion, 3.6%).

In 2022, China (€2,579 billion, 12.7%) was the third largest importer in the world, preceded by the United States (€3,206 billion, 15.8%) and the EU (€3,007 billion, 14.8%) (Ref 14).

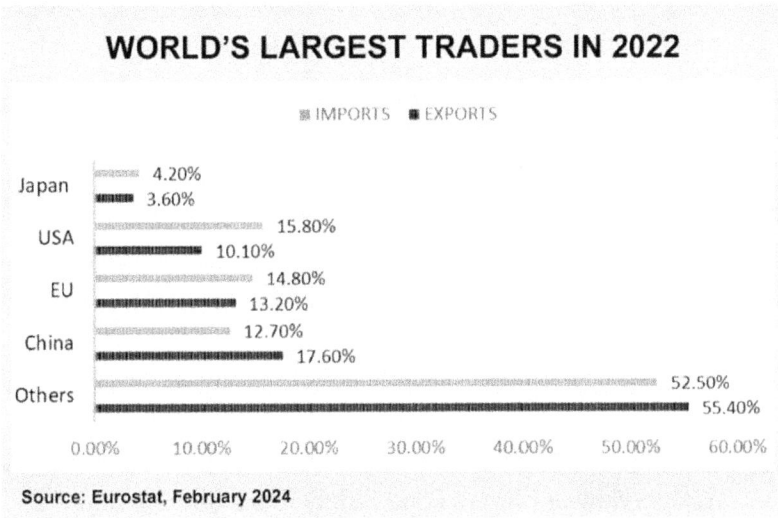

WORLD'S LARGEST TRADERS IN 2022

▨ IMPORTS ■ EXPORTS

Japan	4.20% / 3.60%
USA	15.80% / 10.10%
EU	14.80% / 13.20%
China	12.70% / 17.60%
Others	52.50% / 55.40%

0.00% 10.00% 20.00% 30.00% 40.00% 50.00% 60.00%

Source: Eurostat, February 2024

CHAPTER 11

CHINA'S ENVIRONMENTAL CRISIS: HIDDEN DANGERS OF FOOD SAFETY & POLLUTION

—ᗯᗯ—

The chapter unequivocally presents the dangerous landscape that defines China's food supply chain, issuing a stark warning for consumers worldwide. It provides a robust overview of food safety risks and pervasive pollution, exposing the harsh realities of compromised agricultural practices and environmental degradation. The chapter underscores the profound impact of dwindling arable land, soil contamination, and water pollution on the safety and integrity of food produced in China. Additionally, it unveils the rampant over-usage of chemicals and the inherent risks of widespread food processing practices, underscoring the urgent need for heightened awareness and consumer vigilance. Armed with this knowledge, you are empowered to make informed choices and advocate for stricter food safety standards to safeguard public health and well-being.

1. Overview of China's Food Safety Risks and Pollution

The leading causes of China's food safety issues are linked to the country's rapid industrialization and modernization. Water scarcity, overuse of pesticides, and chemical pollutants are the main factors affecting food safety. The growth of the industry has led to increased pollution of soil and water from emissions and waste. About 20 percent of agricultural soil in China contains excessive levels of heavy metals, which has undermined the foundation of the country's food safety. Many of China's farms and food processors are located in heavily industrialized regions, where factories and car emissions pollute water, air, and soil.

Currently, Chinese food safety is not integrated with policies for managing soil and water pollution. The growing harmful effects of water and soil pollution on food safety pose a health risk to humans. For example, soil and water contamination with the heavy metal cadmium can lead to its presence in agricultural products. This toxic metal poses a range of health risks to consumers, from renal failure to an increased risk of cancer.

Primary food processing facilities tend to generate high levels of pollution, leading to higher occurrences of cancer in nearby population clusters. Lung cancer is the most common disease in China for both males and females, and the mortality rate is 1.5 times higher in China than in Japan and South Korea (Refs 1, 2, 9, 13, and 14).

2. China's Most Polluted Cities and Impact on the Global Environment

In 2019, a staggering 48 of China's 400 cities were ranked among the top 100 most polluted cities worldwide, with only 2% meeting the standards for good air quality, according to Greenpeace. Despite the remarkable reductions in pollution achieved in numerous significant cities, China still struggles with the world's most severe air pollution problem. The predominant sources of outdoor air pollution in China include coal smoke, suspended particulate matter (PM), and sulfur dioxide (SO2). Diesel emissions from transportation also play a significant role. Coal continues to account for about 75% of China's energy sources, with the country consuming approximately half of the world's coal and plans to expand new coal power plants further. It is clear that air pollution in China poses a significant threat to public health, and urgent action is needed to address this pressing issue.

California Got Pollution from China

China's smog is notorious and is ten or more times greater than the World Health Organization's maximum safety level (Ref 3). According to the University of California (Irvine), pollution from China is carried across the Pacific Ocean and contributes to air pollution in the Western United States. Powerful global winds called Westerlies can carry airborne pollutants from China across the Pacific within days, especially during the spring. Black carbon is a particular problem because rain does not wash it out of the atmosphere. Therefore, it persists across long distances. Black carbon is linked to asthma, cancer, emphysema, and heart and lung disease.

Los Angeles experiences at least one extra day a year of unhealthy smog because of pollution emitted by Chinese factories. On other days, as much as 25% of pollution on the US West Coast can be attributed to Chinese pollution. Dust, ozone, and carbon can accumulate in valleys and basins in California and other Western states. The United States is producing less air pollution, but smog levels are still rising in the Western states because of pollutants released in Asian countries drifting over the Pacific Ocean (Ref 17).

In 2017, the National Oceanic and Atmospheric Administration and the Environmental Protection Agency (EPA) conducted a comprehensive ozone study. They concluded that the increasing artificial emissions in Asia were the primary driver of increased ozone levels in the western United States for both spring and early summer. Rapid economic growth has led to a tripling of ozone emissions from Asia in the past 25 years. High levels of ground-level ozone can be harmful to people, animals, and crops. Ozone air pollution can aggravate asthma and can inflame and damage cells that line the lungs. (Ref 18).

3. Impact of Lack of Arable Land and Clean Water

Lack of Arable Land

In 2013, the *New York Times* quoted:

> Vice Minister of Land and Resources Wang Shiyuan said that eight million acres of China's farmland, equal to the size of Maryland, had become so polluted that planting crops on it should not be allowed. More than 13 million tons of crops harvested each year were contaminated with heavy metals, and 22 million acres of farmland were affected by pesticides (Ref 14).

China has only 8% of the world's arable land, but it has more than 20% of the global population. Surprisingly, only 40% of its arable land meets the high-quality standards required for crop production. The country is currently dealing with severe soil pollution, mainly due to rapid industrialization and lax regulations. China's chemical and fertilizer industries have been poorly regulated. Alarmingly, about one-fifth of China's factories are located near critical agricultural areas or rivers used for irrigation, leading to chemical spills onto agricultural land. The Chinese government has publicly acknowledged that around 20% of cultivated land in China exceeds pollution standards for heavy metals or inorganic substances.

In 2012, the Hunan province, a major rice producer, also emerged as a significant environmental concern. It produced a massive 17 million tons of rice, accounting for 16% of the national total. The province, known for its nonferrous metals, has a notorious reputation as the leading polluter of cadmium, chromium, lead, and arsenic. Shockingly, data from 2011 collected by the Institute of Public and Environmental Affairs reveals that Hunan is responsible for a staggering 41% of the nation's cadmium pollution through industrial wastewater. This alarming figure has stubbornly remained above 30% since 2004. Studies have linked cadmium to organ failure, bone weakening, and cancer. The approval of around $10 billion worth of 80 new projects in 2015, including lead-acid car battery manufacturers, with a commitment to increase the industry's revenue by a substantial 18% annually, adds to the urgency of the situation. This irresponsible pursuit directly contributes to the cadmium contamination affecting the province's water and soil (Refs 2, 5, 6, 7, 8, 10, and 14).

Lack of Clean Water

In 2009, the World Bank reported that China was facing a severe water scarcity crisis due to high water demands, limited water supply, and deteriorating water quality due to widespread pollution. Greenpeace's 2015 report revealed that 85% of water in major Chinese city rivers was undrinkable, with an additional 56.4% considered unsuitable for any purpose. In addition, a survey by the Chinese Ministry of Water Resources concluded that 80% of groundwater in the mainland's major river basins is unsafe for human contact (Refs 11 and 12).

The severe water crisis is primarily caused by the failure of local governments to control polluting industries and regulate the disposal of chemical waste. There is also a lack of effective monitoring systems to track the transportation of hazardous materials. Additionally, China's inadequate standards for sewage treatment have led to widespread pollution from wastewater in both residential and commercial areas, especially in densely populated urban areas. Most waste sludge ends up in lakes and rivers and eventually contaminates fields. A study by the Chinese Center for Disease Control and Pollution in 2013 found a direct link between pollution in the Huai River and high cancer rates among people living nearby. This underscores the need for the Chinese government to take more decisive action. Even after a 2015 directive from China's Ministry of Environment requiring provinces to meet water quality targets, almost half of the country failed to do so within the specified timeframe (Refs 6, 12, and 14).

In 2017, the Economist reported a disturbing trend: a growing shortage of fresh water in China leading to a significant increase in the use of wastewater and industrial sewage for irrigation. China produces over 60 billion metric tons of sewage annually, but only 10% of it is treated in rural areas. The scarcity and poor quality of surface water resources in China have forced a heavy reliance on wastewater irrigation to sustain agricultural production. This, in turn, has led to a massive pollution problem of alarming proportions. Extensive pollution of agricultural land and food is occurring, primarily due to the presence of heavy metals.

A comprehensive study in 2014 found that 39 out of 55 areas using sewage irrigation were contaminated with cadmium, arsenic, and other dangerous substances. The significant increase in heavy metal accumulation in intensely irrigated regions has been well-documented (Ref 6). Furthermore, pollution from human and animal waste exacerbates water quality issues, especially in areas lacking sewage systems. Standard practices such as allowing free-roaming livestock and poultry and using waste in fish hatcheries as fishmeal only worsen these concerns.

4. Overuse of Chemicals and Food Processing Risks

Overuse of Chemicals

In the 1950s, the Chinese government led the Green Revolution to boost agricultural productivity and ensure national food security. However, within a decade, the soil became degraded, water was polluted, and agrochemical residues were found in fresh food, setting the stage for long-term consequences. China's status as the largest pesticide producer means that over 200 million farmers use about half a million tons of pesticide, 60 million tons of fertilizer, and 2.5 million tons of agricultural plastic film annually. The presence of toxic residues in food is a direct result of using chemicals and veterinary drugs to achieve high yields. It is concerning to note that banned toxic agricultural chemicals are still easily accessible through underground vendors. This situation poses a severe threat as even if chemicals are not used on a specific piece of land, nearby chemicals and pollution may still spread.

Processed Food Industry Boom

In the early stages of China's economic reform, 82% of the population lived in rural areas and mostly consumed homemade and minimally processed foods. However, over the past three decades, the rural population has decreased sharply to around 40%. As a result, there has been a significant change in dietary habits, with an increased consumption of processed foods and the rise of food processing companies. In 2017, China's food processing industry saw substantial growth, with revenues reaching $1.47 trillion, marking a 6.3% increase from the previous year. It is worth noting that traditional snacks like instant noodles and beverages are mainly popular among rural and older consumers. In contrast, urban, affluent, and younger consumers show a strong interest in new products, imported ingredients, as well as healthier snacks and beverages (Ref 15). The rapid transformation of China's food industry, characterized by extensive food processing, introduces increased susceptibility to food fraud or adulteration, primarily motivated by profit. This transformation amplifies vulnerabilities for contamination across various stages of the food production process. However, the leading causes of foodborne diseases in China are the lack of clean water and inadequate sanitation during food preparation (Ref 2).

Food Safety Risks in China

Food poisoning in China is primarily caused by pathogenic microorganisms, toxic animals, and plants that enter the food supply, as well as chemical contamination. There are also serious concerns about illegal additives and toxic industrial waste contaminating the food supply. Although the Chinese Government has expressed a strong commitment to reforming laws, establishing monitoring systems, and strengthening food safety regulations, the weak implementation of these laws remains a significant issue (Ref 2).

According to a comprehensive report by the United States Department of Agriculture (USDA), many safety risks associated with foods imported from China stem from the manufacturing and handling processes. Poor handling and storage can introduce bacteria, viruses, parasites, fungi, and their toxins. Perishable vegetables and meat are traditionally sold by small vendors who typically transport them in small open trucks. Refrigerated storage and transport equipment are relatively scarce. When temperature-controlled infrastructure is available, power outages or inadequate temperature may lead to spoilage. Awareness of foodborne illness risks is relatively low in China. Many food processors use unsafe additives, toxic dyes, or fake ingredients to preserve food, cut production costs, or improve product appearance.

China has about 200 million farming households with average land holdings of 1-2 acres per farm and at least 400,000 small food processing enterprises, most with ten or fewer employees. In China's food sector, farmers and entrepreneurs frequently enter new industries, and worker turnover is high. As a result, many participants in food supply chains are unaware of standards and proper practices. Some producers and merchants cut corners, add toxic substances, or skimp on safety controls to increase profit margins or gain another competitive edge (Ref 4).

5. Poor Understanding of Food Safety and Consumer Risks

In the past several years, the Chinese government has developed stricter food safety laws and regulations at the state level; however, implementation is still weak. Food safety incidents still occur because of a poor understanding of food safety and its implications. Violations include abuse of food additives, adulterated products, contamination by pathogenic microorganisms, pesticides, veterinary drugs, and heavy metals residues (Ref 5). Only about 10% of enterprises are certified for Hazard Analysis Critical Control Point (HACCP), a universal system used in several food industries worldwide to monitor food safety. Since the 1990s, food safety regulations have evolved worldwide, and food producers are more responsible for monitoring the safety of their products (Ref 5). Finally, Chinese food inspectors do not have sufficient training on food safety regulations and utilize conflicting inspection standards as opposed to one uniform system. These problems are particularly acute in less developed provinces, which often lack the tools to inspect all food products (Ref 16).

CHAPTER 12

UNMASKING CHINA'S FOOD DYSTOPIA: THE QUEST FOR ORGANIC FOOD

—⟋⟍—

This chapter boldly illuminates the stark realities of China's food situation. It underscores the significant challenge of avoiding food products from China amid alarming reports. Additionally, it delves into China's determined pursuit of food sources abroad, prompting you to carefully consider the ethical and environmental implications in a time of escalating global demand and dwindling resources.

1. Impossible to Avoid Food from China

The United States requires a country of origin label on most food. However, with most processed food, companies are not obligated to label where ingredients come from, only where the food was packaged or processed. Unfortunately, the FDA only inspects less than 2% of incoming goods. Experts say that it is nearly impossible to avoid ingredients from China. You can lower your chances of eating foods with Chinese ingredients by staying away from all processed foods and eating fresh whole foods, such as fruits and vegetables.

2. Dangerous Foods

China indisputably holds the title of the world's most polluted country, with its environment suffering immense degradation. The chemical and steel industries are undeniably contributing to this environmental catastrophe. China's prioritization of profit over environmental protection is both reckless and unacceptable. Water pollution in China poses a significant threat to food safety due to its use in crop irrigation and fish farming. Moreover, China's status as one of the largest pesticide producers, consumers, and exporters involves the overuse of fertilizers and pesticides, resulting in cancer-causing residues. Many farmers in China are openly using banned pesticides, while fish farming requires an excessive amount of antibiotics, leaving hazardous residues on seafood.

The pervasive food safety issues in China made headlines with the widespread contamination of global food supplies with melamine-laced products, even infiltrating well-known brands. The appalling incidents involving melamine-tainted infant formula and dog biscuits, which tragically led to the deaths of numerous children and dogs, are utterly incomprehensible.

In 2001, China joined the World Trade Organization (WTO), which eased restrictions on US import barriers and enabled China to trade more freely with the United States. As a result, Chinese imports have been flooding the shelves of American supermarkets. Unfortunately for American consumers, WTO limits the United States from restricting unsafe Chinese imports. This enables food manufacturers to source cheaper food ingredients in China, where food safety regulations are weaker.

China's agricultural practices are raising concerns due to the contamination of soils where crops are grown and the pollution of water where fish are farmed. The Food and Drug Administration (FDA) has faced criticism for inspecting less than 2% of cargo arriving from China despite growing concerns about the safety of food imports. Moreover, the extensive American corporate relationships and investments in China have led to business pressures that prioritize the quick import of potentially hazardous food.

Notably, major American companies, such as Tyson Foods and Keystone Foods, have made substantial investments in China's food industry, risking the import of unsafe food products. The approval of Chinese-cooked chicken import by the USDA in 2013 and the unlabeled arrival of the first known shipment of Chinese-cooked chicken in the United States in 2017 have further raised concerns about food safety. The persistence of food safety risks in China, mainly since the melamine scandal, necessitates urgent attention to address the potential threats posed by environmental contaminants and intentionally added toxic ingredients in cooked poultry products.

3. Desire for Organic Food vs. Reality of Land Acquisition

Desire for Organic Food

The Chinese government is challenged by regulating over 200 million farms and food production companies. The country's economic boom began four decades ago when it moved from a state-owned to a private enterprise system. As a result, over 700 million Chinese have become middle-class, many millionaires or even billionaires.

These wealthy Chinese's diet has become similar to those of Westerners, who consume a lot more meat and dairy products. As a result, the demand for organic and imported food has increased significantly. Middle-class Chinese are now purchasing organic food and imported food online, such as Australian beef and Canadian lobsters. The sales of fresh food on the internet have been booming. China's political elite and champion athletes eat from secret organic farms of a specialized military food supply chain.

Due to China's lengthy history of toxic food supply, a rising number of wealthy Chinese have started farms for their food supply. They do not want food tainted with heavy metals and pesticides. Their farms grow organic fruits, vegetables, and herbs. They also raise chickens, ducks, geese, and fish. Their animals walk freely around the farms. The water used to raise fish is tested for toxic contaminants, and the farm soil is free of heavy metals.

In 2016, Chinese Thai billionaire Chanchai Ruayrungruang started an organic farm near Beijing. The farm consists of 2.5 acres of glass greenhouses that protect crops from pollution. The soil used on the farm is imported from Denmark, and pesticides and fertilizers are strictly banned. The farm produces 5,000 kilograms of food annually for ultra-wealthy golf course members.

Overseas Farmland Acquisition

According to a report by the United Nations Food and Agriculture Organization and the Organisation for Economic Co-operation and Development (OECD), China lost 6.2% of its farmland between 1997 and 2008. Additionally, almost 20% of China's remaining arable land is contaminated, and local governments continue to sell farmland for more profitable real estate development (Ref 16).

China is home to 20% of the world's population but has only 8% of the world's arable land. Consequently, it has sought farmland abroad. The countries selling land are poorer nations in Africa, South America, Southeast Asia, and Eastern Europe. In Africa alone, Chinese corporations grow cabbages in the Democratic Republic of Congo, raise fish in Angola, and harvest sesame seeds, cashews, and peanuts in Mozambique. China ranks as the world's most active country in land trade, purchasing land from 33 countries and selling it to only three (Ref 15).

As Chinese incomes have increased, the average Chinese diet has become more Westernized, leading to higher consumption of meat, dairy, and processed food. This shift in diet has led to an increased demand for overseas food supplies. Additionally, the Chinese government has been leasing or buying agricultural land in developing countries to convert them into farms. While it takes about 1 acre (0.4 hectare) to feed the average US consumer, China only has about 0.2 acres of arable land per citizen, including fields degraded by pollution.

For the past four decades, China's factories have polluted prime agricultural land with chemical waste. Farmers have also been using a large amount of chemical fertilizers and pesticides, making China infamous for tainted food, from cadmium-laced rice to fish raised in toxic water and fed antibiotics. Today, Chinese citizens pay more attention to the origin of their food and are willing to pay more for safety. Therefore, Chinese-owned businesses are looking for overseas investments to turn into premium brands on supermarket shelves in China. Due to the rising standard of living in China, the demand for meat is higher (Ref 16).

CHAPTER 13

BEHIND THE LABEL: UNVEILING THE HISTORY OF HAZARDOUS IMPORTS FROM CHINA

—⟵ℳ⟶—

In this chapter, you will uncover the hidden history of hazardous imports from China, exposing alarming revelations that have significantly shaped global trade dynamics. The chapter sheds light on the profound challenges posed by unsafe imports by scrutinizing critical milestones in food and drug safety incidents and the systemic failures of international regulatory frameworks like the WTO. Furthermore, you gain insight into the exponential growth of imports from China, driven by consumer demand for popular items. Through compelling narratives of food safety scares and the prevalence of contaminated products, the chapter underscores the urgent need for comprehensive reforms to safeguard public health and restore trust in global supply chains.

1. Food and Drug Incidence Milestones and WTO Failure

"The safety of food, feed, and drugs from China is a cause for real concern. We have pet treats that may have sickened and killed many pets across America, a virus that may decimate 10 percent of American pigs, possibly from vitamins or feed from China. We have food products, including processed chicken, that may not have been labeled as being made in China. It may have been labeled as made in America US." Congressman Christopher Smith, Co-chairman, Congressional-Executive Commission on China, 113th Congress Session, June 17, 2014.

Food and Drug Incidence

The texts below highlight crucial milestones related to food safety incidents in China. Despite the Chinese government's regulatory efforts and food safety guidelines, persistent violations and fatal incidents continue to plague the country. Media reports have exposed numerous food safety scandals, including contaminated and counterfeit meat and fish products, adulterated fruit and vegetable products, illicit cooking oils, tainted processed foods, and more. These scandals have also involved pharmaceutical drugs and consumer goods. Furthermore, US inspection records reveal China's repeated export of foods that are unfit for human consumption. Since 2001, China has utilized rock-bottom prices to force competitors out of business, while numerous American corporations remain directly or indirectly involved with Chinese imports (Ref 13).

2001: China entered the World Trade Organization, which enabled China to benefit from lower tariffs and fewer trade restrictions.

2005: The illegal use of carcinogenic red dye Sudan Red I in chicken products in China was a severe violation.

2006: The United States imported $4.1 billion of seafood and agricultural products (up from $800 million in 1995); 78% of unground, dry ginger came from China.

2006: A pharmacist in the United States was convicted of trafficking in counterfeit Viagra and Cialis from China.

2006: Nine people in China died of acute kidney failure from using fake drugs made by a Chinese pharmaceutical company in northeast China's Heilongjiang Province.

2006: Chinese officials found excessive cancer-causing residue in turbo fish, including nitrofuran and chloromycetin (antibacterial drugs).

2007: 90% of vitamin C supplements, 60% of apple juice, 50% of garlic, and 10% of shrimp in the US came from China. Apple juice imports from China totaled 420 million gallons.

2007: After years of warnings, the FDA blocked the sale of five types of farm-raised seafood from China because of repeated contamination from banned animal drugs and food additives. The FDA detained more than 1,000 shipments of tainted Chinese dietary supplements, toxic Chinese cosmetics, and counterfeit Chinese medicines.

2007: Chinese tainted contaminated wheat gluten and rice protein with melamine, causing 17,000 sick pets and about 4,000 dead pets.

2007: Sewage water was used in tofu manufacturing in China.

2007: The head of the Chinese State Food and Drug Administration was executed for taking bribes and failing to police the country's food and drug industries properly. China announced a significant food safety crackdown.

2008: The exports of organic products from China to Europe, the United States, and Japan exceeded $500 million.

2008: Chinese suppliers were blamed for the contamination of heparin in the United States after reports of 91 deaths and at least 785 severe allergic reactions.

2008: A fatal incident involving melamine contamination of baby milk powder caused six deaths and several thousands of sick infants.

2008: Tainted Chinese dumplings with pesticides exported to Japan made many people ill.

2008: Tested ginger revealed harmful levels of aldicarb sulfoxide, a pesticide not approved in the United States and China.

2008: Eggs were contaminated with high levels of melamine, the toxic industrial additive at the heart of an adulteration scandal in Chinese milk products.

2009: The number of USDA-certified organic farms in China climbed to 649.

2009: The United States imported 60% of apple juice, 43% of processed mushrooms, 22% of frozen spinach, and 78% of tilapia from China for US consumption.

2009: The Nigerian government intercepted 600,000 counterfeit antimalarial tablets from China labeled "made in India."

2009: A diabetes drug was pulled after samples showed the medicine, which killed two people in the western region of Xinjiang, was six times more potent than it should have been.

2009: Illegal use of clenbuterol hydrochloride in animal feed in China caused several foodborne illnesses.

2010: Chinese food exports to the United States tripled to nearly $5 billion.

2010: China supplied the United States with 88 million pounds of candy.

2010: Dried soybean and snow peas were dyed with bleach and chemicals to produce the appearance of more expensive peas in Hunan province, China.

2010: The Chinese government found 20,000 pounds of toxic vegetables with excessive pesticide residue in the Guangxi Zhuang region.

2011: US garlic cultivation dropped by 30% due to cheap imports of Chinese garlic. China accounted for 7% of the overall US market of frozen fruits and vegetables and became the fourth largest foreign supplier to the United States.

2011: A factory in Dongguan used fake cooking oil to fry noodles to produce instant noodles. The fake oil came from another factory that mixed cottonseed and flavor-enhanced soybean oil and marketed it as peanut oil. The adulterated oil could harm human reproductive cells.

2011: Chinese officials confiscated over 100 tons of "gutter oil," recycled cooking oil, often scooped up from sewage drains and gutters behind cooking establishments.

2011: A Shuanghui International subsidiary bought pigs fed with a meal containing clenbuterol. The illegal additive keeps the animals lean but can kill people if eaten.

2012: Allegations of maggots, excessive bacteria, and illegal additives have plagued China's biggest meat products company, Shuanghui International.

2013: Shuanghui International purchased Virginia-based Smithfield Foods, the world's largest pork producer, for $4.7 billion.

2014: A US-owned meat factory operating in China sold out-of-date and tainted meat to clients, including McDonald's, Starbucks, KFC, and Pizza Hut chains.

2014: Rice in Hunan province contained heavy metals, including excessive cadmium, which is toxic for human consumption.

2015: China added new provisions to existing food safety laws regarding penalties for food safety violations and imposed stricter rules for surveillance.

2016: The Chinese government uncovered 500,000 domestic food safety violations.

2017: Thirteen people got methanol poisoning after drinking fake whiskey at a Muse Bar in Heyuan, Guangdong province.

2017: Guangzhou factory owners were arrested for fabricating cooking oil made from rotting pig carcasses.

2018: United States food imports from China increased to over $6.6 billion.

2019: Major Chinese frozen food producer Sanquan Food Co Ltd recalled products contaminated with the African swine fever virus.

2018-2019: The FDA recalled a series of blood pressure medications containing carcinogenic impurities from China.

2020: Nine people died in China after consuming homemade corn noodles contaminated with a lethal dose of Bongkrekic acid, a deadly poison that is found in fermented food, including wet noodles and press cake from China, Indonesia, and Mozambique.

2020: The FDA asked five American companies to voluntarily recall a diabetes drug after the agency's testing found higher-than-acceptable levels of a cancer-causing contaminant.

2022: Shuanghui, the pork producer that acquired US-based Smithfield Foods, was found to have unhygienic work practices, such as using food that had fallen on the floor.

2024: A major state-owned food company has been cutting costs by using the same tankers to carry fuel and cooking oil without cleaning them in between.

2024: A Chinese restaurant was filmed spraying cancer-causing paint on BBQ meat skewers.

(Refs 2, 3, 4, 5, 8, 9, 10, 11, 13, 14, 15, 16, 17, 18, 19, 20, 21, 22, 23, 24, 25, 26, 27, 28, 33, 34, 37, 38 and 39)

WTO Failure

The World Trade Organization (WTO) has unequivocally failed US farmers and prompted companies to shift food production to countries like China, with low wages and minimal regulatory standards, endangering consumers worldwide. Being a WTO member enables China to benefit from reduced tariffs, encouraging foreign in China and the inflow of Chinese imports by multinational corporations. However, WTO regulations restrict member countries from implementing health, safety, or environmental standards that could impede global trade. The issue persists despite recent attempts in China to enhance food safety (Ref 5).

2. Booming Imports and Popular Items

Booming Imports

China's role in global agricultural trade has grown significantly. It is now a major supplier of fish and seafood, fruits and vegetables, fruit juices, tea, and processed foods. US imports of agricultural products from China totaled $3.6 billion in 2019, making China the United States' sixth most significant supplier of agricultural imports (Ref 13).

Since China became a member of the World Trade Organization (WTO) in 2001, China's food exports to the United States peaked at $6.6 billion in 2018 (US census data). The number decreased to about $4.5 billion in 2020 due to trade tension and the COVID-19 pandemic. The Chinese food imports compete with American-grown crops and expose consumers to food toxins. Chinese fish, fruit, and vegetable prices are as low as one-tenth of those in the United States. Seafood is the fastest-growing food category exported from China to the United States.

In 2019, China remained the world's largest seafood producer, with production stable at 64.5 million metric tons (MMT). China is also the world's most significant producer of apple juice concentrate and garlic. By 2016, China reached 21 million metric tons of garlic production annually (Refs 2 and 5).

In 2020, the United States imported $4.5 billion worth of food from China. Top imports included seafood ($1.6 billion), fruits and frozen juices ($641 million), and vegetables ($551 million). Other imports were spices and tea ($275 million) and bakery products ($171 million) (Ref www.census.gov).

Finding foods that do not contain an ingredient from China is almost impossible. The quantity of food imported from China has grown dramatically in the past two decades. Chinese imports have been replacing produce from the United States and Central America. In 2019, the United States Food and Drug Administration (FDA) dropped the inspection rate from 2% to less than 1%. This virtually guarantees that unsafe Chinese products enter American grocery stores (Refs 2, 4, and 12).

Popular Imported Items

In 2020, according to the United States Department of Agriculture, total imported foods from various countries accounted for about one-fifth of all foods consumed in the United States. It was an even larger share of seafood, fruit, and vegetable products. China is a significant supplier of apple juice, garlic, canned mandarin oranges, tea, and seafood to the United States. The US imports the following items from China (Ref 4):

a) Tilapia, cod, scallops, shrimp, prawns, crab, salmon, tuna, monkfish, squid, jellyfish, octopus, crawfish, abalone, flounder, catfish, dace (carp family), basa (catfish family), eel, mackerel, anchovy, sole, and other fish.

b) Processed chicken, frog legs, and rabbit.

c) Apple and pear juices and canned fruits (mandarins, pears, and pineapples).

d) Garlic, onion, mushrooms, frozen vegetables (sweet corn, green peas, asparagus, spinach, cauliflower, and broccoli), peppers, Napa cabbage, fresh pear, and other fruits and vegetables.

e) Dried and canned black and kidney beans; dried-salted plums, haw (similar to crab apple), goji berries, wolfberries, pickled radish, bamboo shoots, and water chestnuts.

f) Pine and macadamia nuts; bubble gum, almond cookies, and chocolate; candy and confections; honey, tea, spices, and ginseng.

g) Noodles, pastries, baked goods, soy sauce, and tofu; chili powder/paste and ginger; rice, specialty soybeans, and other foods.

h) Vegetable saps and extracts, cocoa butter, malt extract, wheat gluten, starch, carrageenan, and other food preparations.

i) Sweetened water, beer, ethyl alcohol, and vinegar.

j) Various ingredients used in food processing and miscellaneous food preparations (malt extract, protein concentrates, and wheat gluten), citric acid, xylitol, sorbic acid, artificial vanilla, and vitamins added to food products (folic acid and thiamine).

k) Vitamin C, raw ingredients for health supplements, pharmaceutical and generic drugs.

l) Pet food and snacks and animal feed.

Essential foods that form the core of the US diet (grain, meat, or dairy items) are generally not imported from China (Ref 4).

By 2007, imports from China accounted for about 60% of the US apple juice supply and more than 50% of the garlic supply. Imports from China account for 10% of the US shrimp supply, 2% of the catfish supply, and 8% of the basa (a type of catfish) supply.

Some more recent data from the Alliance for American Manufacturing stated that China is responsible for 90% of vitamin C, 78% of tilapia, 70% of apple juice, 50% of cod, 43% of processed mushrooms, and 23% of garlic consumed by Americans. In short, specific imported food from China may vary from year to year, but overall, Americans consume many Chinese imports (Refs 4 and 29).

Number of Imported Shipments to the United States by Exporting Country/Region

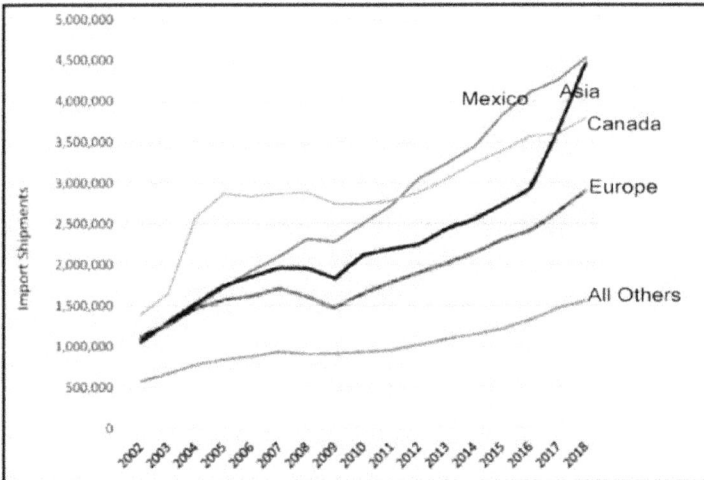

Source: Food & Drug Administration

3. Food Safety Scare and Contaminated Products

Food Safety Scare

Over a decade ago, newspapers published endless articles featuring food scares from Chinese products. In 2011, Fox News reported that 73% of consumer survey respondents were more concerned about their food than ever. A majority said they did not look at the country of origin, especially when the font is tiny and hard to find on the food package. Furthermore, the country of origin does not require multiple ingredients in processed food packages. For example, a granola bar made in the USA could have honey from China.

Unsafe food from China has generated a food scare in the United States and worldwide. Frozen or canned produce, seafood, candy, vitamins, and processed food have increasingly come from China. In China, food manufacturers are known for cutting corners, substituting dangerous ingredients, and compromising safety to boost sales. Despite China's pledge to tighten food safety controls, food scandals remain in the news (Ref 12).

Unsafe Food from China

According to recent data from the Centers for Disease Control and Prevention, about 48 million people in the United States (1 in 7) get sick, 128,000 are hospitalized, and 3,000 die each year from foodborne diseases. China's toxic food supply caught the world's attention. Several highly publicized incidents of food contamination and adulteration in the Chinese domestic food supply and US food imports from China have caused safety concerns (Ref 9).

Between 2001 and 2008, food imports from China to the United States tripled in value. The FDA cites filthy food, unsafe additives, and inadequate labeling for Chinese processed food as the most common problems. Another common problem is potentially harmful veterinary drug residues in farm-raised fish and shrimp (Ref 4).

Since the 1980s, the FDA's import alerts for Chinese products have also included red melon seeds (illegal dyes), bean curd (insect filth), dried mushrooms (filth from animals and insects), fresh garlic (mold, decomposition, and insect filth/damage), and honey (antibiotic fluoroquinolone residues). The FDA also issued import alerts after it detected cancer-causing chemicals and unsafe antibiotic residues in five types of farm-raised fish and shrimp from China. In 2020, the import alert list included candy (lead), fruit juice and fruit juice concentrates (heavy metals), and milk and other food products (melamine) (Refs 5, 7, and 30).

In 2007, the FDA rejection of food shipments from China peaked when the United States encountered widely publicized problems with Chinese imports. Two Chinese companies had illegally exported melamine-tainted wheat gluten and rice protein. Melamine is a chemical used in plastics and fertilizers. The tainted protein was used in pet food, causing 17,000 sick pets and about 4,000 dead pets. Investigations have extended to livestock feed containing melamine, reaching some 6,000 hogs and as many as 3.1 million chickens in the United States (Refs 4 and 5).

In 2008, China's two biggest dairy companies were among those found to have melamine-contaminated products. Six Chinese infants died, and nearly 300,000 children fell ill after consuming melamine-adulterated infant formula. Among the hospitalized babies, 158 were suffering from acute kidney failure. Melamine is an industrial chemical added to raw milk to raise its apparent protein content. The problem spilled over into global markets when Chinese milk and other products (including candy, eggs, and biscuits) containing traces of melamine were found in other countries (Ref 35).

Meanwhile, China had other food safety concerns: toxic dye in chili sauce and other foods; use of industrial bleach to whiten noodles; carcinogenic drugs in fish and shrimp; poisoning from a steroid used in pork production; and the widespread sale of pork from pigs that were sick or had died from illness. Japanese consumers fell sick due to dumplings from China that were poisoned with pesticide residues (Ref 4).

Rice Contaminated with Heavy Metals

Factories, smelters, and mines in Hunan province are located near rice fields. Unfortunately, Hunan is responsible for 41% of China's cadmium pollution in industrial wastewater. Cadmium is commonly found in zinc ores and used in electronic device batteries and coatings. Hunan is also the top rice producer in China, accounting for 17 million tons of rice and 16% of the national total.

Rice absorbs heavy metals from soil and water, and in 2013, the Chinese government found excessive levels of cadmium in 155 batches of rice collected from markets, restaurants, and warehouses. Of these, 89 were from Hunan Province. Researchers for Greenpeace East Asia also sampled soil and rice grown in Hunan province in 2014. They found that it contained cadmium, arsenic, lead, and mercury due to its proximity to smelting and refining industries. In some locations, the soil sampled contained a cadmium level more than 200 times the national health standard. Rice plants absorb heavy metals from soil and water, which are contaminated with these poisons. As a result, researchers found lead, arsenic, and cadmium in the rice they tested. All rice samples (except one) exceeded the maximum level of cadmium in rice for human consumption in China. The Chinese government's report on excessive cadmium levels in Chinese rice is consistent with Greenpeace's findings.

The Chinese government disclosed that one-fifth of China's agricultural land is polluted. Cadmium that accumulates in rice plants gets not only into the rice but also into animals' meat since the husks are fed to farm animals. If too much accumulates in the body, cadmium harms the liver, kidneys, respiratory tract, and bones. It has also been linked to a variety of cancers. Unfortunately, rice is a popular grain for many cultures, from baby food to cereals, and it is a daily diet for the Asian population. Cadmium, arsenic, and lead found in rice, vegetables, and tea from China are toxic and even deadly (Refs 2 and 9).

Cadmium: According to the National Cancer Institute, cadmium is highly toxic and is associated with human lung, prostate, kidney, pancreatic, breast, and bladder cancers. Cadmium accumulates and stays in the body for several decades.

Arsenic: It is linked to cancer, liver disease, diabetes, and nervous system complications, such as loss of sensation in the limbs and hearing problems (Ref 32).

Lead: It is a highly poisonous metal affecting almost every organ in the body. Lead causes severe damage to the brain and kidneys in adults and children. Long-time exposure to lead also causes high blood pressure in old and middle-aged people. The toxicity in children is more severe because their tissues are softer than in adults. Infants and young children are susceptible to even low levels of lead. This contributes to behavioral problems, learning deficits, and lowered IQ (Ref 31).

CHAPTER 14

NAVIGATING THE MAZE: CHINA'S COMPLEX FOOD AND DRUG
SAFETY REGULATIONS

—ɯ—

In this chapter, you embark on a journey through the complexities of China's food and drug safety regulations, gaining invaluable insights into the intricacies of its regulatory landscape. Through a comprehensive exploration of the background and functions of China's regulatory agencies, you gain a nuanced understanding of the institutional framework governing food and drug safety. In deeper investigation, the chapter explains the formidable challenges inherent in monitoring food safety and combating contamination in a vast and diverse market. Moreover, you uncover the regulatory mechanisms employed to oversee small-scale operations and manage pesticide usage, highlighting the government's efforts to uphold safety standards. Finally, the chapter examines the punitive measures imposed for counterfeit drugs, underscoring China's commitment to ensuring the integrity of its pharmaceutical industry.

1. Background and Overview of China's Agencies

Background

The Chinese government has taken steps to improve its food safety since 2006. However, addressing food safety risks in China is difficult because of the wide range of products, millions of small companies, weak enforcement of food safety standards, heavy use of agricultural chemicals, and substantial environmental pollution.

1950s: Food safety concerns mainly came from diseases and foodborne illnesses causing health problems.

1979: The State Council issued regulations on food hygiene management to prevent foodborne diseases.

1982: Food Hygiene Law was implemented, and the food hygiene supervision system was clearly defined. The food production and operation enterprises were responsible for food hygiene management.

2002: The Chinese Center for Disease Control and Prevention (CCDC) and the Health Supervision Center were established by the Ministry of Health.

2003: China's Food and Drug Administration was established to implement laws and regulations on food and drug safety and control (CFDA).

2006: China established the Agricultural Product Quality and Safety Law and the Guidelines for Acceptable Daily Intake of Pesticide.

2009: China implemented the Food Safety Law and created a national surveillance and food recall system.

2010: A National Microbiological Monitoring Network was established to observe major foodborne pathogens.

2013: CFDA increased the number of total employees to nearly 300,000 to supervise about 12 million food production units.

2015: China Food Safety Law was revised to add stricter violation penalties. It gives consumers the right to claim a refund and to seek damage if a product fails to meet safety standards. CFDA established the information inquiry platform for food safety supervision and inspection.

2018: CFDA changed its name to the National Medical Products Administration (NMPA). NMPA is responsible for comprehensive supervision of food, cosmetics, and drug safety management.

2019: China added more provisions to the Food Safety Law, including labeling for genetically modified foods (GMO), hefty fines for severe or intentional illegal acts, and rewards for whistle-blowers. China also released the maximum residue Limits for Pesticides in Foods (Ref 11).

2022: China announced the issuance of 36 new and three revised National Food Safety Standards. The standards cover a wide range of products and specifications, including beverages, food additives, detergents, contaminants, and test methods (Ref 18).

2. Challenges in Food Safety Monitoring and Contamination

China's Food Safety Agencies

No single agency is responsible for China's food safety regulations and enforcement. China's principal food safety authorities include the following:

National Medical Products Administration (previously called China Food and Drug Administration): This agency oversees food production, distribution, and the licensing of food and medical products.

General Administration of Quality Supervision, Inspection, and Quarantine (AQSIQ): Oversees food imports and exports, certifications and standardizations, quality management, and health quarantines.

National Health and Family Planning Commission (NHFPC): This commission conducts food safety risk monitoring and assessment, develops national food safety standards, and reviews the safety of food, additives, and new food products.

Other agencies also play a role, including China's Ministry of Agriculture and provincial government agencies. The Chinese government has taken steps to improve its food safety since 2006, when it created standardization for food production, processing, sales, and supervision. In 2009, China passed a significant food safety law and created a national surveillance and food recall system. The law mandated the creation of a Food Safety Committee reporting to the State Council (Ref 1).

Food Safety Monitoring Is Difficult

Chinese authorities try to control food export safety by certifying exporters. However, monitoring such a wide range of products for the different hazards occurring in the supply chain is difficult for Chinese and US officials (Ref 5).

Despite the 2009 Food Safety Law, food safety incidents persist in China because the regulatory system was ineffective and penalties were too light to deter offenders. As a result, China revised the Food Safety Law in 2015, adding new provisions concerning penalties for food safety violations and establishing stricter risk assessment rules. The revision focused on controlling production in the supply chain and required additional recordkeeping. Under the new law, food producers who do not meet food safety standards must stop production and recall their products from the market. The law further created a system for penalties and gave consumers the right to claim a refund and to seek damages if a product fails to meet safety standards (Ref 1).

Food control and regulation are challenging tasks for the Chinese government. Food safety hazards occur in various foods and even at certified manufacturers. For instance, in the case of melamine adulteration and dumplings tainted with pesticides, incidents occurred at well-known companies that received Hazard Analysis Critical Control Point certifications (HACCP) and inspection exemption from the Chinese government (Ref 5).

From 2009 to 2017, the Ministry of Health integrated about 1,200 food standards. However, resources have not been sufficient to reinforce the rules. It is difficult to assess the seriousness of food safety problems or the degree of progress in China because the Chinese Government closely protects information.

According to an online survey in 2016, food incident statistics in China were reported as follows (Ref 10):

a) 66.18% caused by human factors: 30.71% illegal use of food additives; 19.81% fake and substandard products; 7.6% ingredients that were not listed on food labels; 8.06% other
b) 18.85% caused by natural factors: pathogenic microorganisms
c) 9.29% pesticides and veterinary drug residues
d) 4.33% heavy metals contamination
e) 1.35% impurity of substances

In 2016, Chinese food safety departments conducted about 15 million individual inspections and found more than 500,000 food safety violations. They included false advertising, using counterfeit products and ingredients, and selling contaminated food products. One case involved using industrial gelatin in food, while several cases involved using counterfeit and low-quality salt (Ref 12).

In 2016, a report from Quality Inspection Management (QIMA), an international firm that audits food-processing companies in China, found that 48% of the Chinese plants it inspected failed to meet the standards of its Western clients. Violations included contamination with pesticides, medical drugs, heavy metals, bacteria, and viruses (Ref 20).

Limited technological resources did not cause those incidents, but it was more due to a poor understanding of food safety and its implications. Since the 1990s, food safety regulations have evolved worldwide, and food producers have been given more responsibility to monitor the safety of their products (Ref 10).

The United States continues to be concerned about certain foods that appear to show evidence of poor hygiene and mishandling throughout the supply chain in China. Laboratory tests showed Escherichia coli (E. coli) and Salmonella contamination in processed chicken and seafood from China (Ref 1).

Food Contamination

According to a comprehensive report by the United States Department of Agriculture (USDA), many safety risks associated with foods imported from China came from tainted raw materials and contamination during manufacturing. In some cases, laboratory tests found abnormal levels of pesticides, antibiotics, heavy metals, and bacteria or viruses. Other wrongdoings included mislabeling, abnormal coloring, and soaking seafood in a sodium triphosphate (STPP) solution to make it absorb more water to add weight. Many food processors use unsafe additives, toxic dyes, or fake ingredients to preserve food, cut production costs, or improve product appearance. Problems found in food manufacturers include old rusty equipment, poor control of worker health and hygiene, weak monitoring of raw materials, contaminated water, and nonexistent or fraudulent recordkeeping (Ref 5).

3. Regulation of Small Operations and Pesticides

Very Small Operations

The food processing industry primarily comprises minimal, family-based operations, making it difficult for the government to monitor food production activities to ensure product safety. Almost half of Chinese food-processing plants fail to meet internationally acceptable standards.

On the one hand, several thousand modern, large-scale, multinational, and joint venture corporations/farms use best practices and sophisticated equipment. On the other hand, China has some 200 million farming households with average land holdings of 1-2 acres per farm and about 12 million food production units, 70% of which have fewer than ten employees. Many participants in food supply chains are unaware of food safety standards. Some factories have no basic idea about hygiene standards, and the workers do not wear gloves when handling food. Others cut corners, add toxic substances, or skimp on safety controls to increase profits. These factories could be the third or fourth level of suppliers. Therefore, it is tough for importers to trace the origin (Refs 5 and 15).

Pesticide Management

The maximum residue limits (MRLs) of pesticides in international trade have significantly affected the exports of Chinese agricultural products. In 2006, China promulgated the Agricultural Product Quality and Safety Law and established the Guidelines for Acceptable Daily Intake of Pesticides.

In 2019, China's National Health Commission, the Ministry of Agriculture and Rural Affairs, and the State Administration for Market Regulation jointly released the National Food Safety Standard,

Maximum Residue Limits for Pesticides in Foods. The law sets maximum limits of 483 pesticides in 256 categories of foods (Ref 9).

However, China still faces many challenges, such as complicated cultivation modes. Many farmers are using pesticides but are unaware of pesticide residues and their impact (Ref 2). Government red tape and different standards create confusion. Many local governments do not have sufficient resources to enforce food safety, or they frequently have ties to the industry and ignore regulations (Ref 13).

4. Penalty for Fake Drugs

Fake drugs are challenging to detect in China. People caught making fake drugs usually face small fines. However, they can also face the death penalty, which was used to execute (by lethal injection) the head of the China Food and Drug Administration, Zheng Xiaoyu, for his involvement in a licensing scandal. Zheng Xiaoyu was found guilty of accepting 6.5 million yuan (nearly $1 million) worth of bribes from pharmaceutical companies to expedite the approval of new drugs. According to local media, one antibiotic approved by the agency killed ten patients before it was withdrawn (Refs 7 and 8).

CHAPTER 15

GUARDIANS OF THE PLATE: INSIDE AMERICA'S FOOD SAFETY AND REGULATIONS

—∿∿—

This chapter presents you with a thorough overview of America's food safety oversight, emphasizing the pivotal roles of institutions such as the USDA and FDA. It delves into the background and functions of these agencies, allowing you to gain a deeper understanding of their crucial roles in safeguarding the nation's food supply. The chapter also exposes the inspection protocols for imported food and drugs, highlighting the FDA's insufficient commitment to ensuring product safety. Additionally, you are introduced to significant legislation, such as the 2010 US Food Safety Modernization Act, aimed at improving food safety standards and regulatory compliance. Finally, the chapter unveils the intricacies of the FDA's inspection algorithm, providing crucial insight into the process used to uphold food safety standards nationwide.

1. Background and Role of USDA and FDA

The US Food and Drug Administration (FDA) and the US Department of Agriculture (USDA) are responsible for food safety. The FDA ensures the safety of most domestic and imported food products, including seafood and fish (except catfish). About 212,000 food facilities worldwide are registered with the FDA and are potentially subject to inspection. The USDA's Food Safety and Inspection Service (FSIS) regulates most meat and poultry, some egg products, and catfish. Its jurisdiction covers roughly 1,300 eligible foreign establishments.

Food imports account for about 20% of all US food consumed (by volume or trade value). The percentage for fish, seafood, and fruit and vegetable products is even more significant. Several high-profile food safety-related incidents and outbreaks involving imported foods have generated growing concerns about whether current federal programs sufficiently ensure the safety of food imports into the United States. Several large multi-state outbreaks have been linked to foods regulated by the FDA and the USDA (Ref 4).

Background

For many years, US inspection records show that China has flooded the United States with food unfit for human consumption. The FDA inspectors returned the products they caught to Chinese importers. Many of them reappeared at the US borders, making a second or third attempt to enter the United States (Ref 2).

2007: After years of warnings, the FDA blocked the sale of five types of farm-raised seafood from China because of repeated contamination incidents from banned animal drugs and food additives. In addition, the FDA detained more than 1,000 shipments of tainted Chinese dietary supplements, toxic cosmetics, and counterfeit medicines (Ref 3).

2008: The FDA opened its first overseas office in China but had done little to address the growing concerns about food imports from China, such as chemical adulteration and unsafe drug residues. The FDA inspected less than 2% of imported food and barely visited China food manufacturers.

2009: The FDA conducted only 13 food inspections in China. Inspection reports indicated juices and fruits rejected as filthy, prunes tinted with chemical dyes not approved for human consumption, frozen breaded shrimp preserved with nitrofuran, an antibacterial additive that causes cancer, and swordfish rejected as poisonous (Ref 4).

2005-2013: Fish and seafood, vegetables and fruits, and spices accounted for more than half of all import refusals. The refusals were filthy and decomposed and contained unregistered pesticides or other illegal additives and harmful pathogens and their toxins (Salmonella, Listeria, and aflatoxins). Misleading or missing labels accounted for another 41% of all FDA import refusals during the same period. Overall, the countries with the most shipments refused over this period were Mexico, India, and China (Ref 4).

2013: The FDA approved cooked chicken imported from China.

2017: China's first known shipment of cooked chicken reached the United States. Chicken from China will not be labeled (Ref 6).

2019: Federal officials at the Newark port of entry seized one million pounds of cured pork products allegedly smuggled from China. It was the most significant agricultural bust in American history (Ref 7).

2020: The USDA's FSIS issued a public health alert for raw frozen New Orleans–Roasted Organic Chicken Wings products illegally imported from China and labeled with a false USDA mark of inspection. The products were distributed to 20 retail locations in California, Oregon, and Washington (Ref 8).

2020: The USDA's FSIS issued a public health alert for an undetermined amount of imported cooked duck blood curds from China.

2021: Federal officials caught 48.4 tons of ineligible hot-pot seasoning beef tallow products from China that were smuggled into the United States. These items were shipped to distributors, retailers, and restaurant owners in Arizona, California, Hawaii, Nevada, New York, and Texas (Ref 9).

2. Inspection of Imported Foods and Drugs

The USDA's Food Safety and Inspection Service

In the United States, the US Department of Agriculture's Food Safety Inspection Service (USDA's FSIS) inspectors are present full-time in slaughter plants and at least part-time in establishments that further process meat and poultry products. Inspectors shall ensure that plants are operating in a sanitary manner under an FSIS-approved safety plan. The FSIS is responsible for developing the labeling policy to ensure that meat or poultry products are wholesome, not adulterated, and properly packaged. An adulterated food bears or contains any poisonous or harmful substance that may pose a risk to consumer health.

For imported products, the FSIS is responsible for certifying that foreign meat and poultry plants are operating under an inspection system equivalent to the US system before they can export their product to the United States. The FSIS reviews documents on sanitation control, animal disease, slaughter and processing, residue, and policy enforcement. The FSIS also conducts an onsite audit that assesses risk areas such as plant facilities and equipment, laboratories, training programs, and in-plant inspection procedures.

Eligible countries to export meat, poultry, catfish, and egg products into the United States include many of the countries of the European Union, as well as Argentina, Australia, Brazil, Canada, Chile, Costa Rica, Honduras, Iceland, Israel (processed chicken and turkey), Japan, Lithuania (processed beef and pork), Mexico, Namibia, New Zealand, China (processed chicken and duck and raw catfish), South Korea (processed chicken), San Marino (processed pork), Thailand (catfish),

Uruguay, and Vietnam (catfish). Foreign food importers are responsible for verifying that the products obtained from foreign processors comply with US laws.

Once a foreign country's inspection system has been approved, the FSIS relies on the foreign government to inspect and certify the eligibility of individual exporting establishments. The FSIS periodically reviews foreign government documents and conducts on-site audits at least annually to verify that the eligible country's inspection system is equivalent to the US system. No foreign plant is authorized to ship meat or poultry to the United States unless the country (where it is located) has received an FSIS eligibility determination.

The USDA Inspection of Imported Food

At the United States port of entry, a USDA's Food Safety Inspection Service (FSIS) inspector examines shipments before they are allowed entry. Meat, poultry, eggs, and catfish imports will be visually inspected for appearance and condition. They are also checked for certification and label compliance. Physical inspections of imports may be more random. Products that fail inspection must be refused entry and re-exported, converted to nonhuman food, or destroyed.

The USDA's FSIS inspects imported meat, catfish, poultry (and other birds), and egg products from about 1,300 eligible foreign establishments in nearly 40 countries. In 2019, 3.95 billion pounds of imported meat, catfish, and poultry and 7.5 million pounds of egg products were presented to the FSIS for inspection. The refusal rates were 0.13% for meat, catfish, and poultry and 0.07% for egg products (Ref 4).

The United States Food and Drug Administration

The United States Food and Drug Administration (FDA)'s food regulatory authority came from the 1906 Federal Food, Drug, and Cosmetic Act (FFDCA). The Act demands that domestic and foreign food manufacturing facilities adhere to the FDA's requirements for current good manufacturing practices (CGMPs) and prohibits the adulteration and misbranding of food.

In 2002, the Public Health Security and Bioterrorism Preparedness and Response Act amended the FFDCA to require all domestic and foreign food facilities to register with the FDA. This Act also demands that the FDA regulate imported foods and maintain comprehensive records of suppliers and subsequent recipients of these products. In 2010, Congress further amended the FFDCA by passing a comprehensive food safety law, the Food Safety Modernization Act (FSMA). The FSMA gave the FDA new tools and authorities to ensure imported food meets the same safety standards as those produced in the United States. More than 300,000 domestic and foreign food facilities are registered with the FDA and potentially subject to its inspection and reporting requirements. Of the total number of registered FDA-regulated facilities, about 88,000 are US-based, and another 212,000 are foreign facilities.

In 2020, Congress passed the Protecting America's Food and Agriculture Act. The law authorized Customs Border Protection to hire and train 240 new agricultural inspectors/technicians and 20 new canine units to conduct additional border inspections of foods and goods entering the US ports. This will help the FDA to some extent, but it cannot replace the FDA's food facility inspections in foreign countries (Ref 4).

3. 2010 US Food Safety Modernization Act and Compliance

From 2007 to 2008, China's serious food safety incidents involved melamine as a protein substitute in infant formula, milk products, and wheat and rice protein. Melamine consumption caused many deaths and sick humans and pets. As a result, the United States Congress passed the Food Safety Modernization Act (FSMA) in 2010. This legislation tightened US safety regulations for both domestically produced and imported foods. To help implement the FSMA, congress increased the annual funding for the FDA by $204.3 million (Refs 1 and 2).

Between 2016 and 2021, the FDA's total program budget increased from $4.747 billion to $6.051 billion. Over this time, congressional funding increased by 20%, and user fee revenues increased by 37% (Refs 5 and 10).

User fees: Congress created the Prescription Drug User Fee Act (PDUFA) in 1992 to authorize the FDA to collect fees from companies that produce certain human drugs and biological products.

The FDA Missed the FSMA Target

FDA Inspections of Imported Foods

	2010	2015	2016	2017	2018	2019
Foreign Inspections	354	1357	1269	1548	1638	1747
Import Physical Exams	200,766	266,932	276,502	252,903	206,656	159,675
Field Tests	170,392	245,804	252,766	229,129	185,761	141,905
Labs Samples Analyzed	30,374	21,128	23,736	23,774	20,895	17,770
Import Product Lines (MM)	9.7	13.1	14	15.3	16.9	17.7
% Lines Examined	2.06%	2.04%	1.98%	1.66%	1.23%	0.90%

Source: Congressional Research Service

Mandates vs. Actual Inspections

	2012	2013	2014	2015	2016	2017	2018	2019
Actual Inspections	1,347	1,403	1,339	1,357	1,269	1,548	1,638	1,749
% Mandated	67%	52%	48%	51%	47%	61%	53%	53%
FSMA Mandated	1,998	2,694	2,806	2,678	2,714	2,538	3,096	3,276
Difference		(651)	(1,291)	(1,467)	(1,321)	(1,445)	(990)	(1,458)	(1,527)

Source: Congressional Research Service

The 2010 Food Safety Modernization Act (FSMA) tightened controls on food imports, required certification of imported foods, raised importer accountability, and increased responsibility for US trading partners. The FSMA further required that the FDA increase the number of inspections of foreign facilities and their food safety programs (Ref 4).

In 2019, the FDA inspected 1,747 foreign facilities and oversaw 17.7 million import lines (referring to separate product lines on an entry document). However, the FDA could not keep up with targets set by Congress since the number of import lines had increased by more than 80%. From 2010 to 2019, the total number of import lines rose from 9.7 million to 17.7 million. As a result, the FDA inspection rate dropped from 2% in 2010 to less than 1% in 2019 (Ref 4).

The Food Safety Modernization Act (FSMA) also required that the FDA increase the number of food safety inspectors within the agency to 5,000 by 2014, but the agency only had 3,905 inspectors in 2019. The FDA has continued to experience recruitment challenges in its foreign offices. The agency's food facility inspections in China and India accounted for about one-fifth of all foreign facility inspections. According to the FDA, the average cost of a foreign high-risk food facility inspection is $23,600 per inspection.

In 2019, the FDA missed 1,527 inspections that the FSMA required. The agency only inspected 53% of the FSMA quota (Ref 4). Under the FSMA, food importers must comply with US food safety policy by submitting the Foreign Supplier Verification Program (FSVP) form to the FDA. However, two-thirds failed to submit the form when the FDA inspected their facilities in 2019 (Ref 4).

The WTO Member Compliance

When the FDA inspects a food facility, it evaluates compliance with Current Good Manufacturing Practices (CGMPs) and other relevant food safety regulations. The FDA has established a System Regulation (SR) agreement with Australia, Canada, and New Zealand, as their food safety regulatory systems are compatible with that of the United States. However, under its membership agreement with the World Trade Organization (WTO), the United States must adhere to the trade rules and standards set by the WTO.

4. FDA Inspection Algorithm

The FDA does not randomly sample import shipments for inspection. Instead, it uses a risk-based prediction algorithm to determine whether shipments will be inspected in the field or a laboratory. In practice, import product inspections are relatively infrequent. Product perishability is also challenging because some testing services might not be available locally (Ref 4).

FDA Import Alerts

Import alerts inform the FDA's field staff and the public that the agency has enough evidence to allow for Detention without Physical Examination (DWPE) of products that appear to violate the FDA's laws and regulations. These violations could be related to the product, manufacturer, shipper, and other information. Before importing into the United States, importers should know if their products are subject to DWPE. This allows the agency to detain a product without physically examining it at entry. The FDA posted these import alerts on its website.

FDA Detention without Examination

Date	Import Alert Name
7/12/2024	Cosmetics due to microbiological contamination
7/12/2024	Adulterated human food products
7/12/2024	Seafood products due to salmonella
7/12/2024	Acidified foods due to inadequate process control
7/12/2024	Drug or medical devices without valid registration
7/12/2024	Misbranded food products
7/12/2024	Unapproved new drugs
7/12/2024	Food products containing undeclared added sulfating agents
7/12/2024	Processed human and animal foods for pesticides
7/12/2024	Raw agricultural products for pesticides
7/12/2024	Electronic products that fail to comply with performance standards
7/12/2024	Cosmetics adulterated due to color additive violations
7/11/2024	Drugs from firms which have not met drug GMPs
7/10/2024	Food products containing unsafe food additives
7/10/2024	Food products due to the presence of salmonella
7/10/2024	Misbranded seafood Products
7/9/2024	Acidified food without filed scheduled processes
7/9/2024	Foods containing Illegal and/or undeclared Colors
7/8/2024	Devices without without approval
7/8/2024	Foods due to heavy metal contamination
7/8/2024	Medical instruments from Pakistan
7/3/2024	Dietary supplements from firms not met GMP standard
7/2/2024	Foods Imported from foreign suppliers not in compliance
7/2/2024	Electronic Nicotine Delivery Systems lacking authorization
7/2/2024	Devices from firms not meeting Device Quality System Requirements
7/2/2024	Foods that fail to properly label major food allergens
7/2/2024	Ready-to-eat seafood for Listeria monocytogenes"
7/2/2024	Raw and cooked shrimp from India
7/2/2024	Fish products from foreign processors not in compliance

Date	Import Alert Name
7/2/2024	Condoms
7/1/2024	All milk products from China due to the presence of melamine
7/1/2024	Pig ears and other pet treats due to the presence of salmonella
6/27/2024	Papaya from Mexico
6/25/2024	Fresh produce prepared under insanitary conditions
6/25/2024	Imported soft cheese and soft ripened cheese from France
6/24/2024	Salt-cured, dried, smoked, pickled, or brined uneviscerated fish
6/24/2024	Refrigerated raw fish due to potential for clostridium botulinum toxin
6/24/2024	Imported human foods due to filth
6/17/2024	Crustaceans due to chloramphenicol
6/14/2024	Products imported by debarred entities
6/14/2024	Laser pointers, gunsights, light shows and similar products
6/13/2024	Drugs from foreign establishments refusing FDA inspection
6/12/2024	Seafood products due to nitrofurans
6/10/2024	Cheese due to microbiological contamination
6/10/2024	Aquaculture seafood products due to unapproved drugs
6/6/2024	Surgeon's and patient examination gloves
6/3/2024	Dried mushrooms from Hong Kong and China for filth
5/31/2024	Apple juice products due to patulin
5/31/2024	Food products due to the presence of mycotoxins
5/31/2024	Fresh cilantro from Puebla, Mexico
5/24/2024	Food Products from foreign establishments refusing FDA inspection
5/23/2024	New tobacco products without required marketing authorization
5/23/2024	Cantaloupes from Mexico
5/22/2024	Germanium supplements for human consumption
5/21/2024	External Penile Rigidity Devices
5/13/2024	Tobacco products for non payment of user fee
5/10/2024	Vegetable protein products from China due to the presence of melamine
5/10/2024	Failure to meet nutrient and labeling requirements
5/9/2024	Human food products prepared under insanitary conditions
5/7/2024	Produce due to contamination with human pathogens

Date	Import Alert Name
5/7/2024	Frozen raw and cooked conch meat
5/6/2024	Unapproved products containing xylazine active pharmaceutical ingredient
5/2/2024	Alcohol-based hand sanitizers manufactured in Mexico
5/2/2024	Seafood products due to decomposition
4/24/2024	Ceramicware due to Excessive lead and/or cadmium
4/23/2024	Food products containing Illegal undeclared sweeteners
4/16/2024	Mahimahi from Ecuador and Taiwan due to histamine and decomposition
4/12/2024	Aquacultured seafood from China and Hong Kong for unsafe additives
3/26/2024	Unapproved finished new animal drugs
3/26/2024	Devices without a unique device identifier
3/25/2024	Adulterated powered muscle stimulator devices
3/22/2024	Dried peppers from Mexico
3/20/2024	Honey and blended syrup due to unsafe drug residues
3/19/2024	Foods due to chemical contamination
3/14/2024	Confectionery products containing non-nutritive components
3/12/2024	Food and supplements containing active pharmaceuticlal ingredients
3/12/2024	Guacamole and processed avocado products
3/11/2024	Adulterated medical Devices
3/6/2024	Fish products for importers and foreign processor
2/28/2024	Tobacco products lacking labeling requirements
2/15/2024	New bulk animal drug substances
1/18/2024	Heparin and related products
1/18/2024	Drug products for hazardous microbiological contamination
1/16/2024	Raw Shrimp
12/13/2023	Food products and supplements containing areca nuts
12/11/2023	Medical device firms refusing FDA Foreign Establishment Inspection
11/20/2023	All dried shark fins and dried fish maws due to filth
11/20/2023	Coconut due to the presence of microbiological contamination
11/17/2023	Tamarind products from all countries due to filth
11/8/2023	Enoki mushrooms from the South Korea/China due to listeria monocytogenes

Date	Import Alert Name
11/6/2023	Foreign manufactured unapproved prescription drugs
11/2/2023	Smokeless tobacco products without warning label
10/18/2023	Dates from China and Hong Kong due to filth
10/16/2023	Contact lenses due to microbiological contamination
10/16/2023	Medical devices with false or misleading labeling
10/16/2023	Feeds containing monensin
10/12/2023	Foods containing Siberian ginseng
10/11/2023	Ear Candles
10/4/2023	Juice from foreign processors not in compliance
10/2/2023	Stevia leaves and foods containing stevia leaves
9/11/2023	Drugs based upon analytic test results
9/8/2023	Dietary supplements containing new ingredients
9/1/2023	Whipworms and hookworms including eggs and larvae
8/11/2023	Unapproved human growth hormone (HGH)
8/9/2023	Tobacco products using descriptions as light, mild, or low
7/31/2023	Misbranded drugs or new drugs without approved applications
7/27/2023	Dietary supplements containing mitragyna speciosa or kratom
6/16/2023	Molluscan bivalve shellfish
5/25/2023	Milk products manufactured under insanitary conditions
4/18/2023	Unlicensed immune globulin intravenous for humans
4/6/2023	Animal foods due to the presence of salmonella
3/30/2023	Sunlamp and sunlamp products
3/13/2023	Flavored cigarettes
3/1/2023	Lobster tails from India
2/15/2023	Ackees due to hypoglycin A
2/13/2023	Certain tobacco products found not substantially equivalent
1/19/2023	Raw agricultural products for pesticides
1/19/2023	Black and white pepper from Brazil
12/20/2022	Filtering facepiece respirators (FFR)
11/22/2022	Excimer lasers manufactured for export

Date	Import Alert Name
11/18/2022	Raspberries from Guatemala due to cyclospora cayetanensis
10/31/2022	Black pepper from India
10/26/2022	Processed seafood products due to E. coli
10/25/2022	Seafood due to hepatitis A contamination
9/30/2022	Acidified foods from commercial processors for failure to provide information
9/28/2022	Canned shrimp from thailand for decomposition
9/22/2022	Aquacultured shrimp products from Malaysia due to unsafe additives
6/8/2022	Skin whitening creams containing mercury
5/26/2022	Drugs or active pharmaceutical ingredients from unapproved facilities
5/23/2022	Morel mushrooms due to adulteration
5/18/2022	Guanabana (Soursop)
5/11/2022	Impact-resistant lenses In eyeglasses and Sunglasses
4/22/2022	Examination of puffer fish
4/4/2022	Papad and farfar wafers from India
3/2/2022	Poultry jerky for pets due to the presence of antibiotic or residues
2/24/2022	Dried or pickled finfish from Thailand
2/15/2022	Frog Legs
1/31/2022	Anchovy or bagoong products from the Philippines
11/2/2021	Sterile dosage form drugs from manufacturers not in compliance
8/13/2021	Dietarys supplements containing ephedrine alkaloids from all countries
7/28/2021	Processed crabmeat from Thailand
7/20/2021	Animal feedsa and feed Ingredients containing ingredients of animal origin
7/20/2021	Cat food products due to the presence of propylene glycol
6/24/2021	Gel candies containing konjac
5/6/2021	Processed Foods for Pesticides
4/2/2021	Plastic bandages and cotton pads due to microbiological contamination
12/10/2020	Dietary supplements products containing aristolochic acid
12/10/2020	Adulterated and misbranded medical foods
12/10/2020	Bulk shipments of high-risk bovine tissue from mad-cow countries
12/9/2020	Food products due to the presence of melamine

CHAPTER 16

USDA CHALLENGE: ORGANIC FOOD FRAUD & INADEQUATE CONSUMER PROTECTION

———〰️———

This chapter is an essential guide to the USDA organic food labeling system, a critical tool for consumers to make informed choices and shield themselves from organic fraud. It will illuminate the USDA organic inspection system, its limitations, and the deception surrounding organic fraud, particularly from China.

With over 80 countries having organic standards and more than 200 seals, logos, and certification claims, you must grasp the significance of organic labels and the country of origin. This knowledge empowers you to make informed choices. The United States, Canada, the European Union, and Japan have comprehensive organic standards that their respective governments oversee. However, in 2020, only 1% of American farmland was organic, yet organic sales accounted for more than 6% of total food sales. As a result, American grocery retailers now rely on imported organic food to cater to the demand. Organic imports from countries like China and Turkey have increased steadily since the 2000s.

1. The USDA's Organic Food Inspection System

The USDA plays a pivotal role in regulating domestic and imported organic food. It is important to note that selling imported foods as organic in the United States is illegal unless the product meets USDA standards. The USDA delegates its authority to equivalent agencies in other countries and third-party certifiers, underscoring the reliance on its standards.

All organic farms and businesses must be certified by the USDA. The certificate does not expire unless the farm or business surrenders its certification or is suspended or revoked. Certified operations must maintain records concerning organic agricultural products' production, harvesting, and handling (Ref 20).

In March 2024, the USDA implemented significant changes to the USDA organic regulations under its Strengthening Organic Enforcement (SOE) rule. Key impacts of this rule on imports and exports of organic products include the following:

a) The National Organic Program (NOP) Import Certificates – Each shipment of organic products into the United States must be associated with a valid electronic NOP Import Certificate. The NOP Import Certificate provides traceability to the port of entry and ensures an auditable record trail.

b) Expanded Certification Requirements – The SOE rule expanded the types of operations in the organic supply chain that must be certified. These include businesses importing organic products to the United States and exporting organic products for sale in the United States.

2. Countries Having Organic Equivalency

In 2024, the United States established an organic equivalency arrangement with Canada, the European Union, Switzerland, Japan, South Korea (for processed food only), Taiwan, and the United Kingdom. This means that organic products certified by these countries can be labeled and sold as organic in the United States and vice versa. The USDA also allows New Zealand and Israel to accredit certifying agents in their countries to the USDA organic standards under a recognition agreement. Exporters from other countries must use a third-party certifier approved by the USDA to obtain organic certification (Refs 12, 15, 16, and 24).

3. Country of Origin Labeling (COOL)

All retailers with an annual gross receipt of over $230,000 must list the country of origin for unprocessed food products they sell. This requirement applies to full-line grocery stores, supermarkets, and club warehouse stores. The law covers muscle-cut and ground meats of lamb, venison, goat, and chicken; wild and farm-raised fish and shellfish; fresh and frozen fruits and vegetables; peanuts, pecans, and macadamia nuts; and ginseng.

In 2016, the USDA eliminated the mandatory Country of Origin Labeling (COOL) requirements for beef and pork muscle cuts and ground meat to adhere to international trade obligations. The COOL rules also stipulate that if raw materials from different countries are mixed in the same package (e.g., frozen mixed vegetables from Mexico and Chile), all countries must be listed. However, ground meats (other than beef and pork) derived from raw materials from multiple countries may be commingled, and the meat package must list all countries involved (e.g., ground goat meat from the United States and Canada).

Retail firms such as fish markets, butcher shops, and small stores with annual gross receipts less than $230,000 are exempt from the COOL Law. Similarly, restaurants and other food service establishments (cafeterias, lunchrooms, and similar institutions) are also exempt. Processed food and dried fruit are not subject to COOL labeling requirements since the cooking or drying process is considered curing, which changes the character of the fruit or vegetables. However, trimming, cutting, chopping, or slicing does not change the product's character (Ref 23).

4. Organic Digit Codes

The small sticker found on loose fruits or vegetables in US supermarkets is known as the Price Look-Up (PLU) sticker. It contains codes that cashiers can scan at the register. The code also indicates whether the product is organic or conventional.

a) A five-digit number that starts with a "9" means the item is organic.

b) A four-digit code beginning with a "3" or a "4" means the produce is probably conventionally grown.

c) A five-digit code that starts with an "8" means the item is genetically modified (GMO). However, since GMO labels are not mandatory, companies can code those items as conventional.

5. Organic Label Definition

According to the United States Department of Agriculture (USDA), organic certification requires that farmers or producers be inspected annually. Organic on-site inspections consist of all components of the entire operation. The inspectors also look at contamination, risk prevention, and record keeping. Genetically modified organisms (GMOs) are prohibited from being used when growing or processing organic foods (Ref 9).

Organic Agriculture Crop

Organic producers rely on natural substances and biologically based farming methods to the fullest extent possible. Produce can be called organic if it is certified to have grown on soil with no prohibited substances applied for three years before harvest. Prohibited substances include most synthetic fertilizers and pesticides. Organic agriculture does not allow ionizing radiation, sewage sludge, and GMO seeds.

Organic Meat and Dairy Products

Regulations require that animals be raised in living conditions accommodating their natural behaviors (like the ability to graze on pasture), fed 100% organic feed and forage, and not administered antibiotics or hormones. During processing, the meat or dairy product should be handled in a facility, inspected by an organic certifier, and processed without any artificial colors, chemicals, preservatives, or flavors before being packaged.

USDA Certified Organic Processed Food

Regulations prohibit organically processed foods containing artificial preservatives, colors, or flavors. The foods must contain a minimum of 95% organic ingredients (excluding salt and water). Up to 5% of ingredients may be non-organic products such as baking soda, yeast, dairy cultures, and vitamins. Any Genetically Modified Organism (GMO) is prohibited.

Made with Organic Ingredients

The food package may contain at least 70% organically produced ingredients. The remaining non-organic ingredients must be produced without using prohibited practices (genetic engineering, for example) but can include substances that would not otherwise be allowed in 100% organic products. The package will not bear the USDA organic seal (Ref 9).

Pesticide Residues in Organic Products

Most pest control materials permitted in organic agriculture are naturally derived from a plant (e.g., pyrethrum), microorganism (e.g., Bacillus thuringiensis), or other natural sources. Organic standards prohibit most synthetic substances commonly used in conventional agriculture for at least three years before the harvest of an organic crop. Synthetic pest control materials permissible in organic crop production include elemental sulfur, insecticidal soap, horticultural oils, and copper hydroxide. The USDA organic regulations allow residues of prohibited pesticides up to 5% of the EPA tolerance.

According to Food Safety News, roughly 40% of the organic food sold in America tested positive for prohibited pesticide residue in two separate studies by the USDA. Only 5% of organic products are occasionally tested for pesticides, but not for pathogens, which account for most foodborne illness outbreaks (Ref 3).

In 2017, the Inspector General Report noted that organic produce automatically received a pesticide bath at the port if pests or diseases were found in a shipment. In response to the Inspector General's comments, the USDA stated that it has begun establishing procedures to notify importers and certifiers that they can no longer sell such shipments as organic (Ref 17).

6. Organic Certification and Inspection

USDA-Accredited Agents

The United States Department of Agriculture (USDA) accredits certifying agents to certify organic farms and businesses according to US organic standards to regulate organic food production. Certifying agents can be state agencies or private enterprises, including foreign entities.

In 2024, the USDA has nearly 80 agents: 47 in the United States and 30 in foreign countries. Most USDA-accredited certifying agents can certify farms and businesses anywhere in the world. Farmers, ranchers, and processors may choose to work with any USDA-accredited certifying agent. The USDA may not have any good way to know whether its accredited certifying agents have issued false certification documents to unqualified foreign suppliers. As a result, intermediary organizations can use actual certification documents for products that are not organic. The USDA has limited resources to catch every unethical, dishonest supplier or operator (Refs 15 and 16).

In 2007, USDA-accredited agents certified 27,000 organic producers worldwide. This certification allows approved foreign products to bear the "USDA Organic" seal and freely enter the US market. By 2021, the number has increased to 45,653. The top three countries with USDA organic certified operations are the United States (28,539), Mexico (2,485), and China (1,616). This increase also means that organic food products from China have been increasingly available on US supermarket shelves.

USDA Certified Organic Operations by Country

	Country	Total			Country	Total
1	United States	28539		18	South Africa	212
2	Mexico	2485		19	Indonesia	185
3	China	1616		20	Dominican R.	182
4	Peru	1392		21	Honduras	178
5	Argentina	1236		22	Italy	176
6	Chile	1179		23	Guatemala	139
7	Ecuador	798		24	Philippines	137
8	Turkey	766		25	Viet Nam	137
9	Brazil	725		26	Madagascar	134
10	Australia	567		27	Japan	120
11	Tunisia	372		28	South Korea	120
12	Colombia	371		29	Nicaragua	119
13	Thailand	332		30	Canada	109
14	Bolivia	308		31	Paraguay	106
15	Ethiopia	264		32	Costa Rica	104
16	Sri Lanka	259		33	India	101
17	Morocco	219		34	Netherlands	91
	Subtotal					43778
	Other Countries					1875
	Grand Total					45653

Source: USDA, as of March 28, 2021

7. Flaws in the USDA Organic Inspection System

In 2017, the USDA Organic Program Inspector General reported weaknesses during the audit of organic imports at New York, San Francisco, Seattle, Los Angeles, Philadelphia, Dallas, and Chicago ports. The Inspector General recommended that the USDA strengthen its controls over the approval and oversight of imports of organic products into the United States. In 2018, responding to the Inspector General report, the USDA highlighted additional challenges that prevented the agency from doing a proper job (Refs 17 and 20).

Lacks Transparency: The process for determining equivalency of organic standards between the USDA and foreign governments lacks transparency. This lack of clarity has suggested that the USDA needs to implement measures to improve transparency in this crucial aspect of the organic certification process.

Limited Capacity: US ports of entry, including New York, San Francisco, Seattle, Los Angeles, Philadelphia, Dallas, and Chicago, are not equipped to verify the required National Organic Program import documents. The United States Customs and Border Protection officials have communicated their limited capacity to take on additional responsibilities and their lack of current authority to review organic imports, underscoring a systemic issue in the verification process.

Lack of Standardization for Transaction Certificates: When products are imported into the United States, the exporting company typically creates transaction certificates to confirm that the shipments are organic. The organic certifier, who supervises the company responsible for the products, authorizes these certificates. These transaction certificates are not standardized under USDA organic regulations (Ref 20).

Lack of USDA Authority at the Port of Entry: The USDA does not have the regulatory authority to establish and implement specific controls on organic products at United States ports of entry. There is no mechanism to consistently discover or block incoming fraudulent organic shipments. The current statute does not allow the USDA to stop sales, hold products, or recall products in the marketplace or at the borders (Ref 20).

No Traceability Back to the Farm: The current system of organic product trade, often through uncertified brokers or intermediaries, poses a significant challenge. While the final importer is responsible for obtaining an organic certificate, the lack of traceability back to the farm is a concern. This loophole could potentially compromise the quality and integrity of organic products. The USDA's initiative to eliminate uncertified brokers and enforce full traceability is a step in the right direction, but the challenges of implementation and enforcement remain (Ref 20).

Certification Flaws: In 2019, according to the Washington Post, Cornucopia Institute (a farm policy research group) found significant variation in how certifiers interpreted regulations and variations that frequently benefited substantial corporate farms. Since the farms and food businesses pay certifiers, the compliance may be questionable or even dishonest at times. The gatekeepers for the USDA organic program are the federally accredited third-party certifiers. Many certifiers started as nonprofit companies established by farmers in the early days of organics but have turned into multimillion-dollar corporations pursuing certification of multibillion-dollar corporate agribusinesses (Ref 11).

USDA's Ban on O.C.I.A. in China: In a significant move in 2010, the USDA prohibited the Organic Crop Improvement Association (O.C.I.A.), a prominent American inspector based in Nebraska, from conducting operations in China. This decision was made due to a conflict of interest, as O.C.I.A. was found to be using employees of a Chinese government agency to inspect at least ten state-controlled farms and food processing facilities. O.C.I.A. has been a critical player in inspecting Chinese organics for the United States market for several years. O.C.I.A. is a nonprofit organization founded by American farmers in the 1980s. It has remained one of the most active certifiers licensed by the USDA National Organic Program (NOP). After the ban in China, its operations remained in Canada, El Salvador, Guatemala, Japan, Mexico, Nicaragua, Peru, and the United States (Ref 18).

Fake USDA Organic Certificates

Any attempt to falsely market, label, or sell non-organic agricultural products as certified USDA Organic is a direct violation of federal law. Such fraudulent activities are punishable by hefty fines of over $20,000 per violation.

From 2011 to 2024, the USDA National Organic Program reported 201 fraudulent USDA Organic Certificates. These certificates may have been created and used without the knowledge of the operator or the certifying agent named in the certificate. Most were discovered within one or two years, but some had gotten away with it for more than five or even ten years. The United States had the most fraudulent certificates (39), followed by China (29) and South Africa (17).

8. Worldwide Organic Fraud

Fraudulent Organic Certificates
2011-2024 (Year Got Caught)

Rank	Country	Total	% Total
1	Unted States	39	19%
2	China	29	14%
3	South Africa	17	8%
4	Mexico	16	8%
5	Thailand	14	7%
6	India	13	6%
7	Pakistan	6	3%
	Subtotal	**134**	**67%**
	Other Countries	67	33%
	Total	**201**	**100%**

Source: USDA, July 12, 2024

China ranks second after the United States for fraudulent organic certificates. The United States, China, South Africa, Mexico, Thailand, India, and Pakistan account for two-thirds of USDA organic fraud worldwide. Organic grain costs more to produce per bushel than conventionally grown crops, and therefore, it is sold at a higher price.

The organic grain is fed to cattle and chickens, whose organic meat is sold at a premium price in stores and restaurants. A growing number of consumers are willing to pay more for protein that comes from animals raised on a natural, organic diet. To earn the USDA organic seal, farmers are not permitted to plant genetically modified organism (GMO) seeds and are prohibited from using chemical fertilizers and synthetic pesticides on their crops. Unfortunately, due to financial motives and unethical behavior, organic food fraud has been on the rise around the world.

2007: The USDA considered pulling the organic certification from Aurora Dairy, a supplier of Horizon Organic, for selling non-organic milk marketed as organic for more than four years (Ref 12).

2009: American retailer Target was caught for falsely advertising soymilk as organic (Ref 12).

2010: The USDA banned a leading American inspector, O.C.I.A., from operating in China because of a conflict of interest.

2010: A Texas farmer was sentenced to two years in prison, three years of probation, and over $500,000 in restitution for fraudulently mislabeling three kinds of beans and millions of pounds of milo as organic.

2011: Two California fertilizer suppliers and an Oregon grain farmer got prison time for falsely claiming their products were organic.

2013: German authorities said they had identified more than 200 farms suspected of selling premium-priced eggs marketed as organic free-range but laid by caged hens (Ref 12).

2013: In Italy, prosecutors identified 23 suspected members of a counterfeiting ring that set up a dozen shell companies across Europe that issued fake organic certificates for conventional food products. In previous fraud cases, conventional foods were brought into the EU and then relabeled as organic (Ref 12).

2016: A man from Idaho was sentenced to three years in federal custody, three-year probation, and a $2 million penalty for misbranding conventional, non-organic alfalfa seed as organic alfalfa seed.

2017: The scale of organic fraud cases is alarming. Three shipments, each containing millions of pounds of corn and soybeans from Romania and Ukraine, were sold to Turkish distributors as conventional crops. However, by the time they reached the United States, they were labeled as organic, highlighting the urgent need for stricter enforcement and traceability measures.

2019: A Missouri man who fraudulently sold over $140 million worth of non-organic corn and soybean grains as certified organic was sentenced to more than ten years in prison and a $128 million penalty. Three farmers from Nebraska who supplied him with non-organic grain were also sentenced to federal prison for their roles in a scheme to defraud customers across the United States. The grain was mainly used as animal feed, primarily for organic chickens and cattle, from 2010 to 2017. This was the most significant organic fraud case in history. The Missouri man committed suicide three days after the sentencing (Ref 21).

Organic Fraud from Turkey Is on the Rise

According to USDA rules, a company importing an organic product must verify that it has come from a supplier with a USDA Organic certificate. However, this verification does not apply to the original farmers who supply the crops to an intermediary. As a result, there has been an increase in fraudulent organic labeling. The United States market is particularly vulnerable to potentially fraudulent organic products because the chances of being caught are minimal. The USDA has not issued significant sanctions for the import of fraudulent grain. In 2024, the USDA implemented significant changes to the USDA organic regulations under its Strengthening Organic Enforcement (SOE) rule by requiring traceability. However, the agency relies on third parties to enforce these regulations.

In 2017, *The Washington Post* uncovered a case of fraud that had a significant impact on organic farms. Three shipments, each involving millions of pounds of organic-labeled corn or soybeans, were sold to Turkish organic-certified distributors as conventional crops. These distributors then labeled them as organic and exported them to the United States. The imported corn and soybean shipments were sold as animal feed for organically raised chickens and cows. Unfortunately, about 21 million pounds of the 36 million-pound shipment had already reached organic farms, which were not aware of the fraud, causing a great injustice.

The United States Foreign Agricultural Service statistics show that Turkey is now one of the largest exporters of organic products to the United States. In 2013, a report by the Research Institute of Organic Agriculture revealed that half of European importers had found pesticide residues on organic products from Turkey. The United States has observed a significant increase in the import of organic corn and soybeans from Turkey. Between 2014 and 2016, the amount of organic corn coming from Turkey rose from 15,000 metric tons to more than 399,000 metric tons, while the amount of organic soybeans arriving from Turkey rose from 14,000 metric tons to 165,000. These sudden increases in organic food production raise concerns because the organic transition process is slow, taking at least three years for conventional land to be converted into organic farmland. The surge in imports has caused prices to drop by more than 25%, adversely affecting US organic farmers (Ref 14).

9. Organic Sales Are Booming

According to the Organic Trade Association (OTA), the United States is the largest organic market in the world, representing more than half of all consumer sales of organic products globally. The European Union is the second-largest market for organic products in the world. United States sales of certified organic products approached $70 billion in 2023, a new record for the sector. Dollar sales for the American organic marketplace hit $69.7 billion in 2023, up 3.4 percent, with organic food sales totaling $63.8 billion and sales of organic non-food products totaling $5.9 billion (Ref 25).

Although organic food still represents only 6% of total food sold in the United States, it has been a booming industry since Congress passed the Organic Foods Production Act of 1990. Because the domestic organic food industry could not meet the growing demand, US grocery stores have increasingly relied on imports. The majority of organic produce and grain are imported because only 1% of American farmland is certified organic. Organic coffee, soybeans, bananas, olive oil, and corn represent 68% of the total value of organic imports. Other imported commodities included organic honey, mangos, ginger, rice, wine, tea, avocados, apples, berries, flaxseed, and garlic (Ref 22).

The United States imports organic products from at least 111 different countries. Mexico has been the leading supplier of organic products to the United States since 2013. A little over half of all the US organic imports came from North and South America. On average, annual imports from Mexico and Canada represent $324 million. South America averages $423 million per year, mainly from Peru ($92.9 million), Ecuador ($71.6 million), Colombia ($64.4 million), Brazil ($64.1 million), and Argentina ($55.3 million) (Ref 22).

China Is the Top Organic Agriculture Exporter to the EU

In 2019, the European Union (EU) imported 3.24 million metric tons of organic agriculture food products from 123 countries: 32% was imported by the Netherlands, 13 % by Germany, 12% by the UK, and 11% by Belgium. China (13.4%), Ukraine (10.4%), Dominican Republic (10%), Ecuador (9.4%), and Peru (6.6%) are the five largest exporters of organic agriculture products to the European Union. About 82% of organic oilcake (animal feed), 21% of soybeans, 13% of oil seeds, and 8.4% of vegetables that the European Union imported came from China. The EU also imported organic vegetables (fresh, chilled, and dried), fruit juice, tropical fruits, nuts, spices, and honey from China (Ref 13).

Top Organic Products Imported from China
Volume in Thousand Metric Tonnes

Rank	Product	2018	2019	% Share
1	Oilcakes	300.2	318	82.4
2	Soybeans	23.5	28.2	21.4
3	Oil Seeds	20.8	21.3	13.3
5	Vegetables	10.6	13.3	8.4
5	Fruit Juices	5.8	2.3	2.7
6	Tropical Fruits, Nuts & Spices	11.4	18.8	2.1

Source: The European Union Commission

Organic Agriculture Food Imports in the EU
Volume in Metric Tonnes

	Top Countries	2018	2019	% Share
1	China	404,623	433,705	13.4
2	Ukraine	265,817	337,856	10.4
3	Dominican Republic	271,801	324,354	10.0
4	Ecuador	276,879	304,297	9.4
5	Peru	204,871	214,240	6.6
6	Turkey	262,722	210,760	6.5
7	India	125,477	176,568	5.4
8	Colombia	63,114	87,341	2.7
9	Kazakhstan	50,250	85,675	2.6
10	Brazil	72,204	78,825	2.4
11	Mexico	69,497	74,857	2.3
12	Argentina	66,838	63,369	2.0
13	Egypt	46,599	56,591	1.7
14	Togo	22,123	44,684	1.4
15	Tunisia	40,126	42,591	1.3
16	Israel	40,610	40,983	1.3
17	Moldova Republic	55,368	40,053	1.2
18	Paraguay	35,121	38,271	1.2
19	Honduras	40,235	37,352	1.2
20	Pakistan	27,091	34,116	1.1
	Subtotal	**2,441,366**	**2,726,488**	**84.1**
	Grand Total	**3,230,675**	**3,242,382**	**100.0**

Source: The European Union Commission

10. China's Organic Agriculture

In the late 1980s, some local Chinese government entities were concerned about environmental degradation and began promoting Chinese Ecological Agriculture. There was no organic sector in China before 1994. Polluted air and water and contaminated soil are the main factors hindering the integrity of organic food in China. Most of the organic food produced for export is grown on large-scale farms, where farmers know little or nothing about organic farming. Most of the early development of Chinese organic agriculture was driven by export opportunities to the European Union, the United States, and Japan. International organic inspectors have faced challenges in dealing with local politics rather than the conventional organic structure (Ref 2).

In 2007, the Chinese government certified about 2,500 organic farms. About two to three million hectares of farmland are certified organic, putting China among the world's top five organic producers in acreage. Meanwhile, concerns about food safety led the Chinese government to introduce two food label types: Pollution-Free Food (grown inside a greenhouse) and Green Food (minimum use of pesticides) (Refs 2 and 4).

Chinese organic exports have skyrocketed from $300,000 in 1995 to about $500 million in 2008. By 2020, China had become the largest exporter of organic products to the European Union (Ref 7). China's organic food sector has overgrown over the past decade, exporting organic canned tomatoes, dried fruit, and tea. Nevertheless, its certifying system is less than reliable. Banned toxic pesticides and other chemicals have appeared several times (Refs 7 and 12).

Tainted Chinese Organic Products History

The United States Food and Drug Administration (FDA), responsible for inspecting most imported foods, samples less than 2% of all regulated products. It often refuses shipments of organic foods because of pesticide residues or unsafe food additives unfit for human consumption. For example, organic soybean meal from China through the Port of Seattle in 2007 appeared to contain "a poisonous or harmful substance which may render it injurious to health," according to an FDA report (Ref 7).

In 2008, Whole Foods, a leading US organic retailer, pulled its house brand 365 organic ginger powder from shelves after an investigation by

WJLA, a local ABC affiliate news channel. The lab test revealed that its organic ginger was contaminated with the toxic pesticide aldicarb. As a result, food distributor Frontier Natural Products Co-Op, under its Simply Organic label, also ordered an urgent recall of the Chinese organic ginger. It affects over two dozen ginger products, including Jamaican Seasoning, Pickling Spice, and Seafood Seasoning. After an investigation, the USDA stated that the ginger came from various farms in China that applied the toxic insecticide (Ref 4).

At the time, Whole Foods carried about 30 private-label items from China, including organic frozen vegetables, sunflower seeds, pine nuts, and bottled teas. In 2010, due to the scare caused by China's food, the company stopped stocking these products except for the shelled and unshelled frozen edamame (young soybeans). Today, Whole Foods no longer sells edamame from China (Refs 5, 7, and 18).

Recently, Chinese organic products, such as tea and frozen broccoli, have increasingly found their way onto American store shelves, typically with the green USDA Organic seal (Ref 11).

USDA Organic Stamp in China

In China, USDA-certified organic operations climbed from 496 in 2006 to 1,616 in 2021. China ranked third globally in terms of the number of USDA organic-certified operations and second for having the most fraudulent USDA Organic certificates.

In 2017, The Washington Post examined public records of pesticide residue testing conducted on organic products in China. The results showed very high levels of pesticide residue on some "organic" Chinese products. The pesticide residue tests were utterly arbitrary, and the results varied greatly from one inspector to another: nearly 40% of samples had pesticide residue at one inspection company versus 1% at another (Ref 14).

China is the leading source of organic tea and ginger in the United States, and its organic food exports have been questionable. Farmers in China seeking the USDA Organic label hire their inspection agency to certify that they meet the organic rules. Most inspectors announce in advance, which takes away the element of surprise. Testing for pesticides is the exception rather than the rule, and the method used could be to the advantage of farmers. Some of the problems are due to pesticides from neighboring farms drifting over. In addition, contamination from China's polluted soil and water leaves pesticide residues (Ref 14).

China's New Organic Standards

In 2020, China revised its national standards on organic products, covering mandatory requirements for food production, processing, labeling, and management (Ref 10).

The new organic standard includes changes to production and processing inputs, such as adding microbial preparations to control and prevent animal diseases and adding detergents and disinfectants in plant production. The standard also changed the requirements for the labeling of organic products. The new organic certification rules have streamlined some certification practices (Ref 10).

CHAPTER 17

CHINESE PRODUCT RECALLS: A BATTLE FOR THE US CONSUMER PRODUCT SAFETY

—⚉—

In 2019, Chinese consumer goods totaled a staggering $451.7 billion, making up a significant 18.1% of all US imports. In 2014, Chinese goods comprised 23% of all US imports under the US Consumer Product Safety Commission's (CPSC) jurisdiction. However, they were responsible for a striking 51% of all product safety recalls reported by the CPSC. Since 2012, Chinese products have consistently dominated CPSC safety recalls (Refs 1 and 13).

1. Federal Agencies Involved in Product Safety

Five federal agencies are responsible for product safety in the United States. Once a product has arrived at the US border, responsibility for safety inspections varies among US agencies according to their jurisdiction. The following are quick descriptions of their areas of responsibility:

The US Consumer Product Safety Commission: Most consumer products.

The US Food and Drug Administration: Most foods, seafood (except catfish), animal foods, cosmetics, drugs, medical devices, tobacco, and radiation-emitting devices.

The US Department of Agriculture: Meat, poultry, catfish, and egg products.

The US National Highway Traffic Safety Administration: Automobiles, motorcycles, trucks, and tires.

The Environmental Protection Agency: Pesticides and fungicides.

Most products imported from China fall under the responsibilities of the United States Food and Drug Administration (FDA) and the United States Consumer Product Safety Commission (CPSC). The FDA estimates that all imported products under its review constitute roughly 20% of the US economy. In 2015, over $754 billion of all imported products at 327 US ports fell under the CPSC's jurisdiction (Ref 1).

2. Import Screening Method

Given limited resources and huge responsibilities, the CPSC and FDA use a risk-based approach to examine imported goods. When a ship containing imported products enters a US port, a customs broker files entry documentation with the US Customs and Border Protection (CBP). The customs document includes the type of product and the identities of the shipper, importer, and manufacturer. The same information is sent to the CPSC or the FDA for review. Subsequently, reviewing agencies apply methodologies that estimate potential safety risks associated with the shipment based on the received information.

If the screening indicates that a shipment has a higher risk of containing non-compliant products, the CPSC or the FDA may deploy onsite inspectors to examine the imported products. If the product contains a defect, fails to comply with a technical regulation, has been banned, or creates an unreasonable risk of injury or death, the CPSC may stop the shipment and prevent it from entering the country. Similarly, if the FDA determines a product to be adulterated or misbranded, the agency may refuse entry for the product. A refused shipment must be destroyed or sent back within 90 days of the refusal.

3. Limited Resources for Product Safety Inspection

Despite the administrative tools available to the FDA and the CPSC, both agencies have limited staff resources against a comprehensive mandate. The CPSC lacks sufficient staff to inspect imported products at all US ports. In 2020, the CPSC had a staff presence at 6% of 327 US ports, covering about 68% of all risk-consumer product imports. The agency has been unable to inspect every shipment identified by its methodology as "high risk," enabling them to enter the United States. In the 2021 Performance Budget Request to Congress, the CPSC stated that the agency previously asked for an additional $4 million to increase staff presence at 22 US ports, but the funding was denied. The funding was for adding personnel at five ports with no physical CPSC staff presence and at significant ports with import volumes vastly exceeding the agency's capacity. The CPSC port investigators are co-located with the United States Customs and Border Protection (CBP) at US ports of entry. Port investigators identify and prevent noncompliant consumer products from entering the United States (Refs 1 and 14).

Both the FDA and the CPSC maintain offices in Beijing. The CPSC has two professional staff members, while the FDA has 23. These offices help the Chinese government and suppliers understand US safety requirements and maintain a relationship between US and Chinese regulators. There are roughly 27,000 FDA-registered Chinese suppliers. However, due to a lack of personnel, the FDA can only inspect a small percentage of facilities in China and relies primarily on US-based screening to ensure product safety (Ref 1).

4. Chinese Goods Represent 51% of Recalls

Chinese consumer exports to the United States pose a product safety risk. Although Chinese safety regulations have improved recently, gaps in China's product safety regulatory structure have led to unsafe consumer products. As of 2020, China is the largest foreign supplier of consumer goods to the United States. At the same time, Chinese products account for a disproportionate number of product recalls in the United States. According to the US Consumer Product Safety Commission (CPSC), in 2014, Chinese goods constituted 23% of all goods in the United States but represented 51% of all product safety recalls. Similarly, Chinese food imports constitute a disproportionate share of the US Food and Drug Administration (FDA) import refusals. In 2015, China accounted for 4.6% of all US imports of food products. However, 9.6% of all food imports in China were denied entrance by the FDA (Ref 1).

5. Unique Safety Problems from Chinese Imports

Chinese imports pose several unique safety problems to US regulators and consumers. These are a few common ones (Ref 1):

a) Chinese manufacturers can rapidly export newly invented products in large quantities before safety standards can be drafted for them in the United States.

b) It can be challenging to take legal action against Chinese companies that ship unsafe products into the United States. Chinese firms often claim that they are not subject to US jurisdiction. Serving Chinese defendants and obtaining discovery is time-consuming and often requires cooperation from the Chinese central government. Additionally, Chinese state-owned enterprises (SOEs) have recently started using the

US Foreign Sovereign Immunity Act (FSIA) to claim they are immune to civil prosecution under US law.

c) Chinese firms have arbitrarily changed their product designs without notifying US retailers, which can cause high-risk products to circulate widely in the United States.

d) Occasionally, Chinese suppliers have cut corners in production to save costs, supplying US importers with defective goods, raising safety risks, and leaving US retailers responsible for recall and replacement costs.

e) The Chinese regulatory structure is weak regarding product safety.

6. Foreign Sovereign Immunity

Under international law, foreign sovereign governments are generally immune from lawsuits in the United States. Due to diplomatic pressure, Congress enacted the Foreign Sovereign Immunity Act (FSIA) in 1976. The FSIA provides comprehensive standards to guide courts concerning foreign sovereign immunity. However, there are two exceptions: commercial activities and tortious or wrongful acts. In these two cases, the foreign state shall be liable in the same manner and to the same extent as a private individual (Ref 17).

7. Exploitation of the Trade Loophole

Imports valued at less than $800, known as De Minimis packages, are not subject to tariffs and customs inspection. This exemption allows Chinese manufacturing companies to ship goods to US consumers directly. It is worth noting that about 60% of all De Minimis shipments to the United States come from China.

On November 17, 2023, CPSC Commissioner Peter A. Feldman announced the first-ever criminal guilty verdicts under the Consumer Product Safety Act against Chinese-owned companies. They were charged with conspiracy and failure to report critical safety information related to defective dehumidifiers that could catch fire. This highlights the severe challenges CPSC faces in dealing with Chinese companies that try to undermine regulatory authorities through litigation or trade strategies.

The rise of online marketplaces has heightened the risk of unsafe Chinese products reaching US consumers. Platforms like Amazon, Shein, and Temu need to take on the responsibility of ensuring product safety. Shein and Temu, in particular, pose significant challenges for CPSC and American consumers. As major sellers of consumer products, including popular clothing, Chinese companies have significant control over the $106.4 billion industry in 2022. Shein and Temu reportedly send almost 600,000 packages to American consumers each day (Ref 19).

8. Case Studies of Major Recalls and Lawsuits

COVID-19 Lawsuits Against China

In 2020, lawsuits against the People's Republic of China (PRC) were filed in California, Florida, Nevada, Pennsylvania, and Texas. These are class-action suits for persons and businesses in the United States who have suffered injury, damage, and loss related to the coronavirus outbreak.

Missouri and Mississippi have sued China on similar grounds for itself and its residents. The lawsuits alleged that the People's Republic of

China failed to promptly inform the World Health Organization and the world about the contagiousness and scope of the disease outbreak in China. The suit stated that during the critical weeks of the initial outbreak, Chinese authorities deceived the public, suppressed crucial information, arrested whistleblowers, denied human-to-human transmission, destroyed critical medical research, permitted millions of people to be exposed to the virus, and even hoarded personal protective equipment. Consequently, these wrongful actions caused an unnecessary and preventable global pandemic. The lawsuits claimed to fall within statutory exceptions to immunity for tortious or commercial acts in the United States.

On July 30, 2020, the Senate Judiciary Committee approved the Civil Justice for Victims of China-Originated Viral Infections Diseases (COVID) Act. This bill would amend the Foreign Sovereign Immunities Act to permit lawsuits against China for claims related to the coronavirus (Refs 17and 18).

Chinese Toxic Formaldehyde Flooring

Lumber Liquidators is the largest retailer of hardwood flooring in North America, with over 360 stores in 46 states. The company's less expensive Chinese laminate flooring, totaling over 100 million square feet, has been regularly installed in American homes each year.

In 2013, a hedge fund manager raised concerns about the significant increase in profit margins at US flooring retailer Lumber Liquidators, suspecting that the company achieved this through the importation of underpriced flooring that did not comply with US law. Acting on a tip suggesting that the company was importing formaldehyde-tainted flooring from China, the hedge fund manager short-sold Lumber Liquidators' stocks. Formaldehyde, a potentially harmful substance, can be present in the glues used in flooring construction and can potentially leak into homes. This tip prompted investigations in

California, where tests on Lumber Liquidators' products revealed that the flooring sourced from China consistently contained formaldehyde levels above California's standards. On average, the Chinese samples contained 6 to 7 times the allowable level of formaldehyde as per state law, and some samples contained up to 20 times the permitted amount. Prolonged exposure to formaldehyde carries known health risks, such as an increased likelihood of developing asthma, chronic respiratory irritation, and leukemia.

Following this testing, the news broadcast network CBS launched an investigation into flooring sourced from China. CBS tested 31 boxes of Chinese-made flooring in several US states and found that while all of them were labeled as compliant with California standards, only one contained less than the amount allowed by California law. Some exceeded the legal limit by a factor of 13. In addition, CBS sent investigators to the Chinese flooring mills that manufactured flooring for Lumber Liquidators, and those suppliers admitted to providing high formaldehyde levels in the flooring, deliberately mislabeling them as compliant with California standards.

In 2016, Lumber Liquidators faced severe consequences in federal court after pleading guilty to egregious environmental crimes related to Chinese flooring. The company was ordered to pay over $13.1 million in penalties, including a staggering $7.8 million in criminal fines, and was placed on a five-year probation.

In 2016, a significant milestone was achieved when Congress passed a US nationwide standard for formaldehyde levels in flooring. This crucial legislation, similar to the standards adopted in California, represents a major shift in the industry and a significant victory for consumer rights (Refs 1, 9, and 10).

Toxic Chinese Drywall Legal Battle

Drywall was imported from China in 2004–2008 because of the housing market boom and substantial rebuilding efforts following Hurricane Katrina in New Orleans. As a result, more than 100,000 US homes had Chinese drywall within their structures. The imported Chinese drywall released sulfuric gases that corroded metal appliances, plumbing, and electrical components in homes. In addition, since the Chinese drywall is very brittle, microscopic pieces of the drywall are released into the air when removed from an environment. These particles found their way into the lungs, similar to asbestos materials. Some health problems related to Chinese drywall were respiratory, irritated sinuses and eyes, dry throat, frequent nosebleeds, incessant coughing, and sleep apnea (Ref 8).

The Consumer Product Safety Commission received more than 4,000 reports of tainted drywall in 44 states. Given the large number of affected homes and the expenses associated with repairs, the total economic costs associated with tainted Chinese drywall are estimated to be as high as $25 billion.

Affected US homeowners sued more than 700 builders, suppliers, and insurers to seek damages. However, given the high costs incurred, only Chinese manufacturers had the resources necessary to fund repairs. In 2009, a lawsuit was filed against two firms that had supplied most of the tainted Chinese drywall: Knauf Plasterboard Tianjin (a Chinese affiliate of a German company) and Taishan Gypsum (a Chinese firm).

In 2011, Knauf agreed to an $800 million settlement with US homeowners. Taishan initially claimed that, as a China-based company, it was not subject to litigation in the United States and had stopped appearing in court. In 2014, a US judge took the exceptional step of preventing Taishan or any of its affiliates from doing business in the United States and issued a penalty equal to 25% of its profits. This action prompted Taishan to start cooperating. In 2015, Taishan settled the $2.7 million case brought against it but still has not agreed to pay thousands of other affected US homeowners.

In 2012, the United States Congress passed the Drywall Safety Act, which set chemical standards for domestic and imported drywalls (Refs 1 and 8).

Dangerous Chinese Copycat Hoverboards

A new product can be sold widely in the United States before safety guidelines can be implemented to protect consumers. This occurred with Chinese hoverboards, a self-balancing two-wheeled skateboard. In 2013, the first hoverboard patent was filed by Segway in the United States. By 2015, an estimated 1,000 Chinese factories were manufacturing hoverboards. About 4.5 million Chinese hoverboards were exported to the United States that year. From 2015 to 2016, the Consumer Product Safety Commission received 52 reports of hoverboards catching fire, resulting in more than $2 million in damage, including the destruction of two homes and an automobile. The incidents were widespread, affecting US consumers in 24 different states. More than 500,000 hoverboards were recalled in July 2016 over fire concerns.

Faulty products can result from copycat manufacturers. Enforcement of intellectual property (IP) rights can screen out these faulty products. The hoverboard market, in particular, has been subject to many patent battles. In 2014, Segway filed a patent complaint against Chinese hoverboard manufacturer Ninebot. In 2016, the International Trade Commission banned Chinese copycat hoverboards from entering the United States. However, by then, Ninebot had bought Segway and its IP rights. As a result, Ninebot became the only producer allowed to sell hoverboards to the United States, using Segway's patent (Ref 1).

Chinese Candied Ginger with Harmful Level of Lead

In 2013, the California state attorney general and the nonprofit Center for Environmental Health filed a lawsuit against Trader Joe's, Whole Foods, Cost Plus, H-Mart, Safeway, and many other grocers for selling candied ginger containing high lead levels. The tested ginger products revealed an unsafe level of lead. The candied ginger package failed to warn consumers about harmful toxins as required by California Proposition 65.

According to the court settlement document, the defendants agreed not to sell ginger products containing a concentration of more than 17 parts per billion (ppb) lead by weight. They also agreed to withdraw the products named in the lawsuit from the California market and to pay civil penalties and a portion of attorneys' fees. The companies were also required to turn over the contact information of their suppliers (Ref 15).

Fatal Melamine Tainted Wheat and Rice Protein

In 2007, two Chinese companies had illegally exported melamine-contaminated wheat gluten and rice protein for pet food manufacturing, causing animal deaths in the United States. The United States Food and Drug Administration (FDA) has received about 17,000 complaints of sick pets, with about 4,000 deaths reported. Investigations had extended to livestock feed containing melamine-tainted food that made its way to 6,000 hogs and as many as 3.1 million chickens.

Subsequently, the FDA began sampling all wheat gluten shipments from China for melamine contamination. The FDA singled out Xuzhou Anying Biologic Technology as the supplier of the contaminated vegetable protein but discovered that Xuzhou purchased vegetable protein from 25 different Chinese suppliers. As a result, the FDA concluded that it could not determine the origin of the tainted products and issued a US-wide import alert for all vegetable protein imported from China.

The FDA stated that Xuzhou Anying Biologic Technology Development Co. Ltd. evaded quality checks by labeling their products not subject to inspection. Given the possibility of melamine contamination of human food products, the FDA also issued a country-wide detention of all milk products imported from China (Refs 1 and 2).

Chinese Counterfeit Heparin

In 2007, the Children's Hospital in St. Louis, Missouri, observed adverse reactions in their young dialysis patients who were given Baxter heparin. They promptly informed the FDA and Baxter. Three months later, Baxter, a US-based company, initiated an urgent nationwide recall of nine lots of heparin due to severe allergic reactions and low blood pressure in patients. The contaminated heparin from Baxter led to 81 deaths, and at least 785 people experienced severe allergic reactions.

Heparin is a crucial anticoagulant (blood thinner) widely used in surgery and dialysis. It is derived from pig intestines and has been marketed in the United States since the 1930s. The membrane of the intestine is collected and processed to form a dried substance known as crude heparin, which is further refined into an active pharmaceutical ingredient (API).

Baxter, the final manufacturer of the contaminated heparin, has a complex international supply chain that starts in China, where 10 to 12 Chinese workshops make crude heparin. This crude heparin is sold to brokers or consolidators, who then sell it to Scientific Protein Laboratories (SPL). SPL is an American company with a plant in Changzhou, China, and another one in Wisconsin, United States, that produces heparin API from crude heparin. This heparin API is then sold to Baxter, which manufactures finished heparin products at its Cherry Hill, New Jersey plant. Baxter had produced about 50% of the heparin used in the United States.

The FDA's investigation into the cause of the outbreak revealed that heparin API made by SPL China contained an oversulfated chondroitin sulfate, which mimics natural heparin and could not be detected by standard tests. Oversulfated chondroitin sulfate is not an approved drug in the United States and should not have been present in heparin. The evidence suggests that contamination was a deliberate act by Chinese suppliers to cut the raw heparin with a substitute that would pass the standard purity test. Economic incentives drove the fraud. It costs approximately $20/kg ($20/2.2 lbs.) to produce oversulfated chondroitin sulfate versus $2,000/kg to produce crude heparin.

During the United States House of Representatives hearing, the FDA stated that the agency lacked personnel, effective policies, adequate resources, and funding to perform its job correctly. Unfortunately, the FDA did not inspect SPL China (as required by standard policy) before approving the shipments of heparin API to Baxter. Furthermore, this plant was not registered in China as a drug manufacturer, and Chinese officials had never inspected the plant either. According to the FDA, SPL China failed to have adequate systems for evaluating crude heparin to ensure its safety, and the heparin manufacturing equipment was unsuitable for its intended use. Until the recall, Baxter never inspected the SPL China plant.

According to the *Chicago Tribune*, in 2011, a Cook County circuit court jury in Chicago awarded $625,000 to the family of a deceased man who was given the tainted Baxter heparin. This was the first of 300 lawsuits against Baxter and Scientific Protein Laboratories (SPL). The

Chinese criminals who sold fake crude heparin to SPL used by Baxter have not been caught (Refs 1, 12, and 16).

Lead-Tainted Toys from China

China has been the largest supplier of toys to the United States market for over two decades and accounted for 85% of all US toy imports in 2015. The recalls associated with Chinese toys coated with lead paint in 2007 exposed shortcomings in the US product safety defense and improved how the Consumer Product Safety Commission monitors imports for safety (Ref 1).

In 2007, Mattel, the world's largest toymaker, faced three toy recalls that affected millions of its toys made in China because those toys posed lead poisoning and choking risks to small children. Many of them feature Sesame Street and Nickelodeon. More than 300,000 of the tainted toys have been bought by consumers in the United States. Although the United States has banned the sale of toys made with lead paint since 1978, those products continue to make their way into the US market.

In 2007, China and the United States signed an agreement deepening their cooperation to increase product safety. China pledged to immediately eliminate the use of lead paint in children's products through a paint certification system and agreed to share information about Chinese supply networks in case of a US recall. The Chinese government also agreed to strip manufacturers of their export licenses if they violate safety regulations.

In 2008, the US Congress passed the Consumer Product Safety Improvement Act, which introduced necessary safeguards for children's products. Under the Act, all children's products sold within the United States must be tested by a CPSC-accredited facility, receive safety certification, and contain permanent tracking information.

In 2009, Mattel Inc. and its Fisher-Price subsidiary paid a $2.3-million civil penalty for importing and selling toys that contained excessive levels of lead. The penalty was part of an agreement that the companies had with the Consumer Product Safety Commission for their series of 2007 recalls involving about 95 Mattel and Fisher-Price toy models. These included Barbie doll accessories and Go, Diego, Go! products (Ref 7).

In 2011, the CPSC established its first overseas office to cooperate with Chinese regulators and provide safety training. Total recalls associated with lead in children's products have declined significantly since 2007 (Refs 1, 4, 6, and 7).

Lethal Dog Treats from China

From 2007 to 2015, the FDA received 5,200 complaints reporting gastrointestinal or kidney problems linked to jerky treats (pet food) imported from China. At least 1,140 dogs died. Problems with jerky treats first appeared in 2007, with a rising frequency in 2012 and 2013. The FDA could not identify the contaminant that caused these illnesses but ultimately issued an import alert for Chinese dog treatment companies beginning in 2014. Sure, Chinese jerky treats contain residues of antibiotics and antivirals.

According to the FDA, tracking pet illness outbreaks was not easy. First, it was not easy to collect evidence, as necropsies are not typically conducted on pets. Second, the FDA could not find a definitive contaminant that caused the illness. However, since it began detaining shipments from specific Chinese importers, the reports of jerky-related illness have declined. In 2016, China's animal feed regulations, which pertain to pet food products, were revised to increase pet safety. However, it may take China time to enforce these rules (Refs 1 and 3).

Chinese Ginger with Harmful Pesticide Residue

In 2007, State health officials warned Californians to avoid ginger grown in China after testing it from two dozen Albertsons grocery stores in California. Ginger imported from China contained harmful levels of aldicarb sulfoxide, a pesticide not approved for use on ginger by both the United States and China. Symptoms of aldicarb poisoning include nausea, headaches, blurred vision, muscle spasms, and difficulty breathing. In high doses, aldicarb can be fatal.

The complexity of global supply chains has made it difficult for some US companies to trace the origin of their products. When American companies purchase agricultural products from China, they often demand low prices, making it impractical for importers to run proper tests on the produce. Tainted ginger was traced back to Christopher Ranch, a major US garlic grower, who had acquired about 19,000 pounds from another California company, Modern Trading Inc. California authorities found that Modern Trading did not have the necessary health license to operate and was shut down during the investigation.

Modern Trading imported ginger from Modern Organic Ginger Co., which is located in Shandong Province in China. Modern Organic bought ginger from thousands of Chinese farmers, packaged it, and then shipped it around the world. China accounted for the majority of ginger imported into the United States. CBS News reported that despite the Chinese government's efforts to ban pesticides containing aldicarb on certain produce, it is still very popular with farmers. Some of these pesticides were labeled as the "Gold Farmer Pill" and sold for $2 per kilogram (Ref 11).

Unsafe Chinese Tires: Importer's Responsibility

Chinese suppliers have occasionally altered the design of their products to cut costs, and if importers do not take action quickly, these products can circulate widely through the United States. In 2000, US retailer Foreign Tire Sales (FTS) began buying Hangzhou Zhongce's radial truck tires after their initial tests showed that they performed well. A few years later, Hangzhou Zhongce unilaterally changed their tires by removing gum strips between tire belts, a safety design to keep tires from separating and causing accidents. In 2005, FTS found out about the defective tire after noticing a series of warranty claims. FTS did not alert federal authorities until a lawsuit was brought against the company in 2007, when a Zhongce tire allegedly separated on a van in New Jersey, resulting in two deaths and one serious injury.

Under US law, FTS was responsible for replacing the defective tires. However, as a small company with only seven employees, FTS claimed it would go bankrupt. Finally, FTS recalled 255,000 tires, which cost the company $51 million. Then, FTS sued Hangzhou Zhongce in US court and got a settlement. Zhongce was China's second-largest tire manufacturer and had significant resources to reimburse FTS, but it is unknown to what extent FTS was able to recoup its losses (Ref 1).

Note: The United States Consumer Product Safety Commission has a website that explicitly lists recalls of products made in China at https://www.cpsc.gov, Recalls—Chinese Monthly Listing.

CHAPTER 18

UNVEILING THE DARK SIDE OF POULTRY AND MEAT FROM CHINA

—♈︎—

The chapter offers a thorough exploration of the hidden aspects of China's poultry and meat industry, exposing deceit and potential hazards. It provides historical background and tracks the industry's development, offering valuable insights into its intricate operations and the driving forces behind its expansion. The chapter emphasizes the widespread presence of contaminated chicken, the impact of African Swine Fever, and the rise of harmful meat products, highlighting the severe implications for consumer well-being and safety. It also reveals the illicit practices of smuggling poultry and meat into the United States, posing significant risks to public health and food security. Through rigorous research and compelling analysis, you are urged to demand increased transparency and accountability in the global food supply chain and to push for stricter regulations to prevent malpractice.

1. History & Background of the Chinese Poultry and Meat Industry

History

2004: China submitted a request to export poultry products to the United States.

2005: Hundreds of thousands of pounds of prohibited poultry products from China and other Asian countries were shipped to the United States in crates labeled "dried lily flower," "prune slices," and "vegetables."

2013: The United States approved Chinese processors' re-export of heat-treated/cooked chicken that had been initially slaughtered in the United States, France, Chile, or Canada.

2013: Chinese authorities notified the World Health Organization (WHO) about human infections caused by Avian Influenza (H7N9).

2014: A Chinese meat processor supplied unsanitary and expired meat products to McDonald's, KFC, and other foreign food establishments in China.

2017: The first known shipment of cooked chicken processed in China reached the United States.

2019: The United States approved Chinese imports of fully cooked products from birds raised and slaughtered in China.

2019: China became the sixth largest global poultry exporter at $253 million (3.8%).

2019: China smuggled over 1 million pounds of prohibited pork products into the United States.

2020: Prohibited raw frozen chicken wings from China were smuggled into the United States with a fake USDA approval stamp.

2020: Cooked duck blood curds illegally imported from China.

2021: Over 97,000 pounds of beef tallow products were illegally imported from China and ended up in American supermarkets.

Background of Chinese Poultry

Regulation: The United States Department of Agriculture's Food Safety and Inspection Service (USDA's FSIS) regulates meat and poultry imports by granting equivalency to foreign countries' meat and poultry slaughter and processing systems. Any country that wishes to export meat or poultry to the United States must request that the FSIS review its inspection system to determine if it is equivalent to the one in the United States.

Concern about China's Weak Track Record on Food Safety: Slaughter equivalency would allow China to fill some of the vast US demand for breast meat with excess Chinese supplies. Dark meat, chicken feet, and organs are in high demand in China. Processed poultry meat imported from China has raised concerns about the lax Chinese food safety enforcement. Because China has a long history of food safety violations, many food safety advocates, the public, and Members of Congress continue raising concerns about importing poultry meat from China (Ref 22).

Cheap Labor in China: The United States Bureau of Labor Statistics indicates that American poultry processors are typically paid more than $11 per hour on average. Chinese poultry processing plant workers earn between $1 to $2 per hour. Therefore, it makes good economic sense for American poultry suppliers to ship chicken to China for processing.

Avian Flu: In 2013, Chinese authorities notified the World Health Organization (WHO) about Avian Influenza (H7N9) human infections. The Avian flu killed chickens and infected humans as well. This is China's fifth avian influenza strain since 1997. In 2021, 1,568 laboratory-confirmed human infections with the avian influenza (H7N9) virus have been reported to the WHO since early 2013. Among them, 33 cases were infected with HPAI (H7N9) virus, which has mutations. These 33 cases were from Taiwan and China (Guangxi, Guangdong, Hunan, Shaanxi, Hebei, Henan, Fujian, Yunnan, and Inner Mongolia) (Refs 1 and 10).

2004: The United States denied Chinese chicken import due to avian influenza. China submitted a request to the United States Department of Agriculture's Food Safety and Inspection Service (USDA's FSIS) for initial eligibility to export poultry products to the United States. Animal and Plant Health Inspection Service (APHIS) had classified China as a region affected by highly pathogenic avian influenza subtype (H5Nl) and Exotic Newcastle Disease. As a result, to export products to the United States, China must meet both APHIS and FSIS regulations.

2010: China failed the test to export to the United States. The FSIS comprehensively analyzed China's Food Safety Law and audited China's poultry slaughter inspection system. The FSIS concluded that China was lacking uniform regulatory enforcement across provincial jurisdictions. Furthermore, China was unaware of the FSIS requirements for ready-to-cook poultry and did not require establishments to maintain a Hazard Analysis Critical Control Point (HACCP) system. HACCP is a food safety management system through the analysis and control of biological, chemical, and physical hazards. The system includes raw material production, procurement and handling, manufacturing, distribution, and consumption of the finished product (Ref 19).

Chinese Poultry Approval Process

2013: The US authorized China to export processed, cooked poultry to the United States. The FSIS concluded that the Chinese poultry slaughter system did not meet FSIS equivalence criteria. The auditors reported several discrepancies between the contents of the inspection manual and the actual systems of inspection in operation at the audited slaughter establishments. However, the United States began authorizing China to export processed, cooked poultry to the United States. Poultry imported from China must be sourced from and slaughtered in the United States or from other countries allowed to export raw poultry to the United States (Canada, Chile, and France) (Ref 19).

2015: The United States approved China's poultry slaughter system. The FSIS auditors evaluated the administrative functions of China Inspection and Quarantine (CIQ) offices in the Shandong and Anhui provinces and the two eligible slaughter establishments selected by Chinese officials. Additionally, the FSIS assessed the adequacy of the inspection system's technical support, assessing the functions of two government laboratories (one microbiology laboratory located in the Shandong Province and one chemical residue laboratory in the Anhui Province). Based on assessing only two selected establishments, the FSIS recommended granting China the poultry slaughter system equivalence. This means that the United States will rely on Chinese officials to inspect chicken raised and slaughtered in China for export to the United States (Ref 19).

2017: The first known shipment of cooked chicken from China reached the United States. Chicken from China will not be labeled. A representative from Qingdao Nine-Alliance Group, the first exporter, did not specify the name or brand under which it was being sold. The privately owned chicken company, one of the largest in China, has already supplied markets in Asia, the Middle East, and Europe (Ref 8).

2019: United States approved cooked poultry raised and slaughtered in China. The USDA officially approved China to export fully cooked (not shelf-stable) poultry products from birds raised and slaughtered in China to the United States. China may not export raw poultry because of the risk of animal diseases. However, no USDA inspectors will be present in the Chinese processing plants, meaning American consumers are not guaranteed their chicken is being slaughtered in safe and sanitary conditions. The USDA relies on Chinese officials to certify any poultry establishments within their territories, but they are subject to review by the USDA's Food Safety and Inspection Service (FSIS).

The US Congress Imposed Restrictions on Poultry Products from China: Some Members of Congress have expressed concerns about the USDA-regulated products originating from certain countries, such as China and Southeast Asia. This is due to numerous past incidents of unsafe or tainted food and poor hygiene practices in production. Issues include inadequate regulatory oversight from the Chinese government and persistent evidence of economically incentivized food fraud jeopardizing public health. In response to concerns about China's food safety record, Congress limited imports of poultry products from China in 2020. This does not mean chicken imported from China will not appear at American dining tables.

Poultry from China Will Not Be Labeled: Country-of-origin labeling (COOL) allows consumers to know the origin of their products. However, under the COOL regulations administered by the USDA's Agricultural Marketing Service, processed products are exempt from labeling. Chinese-processed chicken used in restaurants, added to cans of soup and other products, or sent in bulk to be packaged by retailers would not be labeled as it came from China.

(Refs 2, 7, 8, 9, 13, 18, 19, and 22)

2. Tainted Chicken, African Swine Fever, and Toxic Meat

Tainted Chicken

In 2013, fast food giant KFC cut more than 1,000 farms from its supplier network in China to ensure food safety after a scandal over tainted chicken hurt sales. The issue came to light when China's commercial hub of Shanghai and the northern province of Shanxi investigated KFC suppliers over claims of high levels of antibiotics in chicken. KFC stopped using potentially risky chicken farms, improved the screening process of suppliers, and stepped up self-inspections to address food safety concerns. In 2014, a Chinese meat processor supplied unsanitary and expired meat products to McDonald's, KFC, and other foreign food establishments in China (Refs 3 and 22).

African Swine Fever

In 2018, China reported several cases of African swine fever (ASF), a highly contagious, non-curable disease that is deadly to pigs. The disease has spread throughout China and wiped out 50 million of its 428 million pigs in 2018, and that number reached over 100 million in 2021. The ASF also has rapidly spread throughout Asia. Before the outbreak, China produced and consumed about half of the world's pork volume annually.

China's poor food safety regulations and inspection systems contributed to the spread of the ASF virus. The ASF virus could still spread to United States hog farms through contaminated non-pork products or pet food (Ref 24).

In 2020, *The New York Times* reported:

> A new strain of the H1N1 swine flu virus is spreading silently in workers on pig farms in China and should be urgently controlled to avoid another pandemic, a team of scientists says in a new study. The H1N1 was highly transmissible and spread around the world in 2009, killing about 285,000 people and morphing into seasonal flu. The study was a collaboration among China, the World Health Organization, and scientists from China and Britain (Ref 25).

Toxic Meat in China

Diseased Pigs Sold to Consumers: In 2013, more than 16,000 dead pigs were dumped into the river in Zhejiang province, a source of the city's tap water. Early tests showed they carried porcine circovirus, a common disease among hogs. According to Chinese officials, 7.7 million pigs are raised in northern Zhejiang. With a mortality rate of 2% to 4%, up to 300,000 carcasses need to be disposed of each year. While farmers are required by law to cremate animals that die of disease or natural causes, black market dealers intercepted the chain and butchered the dead hogs to sell as pork. In 2012, a Chinese court sentenced three butchers to life in prison who had processed 77,000 carcasses, making almost 9 million yuan ($1.4 million) profit. As a result of the crackdown, black market traders stopped buying the dead stock, and farmers dumped dead pigs into the river.

Rodent Meat Sold as Lamb: In 2013, *The New York Times* reported that Chinese police had caught a gang of 63 traders in eastern China who bought rat, fox, and mink flesh and sold it as lamb. They doused the animals in gelatin, red pigment, and nitrates and sold them as lamb in Shanghai and adjacent Jiangsu Province for about $1.6 million.

Toxic Meat: The Chinese police also arrested 904 people suspected of selling fake, diseased, toxic, or adulterated meat and broke up 1,721 illicit factories, workshops, and shops.

a) Police caught a company in Inner Mongolia with 23 tons of fake beef jerky and unprocessed frozen meat adulterated with flavoring chemicals and swarming with bacteria.

b) Six suspects in Guizhou Province were caught with 8.8 tons of toxic chicken feet marinated in a hydrogen peroxide solution and adulterated with illegal additives. Chicken feet, steamed or boiled with spices, are famous in China.

c) The police in Shaanxi Province arrested a suspect accused of selling a lamb carcass so heavily laced with pesticide that one person died after eating the barbecued meat (Ref 20).

African Swine Fever Contamination: In 2019, a large Chinese frozen food producer, Sanquan Food Co Ltd, recalled products contaminated with the African swine fever virus. The African swine fever is a fatal, incurable disease in pigs that killed up to half of China's hog herd. The disease has spread rapidly across China since 2018, reaching 25 provinces and regions. Samples of processed pork products sold in the northwestern Chinese province of Gansu contained the virus. The infected samples came from 11 companies, including Sanquan, Kedi Group, and Synear (Ref 21).

Cadmium Contamination: One concern about animal meats from China is that Chinese rice fields are likely to be contaminated with cadmium, a toxic heavy metal, from soil polluted by industrial wastewater. Cadmium that accumulates in rice plants gets into the meat of farmed animals that eat the rice husks (Ref 5).

3. Smuggling of Poultry and Meat Products into the United States

2005: Chicken products were smuggled into the United States. The USDA teams seized hundreds of thousands of pounds of prohibited poultry products from China and other Asian countries. Some were shipped in crates labeled "dried lily flower," "prune slices," and "vegetables." It is unclear how much more illegal meat got away undetected. Before 2013, China was not certified to sell chicken to the United States because it had not met food safety requirements. If not correctly processed, Chinese raw chicken could be a source of avian flu, triggering a human pandemic (Ref 11).

2019: Pork products were smuggled into the United States. Federal officials at the Newark port of entry seized 50 shipping containers with 1 million pounds of pork products smuggled from China. This was the most significant agricultural bust in American history. The meat was primarily cured, and the cargo containers were not refrigerated. The Newark port is among the largest ports of entry in the United States and the busiest on the East Coast. It is illegal to import pork products from countries like China (Ref 12).

2020: Duck Blood Curds were illegally imported into the United States. The United States Department of Agriculture's Food Safety and Inspection Service (FSIS) issued a public health alert about imported cooked duck blood curds from China. The total amount of ineligible products was undetermined. A recall was not requested because the FSIS could not contact the importer. The problem was identified through an investigation by the USDA's Animal and Plant Health Inspection Service (APHIS) (Ref 17).

2020: Organic raw chicken wings were illegally imported from China. The United States Department of Agriculture's Food Safety and Inspection Service (FSIS) issued a public health alert for raw frozen New Orleans-roasted organic Chicken Wings products imported from China and labeled with a false USDA mark of inspection. The products were shipped to one retail location and distributed to 20 different locations in California, Oregon, and Washington. The problem was discovered when FSIS received a consumer complaint reporting a product suspected of being illegally imported and sold at a location (Ref 16).

2021: Beef tallow products were illegally imported into the United States. Chino, California-based GLG Trading Inc. recalled almost 97,000 pounds of Ming Yang Hotpot Seasoning beef tallow products that were illegally imported from China, an ineligible country for beef. The products subject to recall did not bear a US federal mark of inspection. These items were shipped to distributors, retail locations, and restaurants in Arizona, California, Hawaii, Nevada, New York, and Texas (Ref 14).

4. The Takeover of America's Biggest Pork Producer

In 2013, China's biggest meat products company, Shuanghui International Holdings, acquired Virginia-based Smithfield Foods (America's largest pork producer) for nearly $4.7 billion, 30% more than the company's market value. It was the most significant Chinese acquisition of a US company. According to *Bloomberg,* the purchase of Smithfield was part of a $52 billion overseas spending spree by Chinese food companies since 2005, as China's population became wary of domestically produced food. Shuanghui's factory in Zhengzhou, China, makes American-style pork products from imported Smithfield meat.

Public Broadcasting Service (PBS) television reported that the Bank of China, a state-owned bank, approved the $4 billion loan to buy Smithfield in a single day. In 2011, the government issued a five-year plan directing food companies like Shuanghui to obtain more meat for their production lines by purchasing overseas businesses. The Chinese government appointed Senior executives at Shuanghui (Ref 23).

Smithfield represents 25% of the pork industry in the United States, and the takeover could threaten the vital American food industry in the long term. Since 2011, China's state-run media has reported allegations of maggots, excessive bacteria, and illegal additives in Shuanghui's meat products. This merger between Shuanghui and Smithfield may only make it more challenging to protect the American food supply (Ref 4).

Since 2019, workers have been shipping frozen pig carcasses to China for further processing. Smithfield's slaughterhouse in Virginia slaughters about 10,000 pigs a day. Since 2018, the African swine fever outbreak has killed millions of pigs and pushed prices so high that Chinese importers are willing to pay hefty tariffs that China imposed on US pork as part of the trade war. China's tariffs are 62% on frozen carcasses and 72% on muscle cuts (Ref 6).

Shuanghui has officially changed its name to W.H. Group. It is now a publicly traded Chinese meat and food processing company headquartered in Hong Kong. However, since the acquisition, it has retained the name Smithfield Foods for that brand. WH Group Limited is the largest pork company in the world.

China used Smithfield to acquire many more businesses. In 2016, Smithfield Foods acquired California-based Clougherty Packing from Hormel Foods for $145 million. The acquisition included brands such as Farmer John and Saag's Specialty Meats. Clougherty had a large selection of pork products and an extensive sales network in the southwestern United States. Smithfield also acquired hog farms in Arizona, California, and Wyoming as part of the deal.

In 2017, Smithfield Foods acquired the remaining 66.5% of the equity in Pini Polonia, which has a slaughterhouse in Poland and facilities in Italy and Hungary. The deal included the acquisition of Pini Polska, Hamburger Pini, and Royal Chicken.

CHAPTER 19

TROUBLED WATERS: UNMASKING THE REALITIES OF SEAFOOD IMPORTS FROM CHINA

———〜〜〜———

This chapter boldly exposes the hidden truths behind seafood imports from China, laying bare a complex web of challenges and risks. You will gain deep insight into the longstanding issues affecting this sector by delving into the historical backdrop of US refusals and the Chinese seafood industry. Furthermore, the chapter fearlessly explores the widespread pollution and abuse in seafood farming practices, vividly highlighting the environmental and health hazards of contaminated products. Through a rigorous examination of regulatory frameworks and FDA inspections, you can confidently make informed choices and advocate for enhanced safety measures when consuming seafood.

1. History of US Refusals and Chinese Seafood Industry

Seafood from China

In general, seafood is an excellent source of protein and omega-3 fats. However, seafood lovers need to know where their food comes from to make a more rational purchase decision. Imported seafood may be more dangerous because the FDA does not have the resources to proactively and regularly inspect foreign facilities and conduct more tests at US ports of entry.

Seafood from China can be found everywhere, from supermarkets to upscale restaurants. American seafood brokers mostly rely on government inspections and importers to ensure the seafood is safe for consumers. However, the FDA has continued to reject filthy and contaminated fish from China at US ports. Due to the agency's limited resources, dishonest businesses continued to mislabel or reroute shipments through other countries. Some American importers have been taking precautions and testing for various antibiotics and melamine (Ref 5).

History of US Refusals of Seafood from China

Seafood products from China faced the most refusals, followed by vegetables and fruit products. Seafood refusals from China doubled from about 20% in 2000-2004 to nearly 40% in 2007-2008. Eels, catfish fillets, and shrimp accounted for most of the refused seafood shipments. Various other products were also refused, including tilapia, tuna, monkfish, squid, jellyfish, crawfish, crab, cod, mackerel, and other fish species. These products were processed-frozen, breaded, filleted, de-boned, and skinless. Many fish and shellfish refusals may reflect increased monitoring of the products in 2006 due to chronic problems with veterinary drug residues and unsafe additives in aquaculture products. During that time, the FDA devoted half of its testing of aquaculture products to shipments from China due to widespread problems (Ref 20).

In June 2007, after years of warnings, the FDA issued an import alert of five types of farm-raised seafood (shrimp, catfish, basa, eel, and dace) from China. While the alert is in effect, these products are refused unless they can be shown to be free of harmful drug residues. During targeted sampling from October 2006 to May 2007, the FDA repeatedly found that farm-raised seafood from China was contaminated with unapproved antimicrobial agents that cause cancer and antibiotic residues. In 2007, a report from the FDA stated that more than 60% of the seafood rejected at the border came from China. The European Union and Japan have also imposed temporary bans on

Chinese seafood because of illegal drug residues. (Refs 8, 9, 10, and 20).

In 2007, officials from the United States and China signed an agreement to improve oversight of Chinese fish farms as part of a more significant deal on food and drug safety. However, regulators in both countries are struggling to keep contaminated seafood out of the US market. In 2024, the FDA is still alerted about these problems with seafood imported from China.

2. Pollution and Abuse in Seafood Farming

Chinese Fish Raised in Toxic Water

Over the past two decades, China's seafood aquaculture industry has expanded significantly, making China the world's largest producer and exporter of seafood. Chinese agricultural statistics show that fish and shellfish production in China doubled from 1999 to 2009, with about two-thirds of the production coming from cultivated sources and a third from wild-caught sources. The Chinese Fishery Bureau reports that there are over 4.5 million fish farmers in China, with most seafood products coming from aquaculture factories in coastal areas. Smaller-scale farmers raise fish and shellfish in ponds, lakes, or reservoirs. In the early 1990s, thousands of peasants began creating fish ponds by carving up large plots and filling them with water, resulting in significant prosperity (Refs 3, 10, and 20).

However, in the mid-1990s, severe environmental issues arose when factories began dumping waste into rivers, polluting the water and making it unsuitable for fish farming. To keep their fish alive, farmers started feeding their stocks with illegal veterinary drugs and adding pesticides to the water in fish farms to kill algae. Consequently, poisonous and carcinogenic residues were found in seafood from

China. Not only that, but wild-caught fish in China are also contaminated because coastal waters are polluted with oil, lead, mercury, and copper, according to the State Environmental Protection Administration in China (Ref 10).

Seafood Raised on Pig Waste

In the November 2012 issue of *Bloomberg Market Magazine*, it was reported that fish at a tilapia farm outside Hong Kong were being fed a diet that included pig and goose feces. This practice is unsafe for consumers because the manure may be contaminated with salmonella. The use of fecal matter is a cheaper alternative to commercial fish food. Some argue that the feces are added to the water to produce an algae bloom, which in turn produces a form of plankton that the fish then eat (Ref 7).

Abuse of Polyphosphates in China

Sodium tripolyphosphates (STPP) is an artificially produced additive that is universally used to add weight to seafood to gain extra profit and mislead customers. It cannot be detected when the seafood is raw because the flesh absorbs it. Shrimps, scallops, flatfish (sole, dap, or plaice), basa or catfish, and other farm-raised fish are commonly soaked in STPP. It is very usual for Alaskan frozen fish to be sent to China for processing and shipped back to the United States. Therefore, Alaskan wild-caught fish may contain STPP. In general, cheaper fish are more likely to undergo the treatment than the more expensive ones, such as king salmon (Ref 6).

After soaking in STPP, a white, watery substance emerges from the frozen fish fillets during cooking, and the fillets shrink. Unfortunately, in the United States, labeling is not required for raw seafood treated with STPP. Some packaged seafood products may list it as an ingredient. As an option, seafood may be labeled as "dry" and has not been treated with STPP. Avoid seafood marked as "wet," meaning they have been soaked in an STPP solution (Ref 6).

The European Union, Canada, and Brazil all have limits on the total STPP allowed in seafood products, generally between 0.1% and 0.5% of the final product. The EU also mandated that the use of STPP must be declared. The United States does not have a limit on how much STPP can be present in seafood. Most phosphates are found naturally in foods. However, exceeding a certain consumption level could harm health (Ref 6).

Grow Hormones, Pesticides, and Dyes

Fish farms in China may use hormones to help their fish grow more prominent, pesticides to keep the water clean, and artificial dyes to give their fish a brighter color. Canthaxanthin and astaxanthin dyes are fed to farmed fish (salmon and trout) and poultry to increase pigmentation. Canthaxanthin uptake can cause a deposit in the human retina, which causes visual problems (Ref 18).

Melamine Tainted Food

In 2008, according to *The Los Angeles Times*, industry experts and business people in China confirmed that melamine has been routinely added to fish and animal feed to boost protein readings artificially. Melamine, commonly used in plastics and dishware, can lead to health problems, such as kidney stones and even renal failure. The FDA's Animal Drugs Research Center Laboratory conducted studies of melamine-fed catfish, trout, tilapia, and salmon and found that fish tissues had melamine concentrations of up to 200 parts per million. That is 80 times the maximum tolerable amount set by the FDA for safe consumption. As of 2024, the FDA still has a melamine alert on food products imported from China (Ref 5).

3. China Is the World's Largest Aquaculture Producer and Exporter

World's Largest Aquaculture Producer

According to the Food and Agriculture Organization of the United Nations (FAO), total fisheries and aquaculture production reached a record 214 million tonnes in 2020. This total comprised 178 million tonnes of aquatic seafood and 36 million tonnes of algae. World aquaculture production of seafood grew by 2.7 percent in 2020 compared to 2019.

Asian countries were the primary aquaculture producers, accounting for 70% of the total production. The Americas followed with 12%, Europe with 10%, Africa with 7%, and Oceania with 1%. China was the leading producer, contributing 35% of the total production. Other significant producers included India (8%), Indonesia (7%), and Vietnam (5%). These four Asian countries were responsible for approximately 55% of the world's fisheries and aquaculture production of aquatic seafood in 2020. The production of worldwide aquatic seafood in inland waters increased from 12% of total production in the late 1980s to 37% in 2020.

Since 2016, the expansion of aquaculture areas in China has virtually halted. Chinese producers have been unable to expand due to environmental concerns and government restrictions on the exploitation of water resources and coastal development. Additionally, e-commerce has become a popular venue for Chinese consumers to purchase seafood products, prompting some producers to shift their focus from foreign markets to domestic e-commerce channels.

In December 2019, the Chinese Ministry of Agriculture and Rural Affairs (MARA) announced a 10-year fishing ban in 332 conservation areas in the Yangtze River. Freshwater aquaculture sites have been significantly reduced as the government has banned or limited aquaculture farming in reservoirs and large lakes. Farmers also face higher rental rates for using water resources, including ponds and ocean waters, which decreases profits and limits expansion abilities. Almost half of China's tilapia production was exported, with about 30% of tilapia exports destined for the United States. China is the world's largest producer of farmed tilapia and shrimp (Ref 4).

World's Largest Seafood Exporter

Since 2002, China has been the leading fish producer and has been the world's largest exporter of fish and seafood products. After China, the major exporters in 2016 were Norway, Vietnam, and Thailand. The European Union (EU) represented the single largest market for fish and seafood products, followed by the United States of America and Japan. In 2016, these three markets together accounted for approximately 64% of the total value of world imports of fish and seafood products (Ref 19).

China has 26 major export markets, with Japan being the most prominent destination, followed by the United States. However, exports to the United States declined significantly due to trade tensions, netting 0.44 MMT and $2.4 billion in 2019, compared to 0.55 MMT and $3.29 billion in 2018. China mainly exports processed fishery products. Exports from China declined in 2020 due to the coronavirus pandemic.

China's Fishery Product Exports by Category
(Value in Million USD)

Category/Year	2016	2017	2018	2019
Total	19,311	19,815	20,810	19,224
Fresh Fish	180	115	142	163
Frozen Fish	2,755	2,740	2,893	2,852
Fish Fillet	4,239	4,404	4,472	4,291
Dried, Salted, Brined Fish	486	511	491	475
Crustaceans	1,683	1,495	1,266	1,028
Mollusks and Other	3,672	3,396	3,278	2,944
Packaged Fish and Caviar	2,900	3,083	3,665	3,759
Packaged Crustaceans and Mollusks	3,395	4,070	4,623	3,710

Source: US Census - Data Trade Monitor

China's Fishery Product Exports by Category
(Volume in Metric Tons)

Category/Year	2016	2017	2018	2019
Total	3,989,778	4,121,036	4,091,216	4,023,545
Fresh Fish	27,646	19,844	20,679	24,550
Frozen Fish	1,079,318	1,181,598	1,135,438	1,151,718
Fish Fillet	984,100	982,836	930,307	892,306
Dried, Salted, Brined Fish	78,633	95,388	97,717	84,232
Crustaceans	171,213	161,096	140,153	117,283
Mollusks and Other	639,097	585,999	557,140	510,016
Packaged Fish and Caviar	662,032	702,492	793,915	868,826
Packaged Crustaceans and Mollusks	347,740	391,782	415,866	374,613

Source: US Census - Data Trade Monitor

China's Exports of All Fishery Products
By Country of Destination (Value in Million USD)

Country/Year	2016	2017	2018	2019
World	19,311	19,815	20,810	19,224
Japan	3,339	3,535	3,619	3,550
United States	2,940	3,087	3,285	2,400
South Korea	1,468	1,414	1,717	1,570
Taiwan	1,551	1,711	1,864	1,328
Hong Kong	1,718	1,616	1,478	1,260
Thailand	1,070	797	857	989
Germany	441	402	499	644
Philippines	556	652	712	623
Malaysia	543	537	439	501
Canada	416	423	465	483
Mexico	428	466	535	446
Spain	413	419	469	428
Russia	420	435	477	408

Source: US Census - Trade Data Monitor

China's Exports of Fish Fillet by Destination
(Volume in Metric Tons)

Country/Year	2016	2017	2018	2019
World	984,100	982,836	930,307	892,306
United States	222,004	219,928	205,774	173,245
Germany	129,652	120,172	134,767	164,542
Japan	159,837	167,317	157,301	149,286
United Kingdom	47,820	52,150	51,739	60,047
France	46,425	45,926	46,545	42,508
Canada	32,119	31,634	28,896	32,657
Spain	26,615	27,281	22,458	25,619
Netherlands	19,978	25,107	25,183	25,224
Poland	30,360	27,753	22,973	25,224

Source: US Census -Trade Data Monitor

Common Farmed Seafood

The most commonly farmed seafoods are shrimp, tilapia, shellfish, salmon, rainbow trout, barramundi (Asian seabass), catfish, US striped bass, and flounder. A commonly known farm-raised salmon is Atlantic salmon.

Wild salmons from Alaska, listed from the highest to the lowest price, are king (Chinook), red (sockeye), silver (coho), pink (humpy), and chum (dog). Chum salmon is the least expensive because it is not as firm and rich as the other kinds, but it is still better than farmed salmon.

Farmed Atlantic Cod in China

In 2013, for the first time, Singaporean shrimp farmer Lim Shrimp Organization and a consortium of Norwegian companies formed a joint venture to farm-raise Atlantic cod in Hainan Island, China. The site also farms Atlantic salmon and sea cucumber. The water quality and conditions of the tanks used to raise fish are the main challenges for this project (Ref 11).

US Fishermen Send Catches to China for Processing

In 2018, seafood imports to China exceeded 3.3 MMT, an increase of nearly 13% over the previous year. China's seafood imports have remained historically high in recent years, driven by solid seafood processing capacity and the Chinese middle class's preference for wild-caught fish. Overseas fishermen send catches to China for processing. Imported products include frozen fish (salmon, halibut, plaice, sole, and cod), shrimp/prawn, and high-value live seafood like lobster. Most seafood from the United States is exported to China and then re-imported after processing; typically, wild-caught Pacific Salmon, Alaska salmon, Pollock, and Dungeness crab (Ref 1).

It would cost $1 per pound of labor in the United States compared to $0.20 in China. Fish are gutted on the ship at sea, frozen, and sent to China. Once they reach their destination, they are deboned, skinned, and cut into portions of 2 ounces to 6 ounces (Ref 2).

4. Chinese Regulations on Veterinary Drugs

China has increased government oversight of veterinary drug use in aquaculture production in recent years. In 2019, China issued the National Food Safety Standards, Maximum Residue Limits (MRL) for veterinary drugs in foods. The measure establishes MRL standards for over 20 veterinary drugs in fish. The MRL standard is expected to cover all permitted veterinary drugs in China by 2024 (Ref 4).

In 2019, the USDA Food Safety and Inspection Service (FSIS) listed China as a country eligible to export catfish and fish products to the United States. The safety of imported seafood, particularly seafood from China and some Southeast Asian countries has continued to be an active congressional issue (Ref 3).

5. FDA Regulations and Inspections

FDA Inspects Less than 2% of Imports

The Food and Drug Administration (FDA) inspects most imported seafood in the United States. The FDA reviews the information a seafood company provides. If the agency determines a possible risk, based on the company's history or records, it could test the seafood. The most common reason for refusal was seafood found to be filthy or decomposed, unfit for human consumption. Overall, seafood from China, Vietnam, and Indonesia was most commonly refused at US ports.

The United States Food Safety Modernization Act of 2010 (FSMA) mandated more foreign facility inspections for all types of food processing. However, the FDA has consistently missed the target due to funding issues. The FDA only looks at less than 2% of imports for issues and tests the seafood for illegal antibiotics or steroids. The FDA usually finds evidence of banned drugs in around 10% of its tests. Foreign farmers are using prohibited steroids to grow bigger fish and use banned antibiotics to keep fish alive in dirty water conditions. Those fish are then quickly slipped into the United States and sold for a lot cheaper than the cost of raising fish locally. Therefore, the lack of inspections will likely harm the American fishing industry and consumers (Ref 15).

In 2016, the catfish industry successfully lobbied to transfer the regulatory oversight for catfish from the FDA to the USDA. However, the problems with imports persist under the USDA's control. The US domestic catfish has to meet the USDA's drug limits. However, other countries can use their countries' standards, where drug residues often far exceed the USDA's threshold (Ref 15).

Seafood rejected in Europe is accepted in the United States. While the United States tests a few imported seafood for issues like salmonella and unsafe drugs, the European Union tests much more. A study by researchers from the Johns Hopkins Bloomberg School of Public Health indicated a lack of inspection in the United States compared to the European Union and Japan, the top two seafood importers. Less than 2% of all seafood imported into the US was inspected for contamination. The European Union and Japan inspected as much as 50% and 18%, respectively. Thirteen drug residues were tested by the FDA in the United States compared to 34 by government officials in the EU and 27 in Japan. This discrepancy suggests that seafood producers can use many drugs for which the United States does not screen. Excessive use of veterinarian drugs can lead to adverse health consequences, including the development of antibiotic resistance (Refs 15 and 21).

Labeling of Imported Seafood

A fish package can be labeled "Alaskan" and "Product of China" if caught in US waters.

For example, when a wild salmon is caught on the coast of Alaska and shipped to China to be fabricated into fillets, the salmon fillets are declared "Wild Caught Product of China" upon import into the United States. However, if the importer can demonstrate that the salmon was caught in Alaskan waters, the packaged salmon fillets are also eligible to say "Alaskan Salmon" instead of "Product of China" (Ref 14).

6. Americans Consume 85% of Imported Seafood

Americans consume nearly 5 billion pounds of seafood annually. According to the Food and Agriculture Organization of the United Nations, the United States is the world's second-largest seafood consumer after China. In 2020, the United States imported 70–85 percent of its seafood, and it is estimated that more than half of this imported seafood is produced through foreign aquaculture. Imported wild-caught seafood includes a significant portion from American fishermen who send their catches to China for processing and then import them back to the United States. Many imported farmed seafood products include shrimp, Atlantic salmon, tilapia, and shellfish such as scallops, mussels, clams, and oysters (Refs 3, 12, 17, and 23).

Mercury in Seafood

Regardless of the origin of the catch, please avoid seafood containing a high mercury level. Mercury is a poison affecting the nervous system. Exposure during pregnancy is of most concern because it may harm the development of the unborn baby's brain. According to the United States Environmental Protection Agency (EPA), the highest allowable average mercury concentration in fish per serving is 0.15 ug/g, up to three servings per week (0.45 ug/g). Exceeding this limit per week is harmful to health. Fish containing mercury levels below 0.15 ug/g is considered a good choice.

Seafood with Most Mercury
Mercury Concentration Average

Fish Species	µg/g or PPM
Tilefish (Gulf of Mexico)	1.45
Swordfish	1.00
Shark	0.98
Mackerel (King)	0.73
Tuna (Bigeye)	0.69
Orange Roughy	0.57
Marlin	0.49
Grouper	0.45
Bluefish	0.37
Sablefish (Black Cod)	0.36
Chilean Seabass	0.35
Markerel Spanish (Gulf of Mexico)	0.35
Tuna (Canned Albacore, Yellowfin)	0.35
Halibut	0.24
Rockfish	0.23
Mahi Mahi/Dolphinfish	0.18
Snapper	0.17
Perch	0.15
Black Seabass	0.13
Tuna (Canned Light, Skipjack)	0.13
Cod	0.11
Lobster	0.10

Source: www.EPA.gov   3/19/2021

7. Promoting American Seafood Competitiveness

In 2020, President Donald Trump signed a new Executive Order promoting American seafood competitiveness and economic growth. This Executive Order propels the United States forward as a seafood superpower by strengthening the American economy and improving the competitiveness of the American seafood industry. The Order also ensures food security, provides environmentally safe and sustainable seafood, and supports American workers. Specifically, the Executive Order calls for (Ref 16):

a) More efficient and predictable aquaculture.
b) Cutting-edge research and development.
c) Regulatory reform to maximize commercial fishing.
d) Enforcement of common-sense restrictions on seafood imports that do not meet US standards.

CHAPTER 20

SWEET DECEPTION: UNVEILING THE TRUTH BEHIND CHINESE HONEY IMPORTS

—⟋⟋⟋—

The chapter uncovers the intricate web of deception enveloping Chinese honey imports, revealing the journey from historical demand to modern-day controversies. By unraveling the complexities of transshipping and contamination, you gain a comprehensive understanding of the challenges haunting the honey industry. The chapter sharply highlights the significant role of the EU and US in regulatory scrutiny and decisive actions taken to combat fraudulent practices and safeguard consumers globally. Equipped with this knowledge, you can confidently navigate the deceptive realm of Chinese honey imports and advocate for transparency and accountability in the global marketplace.

1. History and Demand for Honey

Chinese Honey

Honey fraud has become a nearly out-of-control phenomenon. According to the US Pharmacopeia's Food Fraud Database, honey is the third favorite food target for adulteration, only behind milk and olive oil (Ref 8).

Honey: A Miracle of Nature

Except for a small portion of the population who is allergic to honey, studies found that consuming minimum-processed natural honey is far more beneficial than sugar or corn syrup. Honey is a miraculous food produced by hardworking bees, using a complex and lengthy process. Pure natural honey mainly contains sugar but has many other beneficial nutrients. Unlike sugar, honey contains proteins, enzymes, amino acids, vitamins, and minerals. To gather a full-crop load of nectar, a worker bee must visit up to 1,000 flowers and make around ten daily trips. The bees, with their incredible work ethic, collect and transform the nectar with specific substances of their own. Then, they deposit, dehydrate, and store the nectar in honeycombs to mature into honey. In addition to producing honey, bees pollinate crops and are vital to agriculture. Recently, bee pollen has gained traction in the health community because it contains nutrients, amino acids, vitamins, and over 250 other active substances. Furthermore, researchers found that pollen promotes healing and has beneficial effects against inflammatory and infectious diseases. This underscores the importance of incorporating honey into our diets for its nutritional benefits (Refs 6, 9, 11, 27, 28, and 29).

Increase in Honey Demand in the United States

According to the USDA, US honey domestic production increased by 11% from the previous year to 139 million pounds in 2023. The top three honey-producing states remain North Dakota, California, and South Dakota, contributing to half of the total US production. Honey imports in 2023 totaled 439 million pounds, indicating a significant increase in honey demand. Honey imports have consistently exceeded domestic production since 2005.

According to the National Honey Board, in 2023, the per capita consumption of honey decreased to 1.6 pounds per year from the previous record of 1.9 pounds in 2021. They reported that per-person honey consumption in the United States has doubled since the 1990s. However, domestic honey production in the US has decreased by 40% compared to 30 years ago.

The United States has seen a mismatch between production and demand, increasing honey imports. Over the past decades, the United States has become the world's largest importer of honey. In the 1990s, China emerged as a significant honey supplier to the US, reaching a peak of 57% share of all US honey imports in 1993. However, starting in 2009, China's share of honey imports to the US dropped to nearly zero and was replaced by honey from India and Vietnam. In 2023, nearly half of US honey imports came from India (39%), Vietnam (6%), and other Asian countries (3%). It is important to note that some Chinese honey may have been routed through India or Vietnam to avoid high import tariffs in the US and then labeled as Indian or Vietnamese honey. This topic will be further discussed in the upcoming conversation (Ref 33).

The United States Is the World's Largest Importer of Honey

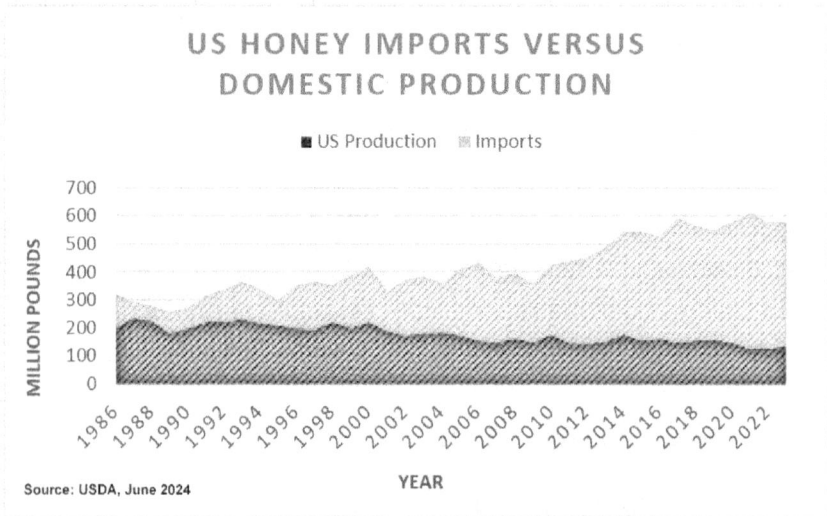

Source: USDA, June 2024

US Honey Imports: China, India, and Vietnam

━━China   ━━India   ━━Vietnam

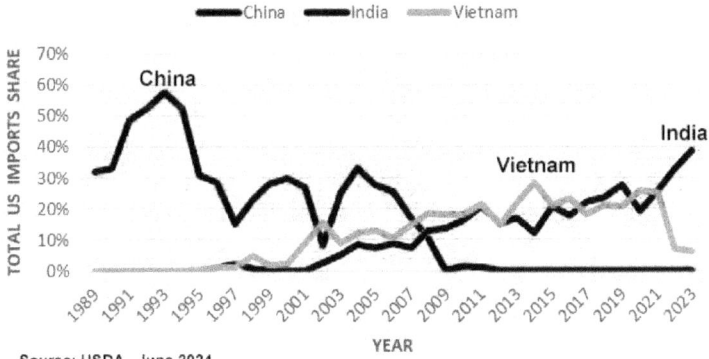

Source: USDA, June 2024

US Honey Imports by Country in Metric Tons

	Country	2019	%	2020	%	2021	%	2022	%	2023	%
	Country	2019	%	2020	%	2021	%	2022	%	2023	%
	World Total	178,964	100%	196,507	100%	219,845	100%	205,508	100%	199,334	100%
1	India	49,657	28%	37,578	19%	56,581	26%	67,528	33%	77,128	39%
2	Argentina	36,468	20%	39,805	20%	43,245	20%	42,493	21%	45,315	23%
3	Brazil	23,913	13%	34,198	17%	34,493	16%	27,824	14%	22,598	11%
4	Vietnam	36,980	21%	50,669	26%	55,515	25%	14,414	7%	12,544	6%
5	Mexico	3,239	2%	3,465	2%	4,125	2%	11,782	6%	6,947	3%
6	Uruguay	1,362	1%	4,063	2%	4,229	2%	8,550	4%	6,167	3%
7	Turkey	826	0%	1,062	1%	2,268	1%	6,597	3%	5,186	3%
8	Ukraine	8,739	5%	11,084	6%	5,953	3%	4,352	2%	4,075	2%
9	Canada	7,872	4%	4,143	2%	2,992	1%	5,774	3%	3,383	2%
10	Thailand	1,579	1%	1,039	1%	720	0%	2,191	1%	2,501	1%
11	New Zealand	1,660	1%	1,898	1%	2,740	1%	2,582	1%	2,154	1%
12	Taiwan	1,651	1%	831	0%	1,100	1%	3,126	2%	2,102	1%
13	Cambodia	0	0%	0	0%	0	0%	718	0%	1,960	1%
14	Australia	676	0%	518	0%	753	0%	1,251	1%	1,900	1%
15	Spain	658	0%	1,211	1%	1,031	0%	1,078	1%	936	0%

Source: USDA, June 20, 2024

2022 World Top Importers of Honey

#	Country	USD Million	% Share
1	United States	794.3	28.8
2	Germany	302.2	11
3	Japan	168.9	6.1
4	France	140.3	5.1
5	United Kingdom	127.6	4.6
6	Italy	106.2	3.9
7	Belgium	102.5	3.7
8	Spain	89.6	3.3
9	Poland	71.7	2.6
10	China	71.4	2.6

Source: worldstopexports.com

China Is the World's Largest Honey Exporter

2022 Top Exporters of Honey

#	Country	USD Million	% Share
1	China	277.7	10.5
2	New Zealand	266.7	10.1
3	Argentina	229.5	8.7
4	India	229.3	8.7
5	Ukraine	137.9	5.2
6	Brazil	137.9	5.2
7	Germany	137.3	5.2
8	Spain	117.5	4.4
9	Mexico	109.1	4.1
10	Belgium	94.2	3.6

Source: worldstopexports.com

In 2001, China's domestic honey production was 252,000 metric tons. By 2016, the yield of honey was 700,000 metric tons. In 2022, China was the world's largest honey exporter, with $277.7 million in value and 10.5% of the global honey export. However, in 2020, the COVID-19 lockdown hindered operations for some 250,000 beekeepers in China, who produce roughly one-quarter of the global supply. Traditionally, many routinely move their colonies around the country as far as 3,000 km (1,900 miles) in a single season in search of pollen and nectar to feed their bees (Refs 2 and 10).

Chinese Honey Floating the US market.

In 2001, China joined the World Trade Organization (WTO), which opened the door for China to trade freely with its members, including the United States. The United States Department of Commerce soon realized that Chinese-origin honey was being sold in the United States for less than fair market value, threatening to force hundreds of American beekeepers out of business. Consequently, the United States government imposed an anti-dumping tariff on Chinese honey. In 2020, the anti-dumping duty (AD) rates ranged from $0.98 to $2.63 per kilogram and 183.80% to 221.02% ad valorem (proportionate to the estimated value of the goods). The AD applies to natural honey and artificial honey containing more than 50% natural honey by weight. It also includes honey and rice syrup, regardless of the percentage of honey contained in the blend, due to the difficulty in detecting the mixed percentage (Ref 34).

In response, Chinese honey producers began using various illegal methods to conceal their honey's origin to avoid the heavy US import tariff. The constant inflow of cheap Chinese honey has been driving the wholesale price of honey below the levels needed by American beekeepers to operate. If beekeeping becomes unprofitable in the United States, fewer hives and bees will exist. Without bees, many crops in America would not be pollinated, leading to much higher fruit prices (Ref 7).

In 2019, the United States Department of Agriculture reported that the average wholesale price for American-produced honey was around

$2.50 per pound. Chinese honey was about $0.57 to $0.90 per pound, including freight and insurance (Refs 1 and 12).

2. Transshipping and Contamination of Chinese Honey

Transshipping

Transshipping and mislabeling Chinese imports to the United States can complicate US product safety agencies' efforts to keep out dangerous products.

Chinese honey producers are strongly incentivized to ship their honey to a third-party country, relabel it as originating from that third-party country, and then export it to the United States to avoid heavy tariffs. This method is called transshipment.

While Chinese Honey imports to the United States have gradually declined, imports from India, Malaysia, and Vietnam (where industry experts say transshipping of Chinese honey occurs) have increased dramatically following the imposition of heavy duties on Chinese honey in 2001.

Very large US honey-packers knowingly buy them because they are cheap, and their chances of getting caught are slim. As much as one-third of all the honey sold in the US may be illegally imported from China (Refs 3, 7, and 30).

Chinese Honey Is Tainted with Illegal Antibiotics

Chinese beekeepers used several Indian-made animal antibiotics, including chloramphenicol, to fight diseases that wiped out their bee colonies. Medical researchers found that children given chloramphenicol as an antibiotic are susceptible to DNA damage and cancer. The FDA banned its presence in food.

In August 2002, the FDA and the United States Customs and Border Protection announced that they had discovered bulk imports of Chinese honey that were contaminated with low levels of chloramphenicol. The contaminated honey was detected during an investigation into a widespread scheme to evade payment of US anti-dumping duties on bulk imports of Chinese honey (Ref 5).

Chinese Honey Is Contaminated with Lead

Chinese honey is also contaminated with lead. Lead is a poison affecting virtually every organ system, primarily the central nervous system, particularly the developing brain. Consequently, children are at a greater risk than adults of suffering from the neurotoxic effects of lead. The lead contamination in some Chinese honey has been attributed to thousands of mom-and-pop vendors, who use small, unlined, lead-soldered drums to collect and store the honey before it is delivered to honey brokers for processing (Ref 3).

Between 2002 and 2004, Chinese honey was banned in the European Union due to its lack of origin labeling and risk of lead contamination. However, the ban was lifted due to the increased demand for honey in Europe.

Chinese Honey Is Low Quality and Adulterated

Bees require additional feeding during specific seasons, such as winter, when blooming flowers are not available. Nectar flows can vary significantly from region to region, so feeding is necessary to maintain breeding activities and prevent starvation.

One way to adulterate honey is to directly add sugar or syrups. Another is to feed bees sugar or syrups during the main nectar flow period when flower nectar is abundant. This is considered indirect adulteration and should not be done using proper beekeeping methods. Indirect adulteration is extremely difficult to detect (Ref 9).

Chinese Honey Pollen Removed to Avoid Detection

The honey industry in China has been under scrutiny due to issues of contamination and adulteration. Chinese honey has been found to lack bee pollen, which makes it difficult to trace its origin. Scientists can detect the origin of honey through a complex analysis of the pollen it contains. This analysis can identify the geographic region of the flowers, as well as detect up to 40 unnatural substances, including antibiotics and pesticide residues. Since there are more than 350,000 different plant species, each with a unique pollen type, knowing the origin of honey is crucial because different countries have varying regulations on pesticide and antibiotic usage.

To avoid detection, some Chinese honey producers have developed a sophisticated process involving high-pressure heating and ultrafiltration to remove all floral fingerprints from the honey. This results in honey with no color or flavor. The producers then blend this honey with natural Indian honey. However, the European Union banned the import of honey from India in 2010 after laboratory tests revealed high levels of lead and antibiotics. Surprisingly, the United States continued importing honey from India during the same period despite the ban by the European Union.

Food Safety News reported that over three-fourths of the honey sold in U.S. grocery stores is missing pollen. Without pollen, it is impossible to determine the legitimacy and safety of the honey. Bee pollen has been highly valued for its flavor and nutritional benefits for centuries. The deliberate removal of pollen is believed to be a tactic to hide the origin of the honey, particularly its connection to China.

In 2011, *Food Safety News* purchased over 60 honey samples from 10 states and the District of Columbia. The contents were analyzed for pollen by Vaughn Bryant, a professor at Texas A&M University and one of the nation's leading investigators of pollen in honey.

a) 100% of the honey sampled from drugstores had no pollen.
b) 100% of the honey packaged in the small individual portions had pollen removed.
c) 77% of the honey sampled from big box stores had the pollen filtered out.
d) 76% of samples bought at the grocery store had all the pollen removed.
e) All samples bought at farmer's markets and natural food stores had a total amount of pollen.

Why Is Asian Honey Cheaper?

Asian beekeepers often harvest unripe honey with high water content and then extensively process it to filter out residues and pollen, remove water, and dilute it with syrup. This processed honey lacks the nutrients found in pure natural honey and may pose health risks to consumers. Cheaper honey is more likely to be adulterated. In recent years, some Chinese shippers have replaced honey with thickened, colored sweeteners labeled as honey.

In 2020, *Business Standard,* a local Indian newspaper, reported that smaller honey companies had gone out of business because they could not compete with the cheaper adulterated honey from China. Standard tests were unable to detect adulteration, prompting investigators to use an advanced laboratory test called nuclear magnetic resonance spectroscopy (NMR) in Germany to detect adulteration in honey from major Indian brands.

Chinese Honey Is Exported from Europe and Asia

Norberto García is a professor of Apiculture at the Universidad Nacional Del Sur in Argentina and chairman of the United States Pharmacopeia Expert Panel on Honey Quality and Authenticity. In recent years, Professor García has worked intensely to raise awareness of honey adulteration at national and international meetings.

In his 2018 report, he demonstrated and highlighted the following points (Ref 6):

a) Five countries (China, India, Ukraine, Vietnam, and Thailand) experienced an increase in their total honey exports without parallel growths in the number of bee hives. Adulteration may explain such an increase in export volumes. In addition, some Asian countries, like Thailand, augmented their honey exports to the United States by increasing their imports of Chinese honey. Thus, they generated new possible routes of transshipping to the United States to avoid the hefty tariff from the United States.

b) Cheap Chinese honey could have incentivized several European countries to import honey from China and re-export it as locally produced in Europe. Spain, Belgium, Poland, Italy, and Portugal have shown a 200% increase in their honey export volumes over ten years. That expansion cannot be explained by an increase in the number of beehives, which only grew by 2.7% over that period.

3. EU and US Regulations and Actions

The European Union found that 14% of Honey Had Added Sugar

In 2015, the European Commission organized an EU Coordinated Control Plan to assess the presence of honey adulterated with sugar and mislabeled regarding its geographical origin. The findings revealed that 14% of the tested samples contained added sugar. Overall, the results suggest that the practice of adding sugars to honey is occurring, both within the European Union and in third-world countries.

During the coordination, all 28 EU countries, along with Norway and Switzerland, participated in the plan. They gathered 2,264 honey samples from all stages of the supply chain, with 45% coming from retailers. The European Union countries examined all samples for sensory characteristics and pollen profiles. Compliant samples were then subjected to chemical sugar analysis to determine whether additional sugar was present in the honey. This was further categorized based on geographical origin, collection point (producer, packager, or retailer), and type of honey (Refs 9 and 19).

The EU Actions and Scope of the Coordinated Control Plan

In December 2015, the EU came up with the Actions and Scope of the Coordinated Control Plan to carry out official controls to establish the prevalence in the European Union market. The plan targets (Ref 9):

a) Honey is mislabeled because of its geographical and botanical origin.
b) Products declared or presented as honey but containing added sugar or sugar products.

The Honey Directive regulates honey in the European Union, but the requirements for declaring its origin are shallow. Labels can read "blend of EU honey," "blend of non-EU honey," or "blend of EU and non-EU honey." Most honey is labeled "blend of EU and non-EU honey" (Ref 19).

The United States Law Enforcement Do Not Protect Consumers

The U.S. Customs and Border Protection (CBP) is unable to inspect all imported honey due to limited resources. Their strategy involves developing a risk-based model to identify high-risk areas for noncompliance and targeting shipments for potential inspections and testing. The agency can pursue honey smugglers by enforcing antidumping tariffs and prosecuting violators. However, consumer protection falls under the jurisdiction of the United States Food and Drug Administration (FDA), which unfortunately lacks the resources to address this challenge entirely. In 2018, the FDA recommended that additional ingredients like syrup or flavor be listed on honey labels, but it does not enforce this rule legally. Imports of Chinese honey and honey products are harmful to the US domestic honey industry and unregulated product safety can pose a threat to American consumers' health and food safety (Refs 8, 23, and 34).

Trade Facilitation and Trade Enforcement Act

In 2015, Congress passed the Trade Facilitation and Trade Enforcement Act (TFTEA) to address the risk posed by industries and companies that evade US laws and regulations and to enhance the nation's economic security. One of the key provisions of the TFTEA is the requirement for the United States Immigration and Customs Enforcement (ICE) and the Customs and Border Protection (CBP) agencies to work together to strengthen trade enforcement. This collaboration is specifically focused on addressing the illegal importation of honey into the United States, which violates US customs and trade laws.

$1.5 Million Request to Detect Chinese Honey Fraud

In a 2020 report to Congress, the US Department of Homeland Security's Customs and Border Protection (CBP) unit requested $1.5 million to purchase advanced machines for detecting Chinese honey fraud. The CBP is responsible for regulating these imports and enforcing antidumping orders. They are working to improve efforts to target and test fraudulent honey imports but face legal, resource, and interagency challenges. The funds were used to develop a comparison database and purchase nuclear magnetic resonance spectroscopy (NMR) equipment. The NMR enhances CBP's testing capabilities to detect substances other than honey by analyzing the organic chemical composition of honey to determine its country of origin. The CBP also collected honey samples in Vietnam and India for its honey reference sample database (Ref 34).

Navigating Honey Imports: A Multi-Agency Regulatory Approach

Different federal agencies enforce various regulations regarding honey imports based on their statutory and regulatory authorities. For instance, the Customs Border Protection (CBP) enforces the honey order and determines tariff classification. The Department of Commerce establishes Anti-Dumping (AD) tariff rates under the honey order and directs the CBP to collect the AD duties. The Food and Drug Administration (FDA) oversees product safety, while the US Department of Agriculture's Agricultural Marketing Service enforces marketing orders. Each agency has distinct legal and regulatory requirements.

Busting Illegal Chinese Honey Imports

In Savanah, Georgia, the United States Customs and Border Protection's laboratory has the following mission:

a) Determine whether the honey samples are adulterated with sweeteners or syrups.
b) If the samples contain natural honey, the lab will try to figure out the origin.
c) The entire shipment may be subject to additional taxes if the honey comes from China.

Around 2006, dishonest importers started mixing honey with rice syrup (a sweetener) to pass off the mixture as pure honey. Lab tests were unable to determine the exact ratio of honey to syrup. This allowed importers to claim that their product contained less than 50% natural honey, helping them avoid paying the honey import tariff. As a solution, an anti-dumping tariff has now been imposed on rice syrup, regardless of the honey percentage in the blend.

Chemists at the lab here have tested thousands of samples pulled from barrels and containers at ports across the Southeast. In 2008, the lab demonstrated that honey imported from Thailand, the Philippines, and Russia had originated in China. The evidence helped federal prosecutors build a case against two large American importers suspected of buying illegal Chinese honey to avoid more than $180 million in duties (Ref 13).

Successful Cases Reported by the United States Department of Homeland Security

2008: Federal authorities began investigating honey brokers evading anti-dumping duties through illegal imports, including transshipment and mislabeling on the supply side of the honey industry. The second phase of the investigation involved allegations of illegal buying and trading of honey smuggling into the United States on the demand side of the industry. Some of that honey was contaminated with antibiotics banned in food by the FDA (Ref 24).

2011: A Chinese business agent for several honey import companies was arrested in Los Angeles on federal charges of illegally importing honey of Chinese origin. The honey was falsely identified as having originated in South Korea, Taiwan, and Thailand to avoid the high anti-dumping tariff (Ref 16).

2011: Three people of Chinese origin have been charged with smuggling honey into the United States via eleven ports and providing false descriptions of the merchandise. Chinese honey containers were labeled as rice fructose to avoid more than $1 million in duties. Once the honey containers passed through customs, they were forwarded to a warehouse, washed off all markings, and relabeled as amber honey. Then, the honey was sold to domestic purchasers (Ref 14).

2012: Chinese-origin honey was falsely identified as originating in South Korea to avoid US high anti-dumping tariffs. The Chinese importer pleaded guilty to the charges and was required to pay $1.48 million in restitution. This case investigates the honey-importing practices of Alfred L. Wolff Inc. (ALW), a German international trading company whose US subsidiary was based in Chicago. In 2010, a federal grand jury in Chicago indicted eight ALW executives and one non-ALW executive in an $80 million honey fraud importation ring – all foreign fugitives (Ref 17).

2013: Two of the nation's largest honey suppliers were accused of flooding the market with cheaper honey from China and avoiding $180 million in duties. Baytown, Texas-based Honey Holding and Michigan-based Groeb Farms agreed to pay $1 million and $2 million in fines, respectively.

Groeb Farms filed for Chapter 11 bankruptcy protection after it was caught. The company's bankruptcy filing halted several lawsuits filed earlier by honey producers and distributors who claimed they were harmed in the scandal. According to court papers (Refs 18, 24, and 31), Groeb Farms sold $137.9 million worth of honey and other products in 2012.

2013: A Chinese-origin broker from Temple City, California, pleaded guilty to three counts of violating US importation laws by falsely declaring that the honey shipments contained sugar syrup and apple juice concentrate to avoid $39.2 million in anti-dumping duties (Ref 15).

2013: A Texas honey broker was sentenced in Illinois to three years in prison and $2.89 million in penalties for evading nearly $38 million in tariffs on Chinese-origin honey. The honey was misrepresented as having originated in India or Malaysia to avoid anti-dumping duties when it entered the United States.

In addition, the broker admitted that he sold Vietnamese honey that tested positive for Chloramphenicol, an antibiotic not allowed in US honey or other food products (Ref 21).

2015: Officers from the United States Immigration and Customs Enforcement (ICE), the Homeland Security Investigations (HSI), and the Customs and Border Protection (CBP) seized 660 barrels of illegally imported Chinese honey valued at $2.45 million. The confiscated barrels weighed 203.28 metric tons (448,156 lbs.). The containers' shipping documents falsely indicated that the bulk honey came from Latvia, a country in the Baltic region of Northern Europe (Ref 25).

2016: The Homeland Security Investigations (HSI) in Chicago seized nearly 60 tons of honey illegally imported from China. The three shipping containers (195 barrels) of bulk honey smuggled into the United States were falsely declared as originating from Vietnam to evade anti-dumping duties. The HSI Chicago was notified of the suspect honey by a domestic honey packer located in the Midwest. Then, HSI sent honey samples to the United States Customs and Border Protection (CBP) laboratory in Savannah, Georgia, for analysis. CBP determined that the honey was of Chinese origin (Ref 22).

4. Honey Awareness

It is safer to purchase honey at natural food stores or local farmer's markets. Look for raw, unprocessed honey with pollen and carefully review the country of origin. Since it is impossible to identify the origin or quality of honey used in processed food, eat less processed food!

Red flags

a) Highly processed and ultra-clear honey
b) Cheap honey
c) Honey without pollen
d) Honey without flavor
e) Watery honey
f) Non-EU sources or blended with non-EU sources (for Europe)
g) Product origin not mentioned

Questionable Honey Sources

a) China (illegal antibiotics, lead, and syrups found in honey)
b) India, Latvia, Malaysia, the Philippines, Vietnam, South Korea, Taiwan, Thailand, and Ukraine (transshipments from China)
c) Spain, Belgium, Poland, Italy, and Portugal (export Chinese honey from Europe, Ref 6)
d) Cheap honey purchased from big box stores, drugstores, and regular supermarkets (Ref 4)
e) Individually packed honey and honey served at fast food places (Ref 4)

Honey Differentiation

Australia and New Zealand have developed and marketed Manuka honey to differentiate high-quality honey from adulterated honey. Brazil and Mexico export organic honey.

The traditional countries that export conventional honey to America and Europe (Argentina, Mexico, Canada, Uruguay, Hungary, and Chile) have suffered from the growing honey exports from Eastern countries. Unfortunately, honest beekeepers receive less and less money for their pure honey, causing many of them to abandon their operations.

TrueSourceHoney.com

The website was launched in 2010 to educate and provide information about honey. Four North American honey marketing companies and importers (Golden Heritage Foods, LLC, Burleson's Inc., Odem International, and Dutch Gold Honey) launched the initiative. This group pledged to help protect the quality and reputation of the US honey supply and the sustainability of US beekeepers and honey businesses. About 40% of honey sold in the United States and Canada is True Source certified (Ref 26 and www.truesourcehoney.com).

CHAPTER 21

STEEPED IN CONTROVERSY: EXPLORING THE TRUTH BEHIND CHINESE TEA

—◊◊◊—

In this chapter, you will embark on a journey through the captivating world of Chinese tea. They will delve into its global trade dynamics and local production landscape. The chapter will explore the nuanced balance between the benefits and risks of Chinese tea consumption and its health implications. With a critical examination of contaminants and associated health risks, you will gain valuable insights into making informed choices about their tea consumption habits. By uncovering the truth behind Chinese tea, this chapter will empower you to savor its delights while navigating potential controversies with discernment and awareness.

1. Global Tea Trade and Chinese Production

The United States Is Among the Top Tea Importer Globally

In 2019, the United States was the top importer of tea worldwide, importing $488.4 million worth, followed by Russia at $425.7 million and the United Kingdom at $356.5 million. The top three tea suppliers to the United States were China at 15.6%, Argentina at 12.8%, and Japan at 12.7%. In 2022, the United States was the second largest importer of tea, with imports totaling $559.7 million, trailing behind Pakistan at $649 million. Japan remained the top tea supplier at 15.2%, followed by China at 13% and Argentina at 12.6%. Global purchases of imported tea totaled $7.3 billion in 2022.

2022 World Top Importers of Tea

#	Country	USD Million	% Share
1	Pakistan	649	9.0%
2	United States	559.7	7.7%
3	United Arab Emirates	410.2	5.7%
4	Russia	365.1	5.1%
5	United Kingdom	356.1	4.9%
6	Egypt	272.7	3.8%
7	Morocco	257.1	3.6%
8	Germany	251.6	3.5%
9	Hong Kong	229.4	3.2%
10	Iran	206.7	2.9%

2022 US Tea Imports by Country

#	Country	USD Million	% Share
1	Japan	85.1	15.2%
2	China	73	13.0%
3	Argentina	70.5	12.6%
4	India	70	12.5%
5	Sri Lanka	52.2	9.3%
6	Taiwan	27.2	4.9%
7	Canada	22.6	4.0%
8	Poland	20.8	3.7%
9	United Kingdom	20.1	3.6%
10	Germany	18.8	3.4%
11	Malawi	14.4	2.6%
12	Vietnam	11.9	2.1%
13	United Arab Emirates	7.9	1.4%
14	Thailand	7.7	1.4%
15	Indonesia	7.6	1.4%

China Is the Top Tea Producer in the World

China has been the world's leading tea producer, with over 2.5 metric tons in 2018. Almost two-thirds of the tea produced in China is green tea. In 2019, China exported approximately $2.02 billion worth of tea, making it the leading exporter worldwide. In 2022, China remained the leader and exported $1.77 billion in tea (Refs 2 and 4).

2. Benefits and Risks of Chinese Tea

Green tea, with its array of health-boosting elements like magnesium, calcium, potassium, phosphorus, and other trace elements, is a reassuring choice. White and green teas pack a punch with their high concentration of antioxidants called catechins, which play a significant role in preventing Alzheimer's disease, hypertension, and obesity. Moreover, let us not forget green tea's strong antibacterial properties that keep tooth cavities at bay.

3. Contaminants and Health Risks

The World Health Organization advises that it is best to limit tea consumption to 5 cups or 1 liter per week and to avoid eating tea leaves. This is because the tea plant is a hyperaccumulator, meaning it can absorb and retain high levels of heavy metals in its tissues when grown in soil or water with high concentrations of heavy metals.

The quality of tea is influenced by factors such as soil quality, environmental contamination, and weather conditions. The presence of toxic contaminants in the soil and air is often linked to factory coal usage. China, which accounts for about half of the world's coal consumption, is planning to expand its coal power plants. Currently, 70% of China's energy comes from coal-burning power plants.

Tea leaves have been found to contain toxic heavy metals like aluminum, mercury, lead, arsenic, and cadmium due to the tea plants' absorption of these elements. Research has shown that these heavy metals can have harmful effects on the body, disrupting the endocrine and immune systems, causing insulin resistance, and permanently damaging vital enzymes, the central nervous system, and the kidneys.

Note: Fenugreek, commonly used in Indian cuisine, is a hyperaccumulator of heavy metals such as cadmium and lead, similar to the tea plant. Fenugreek is renowned for its hormone-balancing properties and other health benefits.

Heavy Metals Found in Tea

Researchers conducted a study on tea and found that drinking more than four cups of tea a day could contribute to a toxic load. The study analyzed 30 different brands of teas purchased at Canadian supermarkets, which are similar to those sold in the United States.

The study revealed that most teas, regardless of whether they were organic or non-organic, contained heavy metals from various origins. Chinese oolong tea had the highest overall amount of heavy metals. Here are the specific findings:

Aluminum: All brewed teas steeped for 3 or 15 minutes contained a significant level of aluminum.

Lead: All tea leaves had detectable levels of lead, with Chinese oolong teas having the highest levels, followed by green and regular black tea.

Mercury: Eighteen out of 30 sampled tea leaves contained mercury, as high as 20 ng/g. It seemed that mercury was bound to tea leaves and was not detected in the tea infusion.

Arsenic: All brewed tea and tea leaves had detectable arsenic, with Chinese oolong teas having the highest levels.

Cadmium: All tea leaves had detectable levels of cadmium. The highest level was 0.067 μgm/L found in standard oolong tea from China.

The study also found that steeping tea for more extended periods increased the levels of these contaminants by 10% to 50% over steeping for 3 minutes. Therefore, steeping for longer than 3 minutes should be avoided.

Harmful Fluoride in Tea

The benefits of fluoride in preventing dental cavities have led to the addition of fluoride to toothpaste, water, milk, and salt. However, more recent scientific evidence suggests that the use of topical fluoride sources, such as toothpaste, is the most effective way to prevent dental cavities. Fluoride has no known essential function in human growth and development. It is not critical for tooth development. Fluoride can contribute to the prevention of caries, but caries is not a fluoride deficiency disease (Ref 3).

Fluoride can be present in rain, with its concentration increasing significantly upon exposure to volcanic activity or atmospheric pollution derived from burning fossil fuels or other sorts of industry. Rapid industrialization has resulted in increased emissions of fluoride. Since the 1930s, many scientific studies have found tea to contain fluoride. Tea plants accumulate and store fluoride by absorbing it from the air and soil. Fluoride accumulates mainly in the leaves of the tea plant. A substantial amount of fluoride is released during hot tea infusion. The gastrointestinal tract can absorb 100% of fluoride from tea, which is similar to that from drinking water.

In a study published by the *International Journal of Environmental Research & Public Health,* researchers found that 96% of the sampled black tea products (infused in non-fluoride, deionized water) had fluoride concentrations that exceeded 1.5 mg/L, and 22% had a fluoride level exceeding 3.0 mg/L. The European Union has set the maximum enforceable limit for fluoride in all drinking waters at 1.5 mg/L (Ref 3).

Black and green tea varieties have the highest concentration of fluoride. High fluoride concentration in tea products can pose a significant health risk if tea is consumed excessively. Fluoride is a cumulative toxin. The rate of increase in fluoride bone levels is almost three times higher among tea drinkers compared to non-tea drinkers. Therefore, drinking more than 5 liters of tea per week may result in dental or skeletal fluorosis, when fluoride accumulates in the bone progressively over many years. In addition, the harmful effects of fluoride include weakening the heart, damaging the brain and nervous system, disrupting hormone balance, and damaging the liver and kidneys (Refs 2 and 3).

Dental Fluorosis

It is the appearance of faint white lines or streaks on the teeth that only occurs when younger children consume too much fluoride. In moderate to severe fluorosis, teeth are weakened and suffer permanent physical damage.

Skeletal Fluorosis

It is a severe condition resulting from chronic ingestion of large amounts of fluoride over many years during bone growth and remodeling. Bone remodeling is a lifelong process where mature bone tissue is removed from the skeleton. Almost 100% of the skeleton is replaced in the first year of life. In adults, remodeling proceeds at about 10% per year. In skeletal fluorosis, the bones are generally weaker than usual, with stiffness and joint pain being the early symptoms (Ref 3).

4. The Tale of Tea: A Journey from China to South Carolina

In the late 1700s, tea bushes (*Camellia sinensis*) arrived in the United States from China. Over the next 150 years, several attempts were made to grow tea in South Carolina, but none succeeded. American-grown tea became a reality in 1888 when Dr. Charles Shepard founded the Pinehurst Tea Plantation in Summerville, South Carolina. He produced award-winning teas until his death in 1915, after which the plantation closed and the tea plants grew wild for forty-five years.

In 1963, Shepard's tea plants were transplanted to a 127-acre farm on Wadmalaw Island in South Carolina's Lowcountry, where research was conducted for the next 24 years.

In 1987, William Barclay Hall purchased the land and transformed the research farm into a commercial operation. A third-generation tea taster trained in London, Hall founded the Charleston Tea Garden. During his seventeen-year tenure, his "American Classic" tea became the first tea made with 100% American-grown tea and has remained popular with tea lovers for nearly thirty years.

In 2003, Hall reached out to his longtime friends, the Bigelow family, founders of the Bigelow Tea Company, established in 1945. A partnership was formed, and the Bigelow Tea Company purchased the garden, bringing extensive experience in specialty tea. Since then, the Charleston Tea Garden has become an American icon, expanding its offerings under the Charleston Tea Garden brand.

Today, the garden offers educational factory tours, a walk through the tea production facility, and a 45-minute trolley ride that includes a stop at their state-of-the-art greenhouse (charlestonteagarden.com).

CHAPTER 22

PILLS, PROMISES, AND PERILS:
THE IMPACT OF CHINESE PHARMACEUTICALS

—〜〜—

This chapter provides an in-depth exploration of Chinese pharmaceuticals, offering you a comprehensive overview of its historical evolution and regulatory framework. It examines the global demand for pharmaceuticals and China's significant role in meeting it while also addressing the alarming risks posed by counterfeit drugs and the opioid crisis. The chapter uncovers the complex story behind Chinese pharmaceuticals with an emphasis on combating illegal trade and ensuring safety. You will gain valuable insights to navigate the pharmaceutical landscape with vigilance and foresight, ultimately developing a deeper understanding of the promises and perils inherent in Chinese pharmaceuticals.

1. History and Regulations of the Drug Industry

Chinese Vitamins, Supplements, and Prescription Drugs

In 2020, Senator Tom Cotton and Congressman Mike Gallagher introduced the bill called "Protecting Our Pharmaceutical Supply Chain from China Act" with the following statement:

> In March 2020, a Chinese Communist Party propaganda outlet insinuated that Beijing could cut off supplies of life-saving medicine to the United States at any time, dooming our country to sink into the hell of a coronavirus epidemic. Unfortunately, this is not an empty threat. The United States

is dangerously dependent on China's pharmaceuticals, whose failures and cover-ups caused this deadly pandemic to spiral out of control. If China stops supplying its pharmaceutical ingredients to the world, military hospitals and clinics will cease to function within months.

This bill requires the United States Secretary of Health and Human Services to maintain a list of the country of origin of all drugs marketed in the United States and to ban the use of Federal funds to purchase drugs manufactured in China.

History of Drug Recalls

Many prescription drugs in the United States come from China. Drug companies rely on China for active pharmaceutical ingredients (API) that go into antibiotics, heart medicines, and many other life-saving drugs. US factories no longer make generic antibiotics. The serious deficiencies in health and safety standards and filthy conditions in many Chinese drug factories pose a health risk to Americans. These are the significant recalls:

2008: Baxter recalled nine lots of heparin (blood thinner) because of severe allergic reactions and low blood pressure in patients. Baxter subcontracted the creation of precursor chemicals of heparin to Scientific Protein Laboratories, an American company with production facilities located in China. Scientific Protein Laboratories used counterfeit precursors to create the chemicals ordered. Baxter then sold this heparin contaminated with counterfeit chemicals in the United States. The heparin killed 81 people and left 785 severely injured.

China produces more than half of the world's heparin, an ingredient derived from hog intestines and used by major pharmaceutical companies in blood-thinning drugs.

2018: The United States Food and Drug Administration (FDA) announced more than 50 recalls of blood pressure medications, potassium, and potassium/hydrochlorothiazide due to a possibly carcinogenic impurity in some batches of the drugs.

2019: Recalls included blood pressure medications valsartan, losartan, and irbesartan, which contain trace levels of the carcinogens NMBA, NDMA, and NDEA.

According to *USA Today*, the FDA admitted that some versions of the drug valsartan contained trace amounts of a carcinogen for four years before regulators detected the impurity in 2019.

2020: Valisure LLC, an online pharmacy, detected high levels of the carcinogen NDMA in metformin products, a widely used diabetes drug. Consequently, the company petitioned the FDA to recall certain metformin products produced by Apotex, Amneal, Lupin Ltd., Actavis Pharma (AbbVie Inc.), and others. The FDA asked five companies to voluntarily recall metformin after the agency's testing found higher-than-acceptable contaminant levels that could cause cancer.

The FDA did not ask the companies that sell a large portion of metformin in the United States to recall their products. The drug is sold under brands such as Fortamet, Glucophage, Glumetza, and Riomet. The agency was assessing whether the drug recalls would cause shortages and only requested these manufacturers to test their products for NDMA before distribution in the United States. Millions of Americans used the drug to control high blood sugar to treat type-2 diabetes.

2020: The FDA ordered the recall of Zantac and some other heartburn medicines after the online pharmacy Valisure LLC had alerted the agency to high carcinogen NDMA levels.

2024: Dozens of CVS drug recalls expose a link to tainted factories in China and India. One factory making CVS-branded pain and fever medications for children used contaminated water. Another made too-potent drugs for kids, and a third made nasal sprays for babies on the same machines it used to produce pesticides.

(Refs 5, 12, 13, and 29)

Drug Regulations in China

The Chinese government does not effectively regulate China's pharmaceutical industry, as the country does not have enough resources to oversee thousands of Chinese drug manufacturers. Meanwhile, the United States Food and Drug Administration (FDA) only has a small number of FDA inspectors in China overseeing many manufacturers. In addition, the FDA has been struggling with cooperation from Chinese officials and fraudulent tactics from many Chinese manufacturers. Consequently, Americans are at risk of exposure to contaminated and dangerous medicines (Ref 11).

According to a report to the United States Congress, in 2016, the China Food and Drug Administration investigated 1,622 drug clinical trial programs and canceled 80% of these drug applications after finding evidence of fraudulent data reporting and incomplete data submissions (Ref 11). In 2018, a scandal over tainted vaccine doses sold in China led to the arrests of Changsheng Biotech executives. Their company was also accused of forging data while producing a rabies vaccine given to infants (Ref 15).

There are no formal regulatory agreements with China regarding dietary supplements and biotechnology. However, the United States and China have Biotechnology and Technical Working Groups that foster bilateral dialogue on trade and information sharing (Ref 16).

The US FDA's Role in Drug Regulations

The United States Food and Drug Administration (FDA) ensures the safety of human and veterinary drugs, vaccines, biological products, medical devices, and radiation-emitting devices. The agency regulates food, cosmetics, dietary supplements, and tobacco products. Imported products must meet the same standards as those produced domestically (Ref 16).

Risk-based Oversight

The FDA uses an automated risk-based system to electronically screen imports and determine if shipments meet specific examination criteria. This system incorporates data from various sources, including product risks, past inspection results, and intelligence data. The prioritization of drug manufacturing surveillance inspections by the FDA is based on factors such as the facility's compliance history, recall trends, time since the last inspection, inherent risks associated with the manufactured drug, and processing complexity (Ref 16).

Due to differences in enforcement tools between foreign countries and the United States, Congress has directed the FDA to develop specific programs to ensure the safety of imported drugs. However, these programs require long-term funding and could potentially reduce resources for other inspections. While the FDA has made substantial progress in registering foreign pharmaceutical manufacturing firms, there still needs to be information gaps related to those manufacturers. For example, in China, approximately 22% of the Active Pharmaceutical ingredients (API) and 14% of finished dosage manufacturing facilities are registered with the FDA, as stated in a 2019 report to Congress (Ref 16).

2. Global Demand and China's Role

A. Chinese Flavorings, Vitamins, and Preservatives

In the past ten years, China has emerged as the leading global supplier of various food flavorings, vitamins, and preservatives. It is the primary producer of vanilla flavoring, citric acid, and several types of vitamin B, including thiamine, riboflavin, and folic acid, commonly used in processed flour products. China is responsible for 80% of the world's ascorbic acid (vitamin C) production. The Ningbo Wanglong Group is the largest producer of sorbic acid, a food preservative, with a third of its output being exported to the United States. In the late 1990s, food additives were predominantly manufactured in Europe and the United States, but in the 2000s, global food companies began using Chinese ingredients to reduce costs. The most common food additives imported into the United States from China are:

a) **Citric acid:** Enhances fruit flavors in soda, fruit-flavored beverages, candy, and flavored syrups.
b) **Sorbic acid:** A preservative used in cheese and other dairy products, baked goods, and wine.
c) **Vanillin:** An artificial vanilla used in chocolates, candies, and cookies.
d) **Xylitol:** A natural sweetener used in sugar-free gum and candy.
e) **Folic acid:** A B-vitamin added to pasta, bread, cereal, flour, corn meal, and rice.

About 90% of all vitamin C and most vitamins A, B12, and E sold in the United States come from China. The United States does not require country-of-origin labels for drugs, processed foods, or supplements (Refs 1 and 2).

B. China Pharmaceutical Industry Boom

Ever since China became a member of the World Trade Organization in 2001, it has experienced increased access to global markets. The country's drug industry relies heavily on its strong chemical industry, which is the largest in the world and makes up 40% of global chemical industry revenues. Chinese chemical companies are capable of manufacturing a wide range of products, from fertilizers to drug ingredients.

The growth of the Chinese pharmaceutical industry has been fueled by factors such as the absence of crucial environmental and labor protections, weak enforcement of intellectual property laws, an abundance of low-wage chemists, and relaxed government regulations. As a result, the US chemical manufacturing industry has gradually shifted to China to produce low-margin active pharmaceutical ingredients (APIs) and generic drugs. Meanwhile, American and global pharmaceutical companies have been concentrating on pursuing potentially lucrative patents and high-value compounds (Refs 10 and 11).

The growth of China's pharmaceutical industry mirrors the patterns seen in the country's chemical and telecommunications sectors. China's government supports domestic companies while creating challenges for foreign competitors. International firms face obstacles in the Chinese health market, such as delays in drug regulatory approvals, restrictions on drug pricing, and intellectual property theft. Chinese drug companies have flooded the global market with low-cost products, displacing United States, European, and Indian manufacturers from the generic drug manufacturing business (Ref 11).

CHINA PHARMACEUTICAL R&D EXPENDITURE

IN BILLION US DOLLARS

Year	Value
2014	64
2015	73
2016	83
2017	99
2018	121
2019	150
2020	187
2021	232
2022	285
2023	342

YEAR

Source: statista.com

In 2008, the Chinese government identified pharmaceutical production as a high-value-added industry and provided substantial subsidies and export tax rebates to encourage pharmaceutical companies to export their products. In 2014, the Chinese government allocated a significant amount, $64 billion, to its pharmaceutical research and development (R&D). By 2023, the amount had increased more than fivefold to $342 billion, demonstrating the scale of investment and its impact on the industry's growth. China's pharmaceutical industry comprises over 4,000 drug manufacturers and generated a total revenue of $127.8 billion in 2017. The country's domestic health expenditures rank as the world's second-largest, behind the United States, and reached $145–$175 billion in 2022. The primary focus of China's pharmaceutical industry lies in producing affordable generic drugs and active pharmaceutical ingredients. By 2020, China and India had become the two largest producers of medical supplies in the world. India, as the leading producer of generic medicines, depends on China for 80% of its active pharmaceutical ingredients (APIs) (Ref 10).

Chinese pharmaceutical companies are rapidly catching up with those in the United States. In 2021, the largest drug company in China, Jiangsu Hengrui Medicine Co. Ltd., boasts a market capitalization of $59.80 billion, in comparison to American Johnson & Johnson's $422.55 billion (Ref 21).

C. China Is the Pharmacy of the World

China is the largest producer of active pharmaceutical ingredients (APIs) globally. According to the United States Department of Commerce, China supplies 80% of the world's API for the blood anticoagulant heparin and an even higher percentage for antibiotics such as amoxicillin, ciprofloxacin, and tetracycline. China also manufactures about 70% of the acetaminophen (pain reliever) used in the United States. Lastly, China also produces 50% of the world's aspirin and 35% of all Tylenol.

Up until the 2000s, the United States was the largest producer of acetaminophen, a petroleum byproduct, with companies including Monsanto and BASF producing it in Texas and Louisiana. However, in 2021, Chinese Anqiu Lu'an Pharmaceutical Co. in Shandong province became the world's largest producer of acetaminophen, shipping 80% of its output to more than 100 countries. In addition, Chinese pharmaceutical companies obtained 77 generic drug approvals from the United States Food and Drug Administration in 2018, up from 38 in 2017 and 22 in 2016, indicating China's ambitions to export generic medication (Refs 10, 21, and 28).

3. US Imports of Medical Products from China

The United States heavily relies on drugs and active pharmaceutical ingredients (APIs) from China, particularly for generic drugs.

According to the FDA, China is the second-largest exporter of drugs and biologics to the United States, following Canada.

There is a significant loophole in US customs law concerning medication country-of-origin labeling. Drug companies are not required to disclose the API country of origin on their product labels. As a result, US consumers are unable to track the sources of the ingredients and related concerns. For example, a drug manufacturer in the United States can collect ingredients from around the world to produce a medication and still label it as made in the USA.

In 2018, 13.4% of Chinese drugs were imported into the United States, with approximately 83% of those drugs being final human drug products and 7.5% consisting of APIs. The remaining imports included animal drugs and medicated animal feed. Additionally, drug products manufactured in other countries, such as India, also contain APIs originating from China. This means that the percentage of imported Chinese APIs into the United States is under-represented.

Significantly, US imports of Chinese biotech products, medical equipment, and pharmaceuticals have increased over the past decade, with the 2018 imports totaling $266 million for biotech, $5.9 billion for medical equipment, and $3.1 billion for pharmaceuticals (Refs 11, 16, and 18).

US Imports of Health Products from China 2010–2018

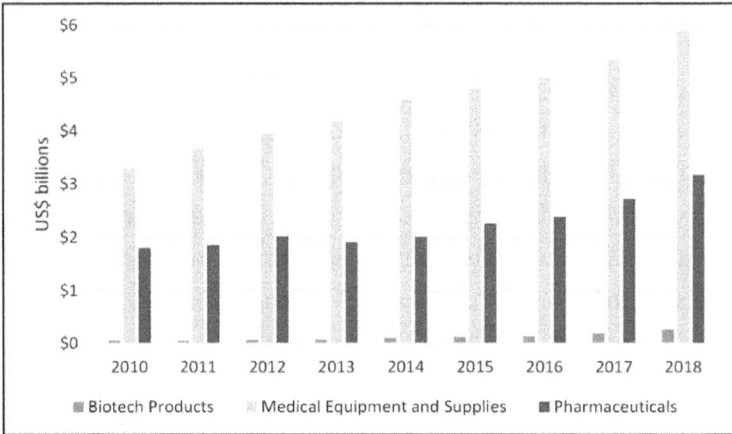

Source: U.S. Census Bureau

United States' Dependence on China for Basic Drugs

America's reliance on China for essential drugs has raised concerns about the safety and security of its citizens. Chinese-produced drugs are known to be low-quality and potentially unsafe, posing a threat to American consumers. China's aggressive tactics, such as state subsidies and relaxed safety standards, have allowed its pharmaceuticals to flood the American market at the expense of domestic drug manufacturers. As a result, China has gained significant control over the global essential drug market. This strategy has led to the closure of American pharmaceutical factories, causing the loss of jobs and the disappearance of high-quality medicines from the US market. Additionally, the US generic drug industry has become unable to produce vital medicines like penicillin and doxycycline, as the necessary active pharmaceutical ingredients (APIs) are primarily sourced from China. This reliance on China for crucial drugs raises the risk of drug shortages in the event of disruptions to the Chinese supply. The US Food and Drug Administration (FDA) also faces challenges in regulating and inspecting these drugs, as the agency is often perceived to have a lenient inspection and regulatory system. For instance, a 2016 congressional investigation revealed that a Chinese company that declined inspections received only a warning letter (Refs 11, 14, and 15).

4. France and the United States Brought Back the API Industry

In 2020, as Chinese factories and exports shut down during COVID-19 quarantine, the flow of medical ingredients declined. As a result, the United States Senate introduced two bills to restore America's capacity to make active pharmaceutical ingredients (APIs). The bills call for more disclosure on drug sourcing by drug makers and authorize $100 million to encourage companies to make more APIs in America. In 2020, the US government loaned $765 million at low interest to Eastman Kodak Company to produce active pharmaceutical ingredients (APIs) for generic drugs. The company expects the production of APIs to make up 30% to 40% of its business volume over time.

In 2020, French giant Sanofi SA created a new company to make APIs for the European market. The new company would rank as the world's second-largest API producer, with approximately €1 billion in expected sales by 2022. It employs 3,100 skilled employees in France (Ref 10).

5. The Crisis of Counterfeit Drugs and Opioids

A. Counterfeit Drugs Are on the Rise

Counterfeit Drug Definition: The United States Food and Drug Administration stated, "Counterfeit drugs may be contaminated or contain the wrong or no active ingredient. They could have the right active ingredient but at the wrong dose. Counterfeit drugs are illegal and may be harmful to your health" (Ref 25).

2006: The Organisation for Economic Co-operation and Development and the European Union Intellectual Property Office reported that counterfeit medications were valued at $4.4 billion. Most of them were fake antibiotics, painkillers, HIV/AIDS, cancer, and diabetes treatments.

2006: A licensed pharmacist was convicted of conspiracy to introduce in interstate commerce counterfeit and misbranded pharmaceutical drugs and trafficking in counterfeit drugs from China. Immigration and Customs Enforcement (ICE) inspectors at the Dallas Fort Worth Airport examined a large package from China with shipping documents identifying its contents as health food. However, inspectors found large quantities of the pharmaceutical drugs Viagra and Cialis instead. Suspecting the pharmaceutical drugs were counterfeit, the ICE agents verified with Pfizer Pharmaceuticals (the manufacturer of Viagra) and Eli Lily (the manufacturer of Cialis). They both confirmed that the drugs were fake (Ref 19).

2009: The Nigerian government intercepted 600,000 counterfeit antimalarial tablets. They were produced and shipped from China but labeled Made-in India (Ref 7).

2009: The International Criminal Police Organisation throughout China and seven other Southeast Asian countries seized 20 million pills of counterfeit and illegal pharmaceuticals. The police arrested 33 people and closed 100 retail outlets. The confiscated drugs were antibiotics, birth-control medicines, and antimalarial drugs (Ref 20).

2016: Law enforcement officers in Lorain County, Ohio, seized 500 pills that visually appeared to be oxycodone. Laboratory analysis indicated that the pills did not contain oxycodone. However, it was instead synthetic opioids unfit for human use, which has caused at least 17 overdoses and several deaths in the United States.

2018: Pfizer identified 95 fake products in 113 countries, up from 29 fakes in 75 countries in 2008. The company warned that the rise in falsified and substandard medicines had become a public health emergency (Ref 27).

2018: The most prominent Canadian online pharmacy, Canada Drugs, was fined $34 million for importing counterfeit cancer drugs and other unapproved pharmaceuticals into the United States. US prosecutors said: "The Canada Drug business model is based entirely on illegally importing unapproved and misbranded drugs not just from Canada, but from all over the world." The company has made at least $78 million through illegal imports, including two that were counterfeit versions of the cancer drugs Avastin and Altuzan that had no active ingredient. Canada Drugs has filled millions of prescriptions by offering itself as a safe alternative for patients to save money on expensive drugs since 2001 (Refs 25 and 9).

2019: The European Union's law enforcement agency seized 13 million doses of counterfeit medicine ranging from opioids to heart medication. This type of counterfeiting is on the rise due to the relatively low risk of criminal detection (Ref 25).

2019: The World Health Organization (WHO) issued a global alert about a fake cancer drug in Europe and America. The counterfeit drug was packaged to look like Iclusig, an anticancer medicine used to treat adults with chronic myeloid leukemia and acute lymphoblastic leukemia. WHO said the pill contained nothing but paracetamol, a common painkiller used to treat aches and pains (Ref 27).

2020: Operation Pangea, Interpol's global pharmaceutical crime-fighting unit, made 121 arrests across 90 countries, resulting in the seizure of fake dangerous pharmaceuticals worth over $14 million. Police officers confiscated tens of thousands of counterfeit fake medicines that claimed to cure coronavirus (Ref 8).

2023: According to the Pharmaceutical Security Institute (PSI), in 2023, law enforcement officials uncovered 6,897 incidents of counterfeiting, illegal diversion, and theft of pharmaceuticals in 142 countries. The crimes involved more than 2,440 different medicines across every therapeutic category. The PSI documented 4,894 arrests for pharmaceutical crime, the most significant number of arrests achieved in 22 consecutive years (Ref 30).

B. China and India Are the Sources of Fake Drugs

China and India are responsible for the vast majority of counterfeit drugs. The total annual global sales of counterfeit pharmaceutical products are at least $200 billion. Africa had the highest percentage (18.7%) of fake or substandard medicines, particularly fake coronavirus medications. The World Health Organization stated that about 10.5% of drugs in low and middle-income countries were fake or substandard. Most of the deaths caused by counterfeit drugs were in countries with a high demand for drugs (Refs 23, 25, and 27).

Counterfeit drugs may look like fundamental medicines but do not contain active ingredients. They often have harmful contaminants (arsenic, cement, printer ink, talcum powder, sawdust, industrial solvents, or paint). In addition to fake drugs, poor-quality medicines that lack sufficient active ingredients to work correctly or degraded/expired drugs have also flooded the market (Ref 27).

Poor surveillance and little regulations have facilitated market penetration for criminal gangs and cartels. Often, counterfeiters face only fines or minor sentences if caught. It is tough to catch counterfeiters because they move the drugs through several nations before reaching their final target. The World Customs Organization (WCO) reports that 50% to 60% of illicit traffic is shipped via sea to Hong Kong, Myanmar, Vietnam, and Thailand as major transit points. Subsequently, many of the fake medicines move west and often pass through the Middle East and Europe. Organized crime entities and terrorist groups are significant producers of counterfeit drugs (Refs 7, 25, and 20).

C. Popular Counterfeit Drugs

Counterfeit medicines have been a significant global problem for many years, typically targeting high-demand, expensive medications. They include (Ref 25):

a) Chemotherapeutic drugs
b) Antibiotics
c) Vaccines
d) Cholesterol-lowering agents
e) Anti-arthritis medications
f) Erectile dysfunction drugs
g) Weight loss aids
h) Hormone replacements
i) Analgesics
j) Steroids
k) Antihistamines
l) Antivirals
m) Antianxiety drugs

D. Market for Counterfeit Drugs

More than 110 countries have reported over 2,000 cases of harmful drugs to WHO's global surveillance and monitoring system. Illegal online pharmacies and medicines sold via social media platforms pose the most significant risk to the public. Approximately 35,000 online pharmacies have set up internet operations over the last decade, and many of them sell unapproved or counterfeit drugs. Eighty-five percent of the drugs being promoted as Canadian came from 27 other countries around the globe. Drugs purchased via mail order or courier are also susceptible to being illegitimate. During a spot check of mail, the FDA and the United States Customs Service found that 88% of drugs imported into the country violated federal safety standards. Smugglers also sold 63 different types of medications to over 3,000 doctors, clinics, and hospitals in the United States since 2012 (Refs 25 and 27).

6. Combating Illegal Trade and Ensuring Safety

A. Preventive Measures

2018: The National Institution for Transforming India (NITI) announced that they would be collaborating with US-based computer technology company Oracle to deploy blockchain technology to advance the traceability of pharmaceutical products. Having a growing database for products enables countries to track pharmaceutical products and prevent counterfeits from entering the system quickly (Ref 20).

2018: Chinese lawmakers began reviewing a draft amendment to the Drug Administration Law, which toughens penalties for offenders as the country cracks down on counterfeit drugs. The draft includes a traceability mechanism and drug recall system (Refs 20 and 26).

2019: The falsified Medicines Directive by the European Union (EU) mandated a new medicine verification law. The EU requires manufacturers to place safety features on all medicines and make financial contributions to a verification system to ensure the validity of pharmaceutical products. Required information on packaging will be a unique identifier in the form of a barcode and an anti-tamper mechanism.

2020: The Indian government has introduced mandatory barcoding of pharmaceutical products for its domestic market. When drugs are scanned, they can be immediately identified. This improves the traceability of medicines for consumer safety (Ref 20).

B. Combating the Opioid Crisis

China is the largest source of fentanyl (a powerful synthetic opioid) in the United States. Opioids are drugs naturally found in the opium poppy plant and are commonly prescribed as painkillers. Although the Chinese government made multiple commitments to control the flow of illegal fentanyl to the United States, it has failed to carry out those commitments. Half the deaths from the current opioid crisis in the United States were from the synthetic heroin fentanyl manufactured in China. Fentanyl has been smuggled across the US Southwest border by Mexican drug trafficking organizations to supply millions of addicted Americans (Refs 11, 20, and 22).

The FDA and its government partners are actively tracking illicit opioid products arriving through International Mail Facilities (IMF) and other illicit networks. In 2019, there were more than 17,000 prohibited drug products destroyed across all nine IMFs. Their value was more than $1.5 million. In addition, the FDA has been cracking down on opioid websites and has seized more than $41 million in assets. The United States Drug Enforcement Administration (DEA) seized 73,000 counterfeit pills containing fentanyl (a synthetic opioid) in Arizona. According to the Centers for Disease Control and Prevention, US prescription drug overdoses reached a record of 72,000 deaths in 2018 (Refs 22 and 24).

7. China Owns GNC

In 2018, China's state-controlled drug maker Harbin Pharmaceutical Group Holding Co. bought about 40% stake in US nutritional supplements retailer GNC Holdings Inc. for $300 million. The two companies started an e-commerce venture together. In June 2020, GNC filed for Chapter 11 bankruptcy protection and indicated that the company plans to close at least 800 stores. In September 2020, the bankruptcy court in Delaware approved the sale of the remaining 60% of GNC to Harbin Pharmaceutical Group for $770 million.

Harbin Pharma produces over 20 dosage forms and over 1,000 drugs, including antibiotics, over-the-counter products, modern Chinese medicines, and animal vaccines. CITIC Capital Holdings Ltd, the private equity Chinese state-owned firm, is a significant shareholder in Harbin Pharma (Refs 3 and 4).

CHAPTER 23

SILENCING DISSENT: REPRESSION AND RESISTANCE IN CHINA

—⟋⟋⟍—

As you ponder over this chapter, you will encounter a poignant exploration of the ways repression and resistance play out within China. It sheds light on the painful realities of religious restrictions and the deliberate dismantling of cultures, showcasing the crackdowns on ethnic minorities such as the Mongols, Muslims, and Uyghurs. You will also come face to face with disturbing human rights abuses, including forced labor, persecution of Falun Gong practitioners, and evidence of forced organ harvesting, urging us to reflect on the ethical dimensions of these unspeakable acts. Additionally, you will grapple with the harsh absence of freedom of speech, democracy, and internet control, underscoring the ongoing struggle for fundamental rights within China's authoritative regime.

1. Restrictions on Religion

In China, only the Buddhist faith is permitted. Many Mongolians follow a Tibetan form of Buddhism that recognizes His Holiness, the Dalai Lama, as a spiritual leader. The Chinese government restricted the Tibetan religion. The Communist Party believes it has the right to control all organized religions, fearing that religious organizations could challenge its political power. Since religious suppression has triggered violence in the past, the government views religion as the primary enemy of the state (Ref 15).

2. History of Mongols and Muslims in China

A. The Mongols

In 1947, the southern part of Mongolia became an autonomous region of China, known as the Inner Mongolia Autonomous Region today. Since that time, the Communist Party of China (CPC) has gradually eroded the culture and independence of the region. The CPC has encouraged Han Chinese to relocate to Inner Mongolia. There are 24 million of Han Chinese versus 5 million of ethnic Mongolians in the region. The official languages are Mandarin and Mongolian (Ref 11).

B. The Muslims

During the Tang Dynasty, which began in 618 AD , many Muslims traveled to China for trade and eventually became significant figures in the import and export industry. These Muslims settled in China and assimilated into Chinese culture. They even adopted Chinese surnames. Those who married Han Chinese women took on their wives' surnames. While they continued to adhere to Islamic attire and dietary regulations, they began speaking the local Chinese dialect. Presently, there are approximately 22 to 23 million Muslims in China, with the Hui and Uyghur ethnic groups being the largest.

The Uyghurs are Turkic descendants, a Muslim minority group of 12 million people who live mainly in the Xinjiang province in northwestern China. In the early part of the 20th Century, Uyghurs briefly declared independence. However, the region was brought under the complete control of the Communist Party of China in 1949. During the Cultural Revolution, the Chinese government attempted to dilute the Muslim population in Xinjiang by settling masses of Han Chinese there and replacing Muslim leaders. Xinjiang is currently designated an autonomous region within China, but the province has little autonomy (Refs 5 and 7).

The Huis are descendants of Arab and Persian traders who settled more than a millennium ago. They are scattered all over China and speak mostly Chinese while maintaining some Arabic and Persian phrases. After centuries of intermarriage, they have become ethnically integrated with Han Chinese (Refs 15).

3. Cultural Genocide: Crackdowns on Mongols, Muslims, and Uyghurs

A. Cultural Genocides

In 2015, China's new leader, Xi Jinping, initiated a policy of "Sinicization of Islam," which aims to bring non-Chinese societies under the influence of Han Chinese culture, language, norms, and ethnic identity. In 2019, the Chinese government announced that literature, politics, and history should be taught in Mandarin in the Inner Mongolian Autonomous Region, Tibet Autonomous Region, and Xinjiang Uyghur Autonomous Region. Over the past 70 years, the government has been gradually limiting the rights of ethnic minorities. Additionally, Han Chinese men are reportedly being incentivized to marry ethnic minority women, including Uyghurs and Mongols. There are also allegations of forced sterilization targeting Uyghur women (Refs 8 and 11).

B. Crackdowns on Mongols

China is cracking down on protesters in Inner Mongolia following the implementation of a new policy that mandates Mandarin-language education in the region. Many Mongolians are upset with the government for attempting to erase their culture. Under President Xi Jinping, the Chinese Communist Party has escalated efforts to encourage the country's ethnic minorities to embrace a uniform Chinese identity. While the government has characterized these policies as promoting bilingual education, activists argue that the true objective is to replace local languages with Mandarin, accelerating the disappearance of ethnic minority cultures (Ref 12).

C. Crackdowns on Muslims

The government has been cracking down on the Muslim religion and destroyed mosques built with domes and others with Arabic architectural characteristics. From Beijing to Ningxia, officials have banned the public use of Arabic script. The goal is to eradicate the Muslim religion, tradition, and belief system. In the state's view, the spread of Islamic customs dangerously disrupts social and political conformity. China fears that Saudi Arabia, in particular, will poison Chinese Islam with Wahhabism, an Islamic doctrine and religious movement often linked with extremism (Refs 11 and 15).

D. Crackdowns on Uyghurs

In 2017, President Xi Jinping announced that Chinese religions must be traditional. This order led to a crackdown on religious practices, mainly affecting the Uyghurs. The Chinese government claims the measures are necessary to combat violence in the region. However, critics argue that this was used as an excuse to justify the repression of the Uyghurs. China has been facing global political criticism over its alleged persecution of the Uyghurs. Many prominent members of the ethnic minority have been imprisoned or sought asylum abroad after being accused of terrorism. The Uyghur autonomous region has been turned into what resembles a massive prison camp. Human rights charities, including Amnesty International and Human Rights Watch (HRW), have long accused China of mass imprisonment and torture.

Evidence shows that many people have been detained for simply expressing their faith by praying or wearing a veil or for having overseas connections to places like Turkey. Many are forced to work in factories and are subjected to constant digital surveillance. Xinjiang is covered by a pervasive surveillance network, including police, checkpoints, and cameras that scan everything from vehicle number plates to individual faces. Chinese police routinely plug pedestrians' smartphones into a device that scans their files and apps. Targeted individuals have been required to submit voice and face scans in addition to DNA samples. Local officials block foreign reporters from moving freely in the region, particularly near the prison camps. The repression of Muslims in the western region of Xinjiang has spread to other parts of China, targeting other Muslims who have been better integrated into Chinese society (Refs 6, 7, 8, 14, 15, and 22).

4. Forced Labor and International Reactions

A. Forced Labor

In April 2018, the Xinjiang government began planning to attract textile and garment companies. Local governments would receive funds to build production sites near the re-education camps (prison); companies would receive a subsidy of $260 to train an inmate and other incentives. State-sponsored forced labor programs often set a quota of working inmates that local officials must meet.

Furthermore, satellite imagery suggests that growing numbers of Muslim detainees are being sent to new factories and production lines built inside some re-education camps. Commercial registration records also show that at least a few companies have addresses inside the camps. They include a printing factory, a noodle factory, a bedding manufacturer, and clothing and textile manufacturers.

Inmates have no choice but to accept jobs for very little pay or no salary and must endure harsh conditions at these factories. The program aims to transform Uyghurs, Kazakhs, and other ethnic minorities into a disciplined, Chinese-speaking industrial workforce loyal to the Communist Party and factory bosses. As many as 1.5 million Uyghurs and other Muslim minorities have been sent to re-education and forced labor camps (Refs 4, 5, 7,9, and 22).

B. International Reaction to Forced Labor

In July 2020, more than 190 organizations from 36 countries issued a call to action to end all sourcing from the Xinjiang region of China, which is well known for forced labor. Roughly one in five cotton garments sold globally contains cotton or yarn from Xinjiang (Ref 5).

Recent investigations by *The New York Times, The Wall Street Journal,* and others have found evidence that connects China's forced detention of Turkic-speaking Uyghurs to the supply chains of many of the world's best-known fashion retailers. According to another BBC News report, between 2017 and 2019, more than 80,000 Uyghurs were transferred out of the western Xinjiang autonomous region to work in factories across China. These factories claim to be part of the supply chain for 83 well-known global brands (Ref 7).

In 2020, the United States Congress introduced the Uyghur Forced Labor Prevention Act bill to ensure that goods made with forced labor in the Xinjiang Uyghur Autonomous Region of China do not enter the United States market. Any goods from Xinjiang would be presumed to have been made using forced labor unless companies could provide clear and convincing evidence that they did not use forced labor. Many Western fashion businesses have remained quiet, fearful of losing the Chinese market or access to a critical manufacturing hub in their supply chains. In addition, they cannot do due diligence to determine whether forced labor is involved. Chinese officials tightly control Xinjiang (Refs 5 and 8).

In March 2021, in a unified statement, the United States, the European Union, the United Kingdom, Australia, Canada, and New Zealand announced sanctions against Chinese officials for serious human rights abuses against Uyghurs. The US and its allies also issued condemnations to isolate and pressure China. The joint statement said:

> The evidence, including from the Chinese Government's documents, satellite imagery, and eyewitness testimony, is overwhelming. China's extensive program of repression includes severe restrictions on religious freedoms, the use of forced labor, mass detention in internment camps, forced sterilizations, and the concerted destruction of Uyghur heritage (Ref 23).

5. Persecution of Falun Gong

Falun Gong is a Buddhist meditation system that was introduced to the public in 1992 by Mr. Li Hongzhi, a Chinese chi-gong master. The practice of Falun Gong entails both spiritual and physical components. The essence of the spiritual component is represented by the guiding principles of "Truthfulness, Compassion, and Tolerance." The physical component of Falun Gong comprises five gentle chi gong exercises, similar to Tai Chi, to improve both health and well-being. Falun Gong follows neither religious formalities nor a membership structure. Its classes and activities are open to the public free of charge.

By 1999, over 70 million people had been practicing it regularly. The Chinese government became cautious of Falun Gong's spiritual aspects and immense popularity. Therefore, the Communist Party banned the Falun Gong and mobilized the state's massive resources to eradicate it. Thus, one of the most brutal human rights abuses in history began.

The primary goal of the Chinese Communist Party is to transform practitioners by destroying their beliefs and conscience. As a result, Falun Gong practitioners have been imprisoned, tortured, and forced to undergo comprehensive medical examinations related to organ function, both in state custody and in their homes. Then, hundreds of thousands of them have disappeared.

In 2006, there were accusations that Falun Gong followers detained in government facilities and hospitals throughout China were being killed on demand to source organs for transplant surgeries. More than a million practitioners of Falun Gong are believed to have been killed by the Chinese government (Refs 1 and 4).

6. Medical Genocide and Evidence of Forced Organ Harvesting

A. Medical Genocide

The following facts are from the China Organ Harvest Research Center:

"Documenting Genocide: The Extrajudicial Killings of Prisoners of Conscience for Organs in China and the Campaign to Eradicate Falun Gong Factual Findings and Analysis Report," September 2019 (Ref 1).

> China now performs more organ transplants than any other country in the world despite having few donations. Where do these organs come from? A decade of research by international investigators has found that the Chinese regime is systematically killing prisoners of conscience on demand to feed its vast organ transplant industry. With patients throughout the world traveling to China for organ transplants, the practice has become a global crime.
>
> The Chinese Communist regime has extra-judicially killed Falun Gong practitioners for organ harvesting on a large scale as part of a state-driven campaign to eliminate Falun Gong. Killing for organs is a crime against humanity and a new form

of state terrorism. The scale, sophistication, cruelty, and longevity of the campaign against Falun Gong make it one of the most hideous human rights disasters of the 21st century.

The Communist regime has also intensified its persecution of other faith groups, including Uyghur Muslims, Tibetan Buddhists, and House Christians (underground churches). More than one million Uyghurs are now detained in political reeducation camps in Xinjiang and subjected to similar transformation techniques as those used by Falun Gong. They have been forcibly blood tested, given other medical examinations, and had DNA data collected. The Communist Party is now expanding its targets for reeducation campaigns, surveillance, and organ harvesting to exploit much larger populations across China.

Since 2001, the Chinese government has prioritized the organ transplantation industry in its national development strategy. It has invested heavily in research, development, and personnel training in transplantation technology to meet the needs of this rapidly growing industry. As a result, China's transplant centers have made breakthroughs in crucial organ transplantation capabilities and technologies to become the worldwide leader in organ transplantation technology in recent years. After the year 2000, China has performed more transplants than any other country in the world despite the lack of a voluntary organ donation system. Organ transplant operations in China are usually conducted on demand with short wait times; they are scheduled in advance and use organs taken from living people who were then killed in the process.

In response to international criticism since 2006, Chinese officials claimed that almost all transplant organs came from death-row prisoners and, later, from voluntary donations.

However, these sources could not have provided enough organs to supply the number of transplants performed. China did not have an organ donation system until March 2010, and the number of dead-row prisoners has reduced to a few.

B. US Resolution on the Forced Organ Harvesting

In July 2019, the United States Senate passed a resolution regarding human rights and the forced organ harvesting of Falun Gong practitioners.

> Expressing solidarity with Falun Gong practitioners who have lost lives, freedoms, and other rights for adhering to their beliefs and practices, and condemning the practice of non-consenting organ harvesting and for other purposes.

> Whereas the United Nations Committee Against Torture and the Special Rapporteur on Torture have expressed concern over the allegations of organ harvesting from Falun Gong prisoners and have called on the Government of the People's Republic of China to increase accountability and transparency in the organ transplant system and punish those responsible for abuses.

> The killing of religious or political prisoners for any purpose, including to sell their organs for transplant, is an egregious and intolerable violation of the fundamental right to life. United States Senate Resolution 274, July 11, 2019 (Ref 20).

7. Lack of Freedom of Speech, Democracy, and Internet Control

A. Tiananmen Square, June 3-4, 1989

Tiananmen, which means "gate of heavenly peace," is located in Beijing. On April 15, 1989, Hu Yaobang, the expelled General

Secretary of the Communist Party, passed away at the age of 73 due to a heart attack. Hu had been working to push China towards a more open political system and had become a symbol of democratic reform. Following his passing, over one million Chinese students and workers occupied Tiananmen Square in Beijing and initiated the most significant political protest in communist China's history. After six weeks of demonstrations, Chinese troops entered Tiananmen Square from June 3 through June 4, 1989, and fired on civilians—estimates of the death toll range from several hundred to thousands (Ref 16).

B. No Freedom of the Press

In a 2020 US Congressional report, China was ranked as the fourth worst country in the world (out of 180) for press freedom. This is due to its censorship, harassment, detention of journalists, and pervasive surveillance. According to the Committee to Protect Journalists (CPJ), China imprisoned the most journalists in the world in 2019. Many of the detained journalists are Chinese citizens, including non-professional or former journalists who use digital media platforms to document rights abuses.

In 2019, the Chinese government expelled or failed to renew the work visas for nearly 19 foreign journalists. The expulsions of US journalists from *The New York Times*, *The Washington Post*, and *The Wall Street Journal* were in retaliation for the US Government requiring that Chinese state-run media outlets register as foreign missions in the United States (Ref 22).

C. Internet Control

The Chinese government maintains strict control over its citizens' freedom of expression and access to information. They have invested significant resources in monitoring and censoring internet content, with the implementation of the Great Firewall in December 1999. Research indicates that the regime blocks a high percentage of political and Falun Gong-related websites while allowing a smaller percentage of pornographic sites. Additionally, the government has developed extensive surveillance systems, including "Skynet," "Safe-City," and "Sharp Eyes," which collectively consist of around 500 million cameras capable of facial recognition and posture analysis.

Furthermore, Chinese companies like Baidu use facial recognition technology for employee entry and exit monitoring. Several international internet companies, including Yahoo!, Microsoft, Cisco, and Google, have been criticized for assisting the Chinese government in censorship and surveillance. This has led to concerns about privacy and freedom of expression, prompting U.S. Representative Chris Smith to propose the Global Online Freedom Act in 2006, which aims to prevent U.S. businesses from cooperating with internet-restricting countries (Refs 1, 13, 18, and 22).

CONCLUSION

—⦚—

As we approach the final chapters of *China's Secret Strategy*, it becomes unmistakably clear that China's rise has significant implications for the United States, India, and the world. Since joining the World Trade Organization in 2001, China has transformed into a global superpower, reshaping the world's economic, political, and technological landscapes.

China's strategic maneuvers, such as intellectual property theft, currency manipulation, and aggressive export subsidies, have given it an unfair advantage, often at the expense of the United States. These tactics have not only hurt US industries but have also changed global market dynamics. The environmental and health problems stemming from China's rapid industrialization, including air pollution, contaminated food, and tainted medications, have far-reaching consequences for all of us.

China's rise has been overshadowed by darker aspects such as human rights abuses, the repression of dissent, and the mistreatment of minority groups. At the same time, its Belt and Road Initiative, coupled with extensive overseas investments, has significantly expanded China's global influence, fostering new dependencies and escalating geopolitical tensions. While these investments are often framed as contributions to economic development, they are, in reality, part of China's broader strategy to enhance its global power.

The emergence of a new Cold War, characterized by China's military build-up and its alliance with Russia, highlights the increased geopolitical stakes. The intense competition for technological supremacy, especially in the semiconductor industry, underscores the global race for innovation and control.

Understanding the complexities of China's rise is crucial for navigating the future. The United States and the world as a whole must confront these challenges with strategic foresight, resilience, and a commitment to maintaining a balance of power that favors freedom and democracy.

China's Secret Strategy has uncovered the mechanisms, strategies, and costs of China's rapid rise, shedding light on the challenges faced by the global community. As we move forward, it is essential to remain vigilant and proactive in addressing the ongoing shifts in global power dynamics.

The story of China's rise is far from over. It continues to evolve, presenting new challenges and opportunities. Equipped with a deeper understanding of the forces at play, we must remain committed to safeguarding our values and interests in this ever-changing global landscape. The dragon has ascended, but our journey to understand its impact has just begun.

ANOTHER BOOK YOU MAY LIKE

—〰—

Healthy Cookbook for Adults: 90 Favorite Easy Recipes from Around the World by Coco Hazel is your go-to guide for cooking delicious meals without complicated steps or boring ingredients. Here is the link to the book on Amazon:

https://www.amazon.com/dp/B0DXBFV7G1

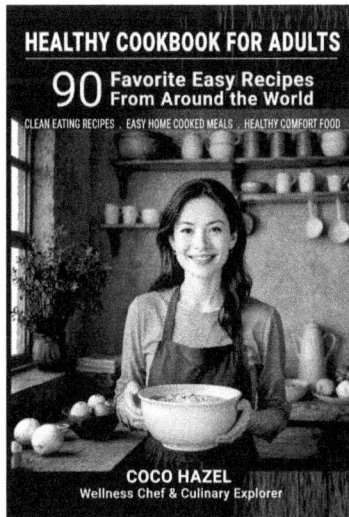

HEALTHY COOKBOOK FOR ADULTS
90 Favorite Easy Recipes From Around the World
CLEAN EATING RECIPES . EASY HOME COOKED MEALS . HEALTHY COMFORT FOOD
COCO HAZEL
Wellness Chef & Culinary Explorer

FEEDBACK IS GREATLY APPRECIATED

———〜〜〜———

If you found *China's Secret Strategy* insightful and compelling, we would greatly appreciate it if you could share your positive experience with others by leaving a review on Amazon. Your feedback will help others discover the depth of this exploration into China's emergence and its impact on the United States. It will also support our efforts to bring critical geopolitical issues to a broader audience.

Here is the barcode that will retrieve the link from Amazon when scanned by a smartphone or other device.

https://www.amazon.com/dp/B0DX41Q9S8

Thank you for engaging with this critical topic and for your support!

Arthur Deperis

R Sampath

REFERENCES

—ᜍᜍᜍ—

Chapter 1 References

1. Gautam Jaggi, Mary Rundle, Daniel Rosen, and Yuichi Takahashi, "China's Economic Reform," Institute for International Economics, 1996

2. Iman Ghosh, "The People's Republic of China: 70 Years of Economic History," *Visual Capitalist*, October 12, 2019

3. "China profile – Timeline," BBC News, July 29, 2019

4. Shibani Mahtani, Anna Field Tiffany Liang, and Timothy McLaughlin, "China to Impose Sweeping Security Law in Hong Kong, Heralding End of City's Autonomy," *The Washington Post*, May 20, 2020

5. Roberto Suro, "Chung Makes Deal with Prosecutors," *The Washington Post*, March 6, 1998

6. Brian Ross, Rhonda Schwartz, and Alex Hosenball, "FBI Arrests Chinese Millionaire Once Tied to Clinton $$ Scandal," ABC News, September 24, 2015

7. James Bennet, "Clinton Says Chinese Money Did Not Influence US Policy," *The New York Times*, May 18, 1998

8. Grace Tsoi and Lam Cho Wai, "Hong Kong Security Law: What Is It and Is It Worrying?" BBC News, June 30, 2020

9. "Top Trading Partners," US Census, December 2019

10. "What is Behind the China-Taiwan Divide?" BBC News, January 2, 2019

11. Anna Field, "China Vows to 'Smash' Any Taiwan Independence Move as Trump Weighs Sanctions," *The Washington Post*, May 29, 2020

12. Wang Sangui, Li Zhou and Ren Yanshun, "The 8-7 National Poverty Reduction Program in China-The National Strategy and Its Impacts," World Bank, May 2004

13. Sophie Williams, "Macau: China's Other 'One Country, Two Systems' Region," BBC News, December 20, 2019

14. "Taiwan Allies International Protection and Enhancement Initiative Act (Taipei)," Public Law 116–135, 116th Congress, March 26, 2020

15. Ilya Somin, "Remembering the Biggest Mass Murder in the History of the World," *The Washington Post*, August 3, 2016

16. Eswar Prasad, "China Stumbles but Is Unlikely to Fall," International Monetary Fund, Finance and Development, December 2023

17. "Countries that Recognize Taiwan 2024," www.worldpopulationreview.com, assessed July 2, 2024

Chapter 2 References

1. "Sun Zhengcai: Former Top Chinese Official Jailed for Life," BBC News, May 2018

2. Yuwen Wu, "Profile: China's fallen Security Chief Zhou Yongkang," BBC News, October 12, 2015

3. "Bo Xilai Scandal: Timeline," BBC News, November 11, 2015

4. "What Does Xi Jinping's China Dream Mean?" BBC News, June 6, 2013

5. Timothy R. Heath, "Xi's Cautious Inching Towards the China Dream," The RAND Corporation, August 7, 2023

6. "Four Comprehensives Are the Road to Prosperity," *China Insight*, March 27, 2015

7. Melissa Albert, "Xi Jinping", *Britannica*, Jun 4, 2024

8. "China's Xi Jinping Unveils New Four Comprehensives' Slogans," BBC, 25 February 2015

9. Tony Saich, "The National People's Congress: Functions and Membership," Harvard Kennedy School, ASH Center, November 2015

10. Yi Zeng and Therese Hesketh, "The Effects of China's Universal Two-Child Policy," National School of Development and Raissun Institute for Advanced Studies, Peking University, May 10, 2018

11. "The Chinese Communist Party: Threatening Global Peace and Stability," US Department of State, January 20, 2021

12. Jie Lin, Kuiyuan Gong, and Chuangbin Chen, "Towards Integrated Sustainability for China's Rural Revitalization: An Analysis of Income Inequality and Public Health," *Public Health*, January 8, 2024

13. Muhammad Asif Noor, "China's Rural Revitalization Strategy," *Beijing Review*, April 2, 2021

14. Tang Renjian, Minister of Agriculture and Rural Affairs, "Steadily Advancing Rural Revitalization," *QIUSHY*, CPC Central Committee Bimonthly, December 2021

15. Katja Drinhausen, "China's Social Credit System in 2021: From Fragmentation Towards Integration," Mercator Institute for China Studies, March 03, 2021

16. "Communiqué of the 19th Central Committee of the Communist Party of China on the Fifth Plenary Session," *Xinhua*, November 1, 2021

17. Jane Perlez, "Xi Jinping Celebrates China's Transformation, but Critics See Stagnation," *The New York Times*, October 1, 2021

18. "The 14th Five-Year Plan (2021-2025) for National Economic and Social Development and the Long-Range Objectives Through the Year 2035," The State Council of the People's Republic of China, March 2021

19. Keith Bradsher and Steven Lee Myers, "Xi Jinping Declares Victory Over Extreme Poverty, but the Fight Continues," *The New York Times*, February 25, 2021

20. "CPC History: Compilation of Historical Resolutions of the CPC Central Committee," *Xinhua*, October 2020

21. Li Keqiang, "The Report on the Work of the Government," State Council of the People's Republic of China, March 2022

22. Chris Buckley, "China's President Xi Jinping Tightens His Grip on Communist Party," *The New York Times*, October 24, 2022

23. "China's Xi Jinping Stresses Party's Leadership in All Aspects of Governance," *Xinhua*, March 15, 2024

24. "China's Legal System and Judicial Reform," *South China Morning Post*, June 20, 2023

25. "China's Rural Revitalization Strategy: A Blueprint for Prosperity," *Reuters*, November 30, 2023

26. "Military-Civil Fusion and the People's Republic of China," US Department of State, 2020

Chapter 3 References

1. Madelyn R. Creedon et al., "America's Strategic Posture, Final Report of the Congressional Commission on the Strategic Posture of the United States," The Congressional Commission on the Strategic Posture of the United States, October 2023

2. Christian Breuer, "The New Cold War and the Return of History," *Intereconomics*, 2022

3. "The China-Russia Gas Deal: Background and Implications for the Broader Relationship," US-China Economic and Security Review Commission, June 9, 2014

4. Mark Cozad, Cortez A. Cooper III, Alexis A. Blanc, David Woodworth, Anthony Atler, Kotryna Jukneviciute, Mark Hvizda, Sale Lilly, "Future Scenarios for Sino-Russian Military Cooperation," *Rand Research Report*, 2024

5. Gita Gopinath, "Geopolitics and Its Impact on Global Trade and the Dollar," International Monetary Fund, May 7, 2024

6. Lloyd Green, "New Cold Wars Review: China, Russia, and Biden's Daunting Task," *The Guardian*, 21 April 2024

7. Dmitri Alperovitch, "How the US Can Win the New Cold War?" *Time Magazine,* May 1, 2016

8. "In Their Own Words Joint Statement of the Russian Federation and the People's Republic of China on International Relations Entering a New Era and Global Sustainable Development," China Aerospace Studies Institute, February 4, 2022

9. Yukio Tajima, "China and Russia Kick-off Military Exercises in the Sea of Japan," *Nikkei Asia,* July 21, 2023

10. Philip Wang, "China Sees Biggest Trade Increase with Russia in 2023, Chinese Data Shows," CNN, June 7, 2023

11. "China-Russia 2023 Trade Value Hits Record High of $240 Billion - Chinese Customs," *Reuters,* January 11, 2024

12. "The Sixteenth Meeting of Space Cooperation Sub-Committee Was in Moscow," China National Space Administration, September 16, 2015

13. Yew Lun Tian, "China, Russia to Start Joint Air and Sea Drill in the Sea of Japan," *Reuters,* July 16, 2023

14. Iacob Koch-Weser, "The China-Russia Gas Deal: Background and Implications for the Broader Relationship," US-China Economic and Security Review Commission, June 9, 2014

15. "China and Russia Signed New Bilateral Local Currency Settlement Agreement," The People's Bank of China, www.pbc.gov.cn, accessed June 17, 2024

16. "Military and Security Developments Involving the People Republic of China Annual Report to Congress," The US Department of Defense, 2023

17. Alec Luhn and Terry Macalister, "Russia Signs 30-Year Deal Worth $400 billion to Deliver Gas to China," *The Guardian*, May 21, 2014

18. "China and Russia Sign a Memorandum of Understanding Regarding Cooperation for the Construction of the International Lunar Research Station," China International Space Administration, March 9, 2021

Chapter 4 References

1. Michele Ruta, Matias Herrera Dappe, Somik Lall, Chunlin Zhang, Erik Churchill, Cristina Constantinescu, Mathilde Lebrand, and Alen Mulabdic, "Belt and Road Economics: Opportunities and Risks of Transport Corridors," World Bank, 2019

2. Nedopil Christoph, "Countries of the Belt and Road Initiative," Green Finance and Development Center, FISF Fudan University, www.greenfdc.org, 2023

3. "The World by Income and Region," World Bank, accessed June 5, 2024

4. "The Asian Infrastructure Investment Bank," www.aiib.org, accessed June 6, 2024

5. "Asian Infrastructure Investment Bank," Standard and Poor Global Ratings, RatingsDirect, January 20, 2023

6. "The Regional Comprehensive Economic Partnership (RCEP)," The Association of South East Asian Nations, www.asean.org, accessed June 7, 2024

7. Daniel C.K. Chow, "Why China Established the Asia Infrastructure Investment Bank," *49 Vanderbilt Law Review* 1255, 2021

8. "What Is the South China Sea Dispute?" BBC News, July 7, 2023

9. Jesse Johnson and Gabriel Dominguez, "US and Chinese Defense Chiefs Agree on the Importance of Military Talks," *The Japan Times*, May 31, 2024

10. "China's Military Strategy," The State Council Information Office of the People's Republic of China, May 27, 2015

11. "US-China Strategic Competition in South and East China Seas: Background and Issues for Congress," Congressional Research Service, December 21, 2021

12. "Forum on China-Africa Cooperation," www.focac.org, accessed June 7, 2024

13. Xi Jinping, "Further Deepening Cooperation and Moving Forward to Step up the Building of a China-Arab Community with a Shared Future," Ministry of Foreign Affairs of the People's Republic of China, www.fmprc.gov.cn, May 30, 2024

14. "China's Engagement with Latin America and the Caribbean," US-China Economic and Security Review Commission, October 17, 2018

15. "Basic Information about China-CELAC Forum," Department of Latin American and Caribbean Affairs, Ministry of Foreign Affairs of China, April 2016

16. Michael R. Pompeo, "US Position on Maritime Claims in the South China Sea," US Department of State, July 13, 2020

17. Jenni Marsh, "China's President Xi Pledges Another $60 Billion for Africa," CNN, September 4, 2018

18. "China-Africa Economic Bulletin," Global Development Policy Center, Boston University, 2024

19. Rachel Savage and Clare Baldwin, "China Lent $1.34 Trillion in 2000-2021, Focus Shifts from Belt and Road to Rescue Finance-Report," *Reuters*, November 6, 2023

20. "G7 Japan 2023 Foreign Ministers' Statement," United States Department of State, November 8, 2023

21. "Military and Security Developments Involving the People Republic of China Annual Report to Congress," The US Department of Defense, 2023

Chapter 5 References

1. Ana Swanson, "Trump Administration Blocks Chinese Acquisition of Hotel Software Company," *New York Times*, March 6, 2020

2. David McLaughlin, "Trump Blocks Chinese Deal for US Software Firm StayNTouch," *Bloomberg*, March 6, 2020

3. Holger Hansen and Michael Nienaber, "With Eye on China, Germany Tightens Foreign Investment Rules," *Reuters*, December 19, 2018

4. Ana Swanson and David McCabe, "Trump Effort to Keep US Tech out of China Alarms American Firms," *New York Times*, February 16, 2020

5. "2019 Special 301 Report," Office of the United States Trade Representative, April 2019

6. "The Theft of American Intellectual Property: Reassessments of the Challenge and the United States Policy," The Commission on the Theft of American Intellectual Property, February 2017

7. Kate O'Keeffe and Aruna Viswanatha, "Chinese Diplomats Helped Military Scholars Visiting the US Evade FBI Scrutiny, US Says," *The Wall Street Journal*, August 25, 2020

8. Kate O'Keeffe and Aruna Viswanatha, "FBI Sweep of China Researchers Leads to Cat-and-Mouse Tactics," *The Wall Street Journal*, September 7, 2020

9. Eric Rosenbaum, "1 in 5 Corporations Say China Has Stolen Their IP within the Last Year: CNBC CFO Survey," CNBC, March 1, 2019

10. Kate O'Keeffe Aruna Viswanatha, "How China Targets Scientists via Global Network of Recruiting Stations," *The Wall Street Journal*, August 20, 2020

Chapter 6 References

1. David Meyer, "As Chinese State-Backed Firms Eye Overseas Acquisitions, Europe Considers New Ways to Block Them," *Fortune*, June 17, 2020

2. "CNOOC Completes Contentious $15.1-Billion Acquisition of Nexen," *Reuters*, February 25, 2013

3. Agatha Kratz, Mikko Huotari, Thilo Hanemann, Rebecca Arcesati, "Chinese FDI in Europe: 2019 Update," Rhodium Group (RHG) and the Mercator Institute for China Studies (MERICS), 2019

4. "Who is Behind the Chinese Takeover of World's Biggest Pork Producer?" PBS News, September 12, 2014

5. Jane Perlez and Ryan Mcmorrow, "A Deal for an Australian Dairy Wrapped in Layers of Chinese Loans," *The New York Times*, August 2, 2017

6. Hollie Mckay, "How Much of the United States Does China Really Own?" Fox News, June 30, 2020

7. Holger Hansen and Michael Nienaber, "With an eye on China, Germany Tightens Foreign Investment Rules," *Reuters*, December 19, 2018

8. Esther Fung, "Chinese Exiting US Real Estate as Beijing Directs Money Back to Shore Up Economy," *The Wall Street Journal*, January 29, 2019

9. 116th Congress, "Holding Foreign Companies Accountable Act," Public Law No: 116-222, December 18, 2020

10. Alan Rappeport, "In New Slap at China, US Expands Power to Block Foreign Investments," *The New York Times*, October 10, 2018

Chapter 7 References

1. James T. Areddy, "In Allowing Yuan to Devalue, China Policy Makers Concede Economy Needs a Boost," *The Wall Street Journal*, August 7, 2019

2. Joanne Chiu Steven Russolillo, "China's Yuan Breaches Critical Level of 7 to the Dollar, Prompting Trump Critique," *The Wall Street Journal*, August 5, 2019

3. William Mauldin, Nick Timiraos, and Paul Kiernan, "US Designates China as Currency Manipulator," *The Wall Street Journal*, August 5, 2019

4. Shawn Donnan and Lucy Hornby, "US Challenges Illegal Chinese Export Subsidies," *Financial Times*, February 11, 2015

5. Peter Navarro, "Death by China: How America Lost Its Manufacturing Base," a documentary film on Netflix, 2016

6. "EU, US, and Japan Agree on New Ways to Strengthen Global Rules on Industrial Subsidies," European Commission Directorate-General for Trade, January 14, 2020

7. David Meyer, "As Chinese State-Backed Firms Eye Overseas Acquisitions, Europe Considers New Ways to Block Them," *Fortune,* June 17, 2020

8. Christopher S. Chivvis and Hannah Miller, "The Role of Congress in US-China Relations," The Carnegie Endowment for International Peace, November 2023

9. "Fact Sheet: President Biden Takes Action to Protect American Workers and Businesses from China's Unfair Trade Practices," The US Department of Commerce, Office of Public Affairs, May 14, 2024

10. Jim Tankersley, "Biden Will Raise Tariffs on Chinese Electric Vehicles, Chips, and Other Goods," *The New York Times*, May 14, 2024

11. "Department of Commerce Issues Final Determination of Circumvention Inquiries of Solar Cells and Modules from China," US Department of Commerce, August 18, 2023

Chapter 8 References

1. "Coming Home," *The Economist*, January 17, 2013

2. Evan Comen, "Which Manufacturers Are Bringing the Most Jobs Back to America?" *USA Today*, June 28, 2018

3. "Apple Explores Moving 15-30% of Production Capacity from China: Nikkei," *Reuters*, June 19, 2019

4. Niharika Mandhana, "Manufacturers Want to Quit China for Vietnam. They are Finding It Impossible," *The Wall Street Journal*, August 21, 2019

5. Siddhartha, "Apple Vendor Eyes Production Shift to India," *Times of India*, August 2, 2020

6. Masamichi Hoshi, Rei Nakafuji, and Yusho Cho, "China Scrambles to Stem Manufacturing Exodus as 50 Companies Leave," *Nikkei Asian*, July 18, 2019

7. Hiroyuki Akiyama, "Japan Companies Line up for 'China Exit' Subsidies to Come Home," *Nikkei Asia*, September 9, 2020

8. Taylor Telford, "More than 50 Major Companies, from Google to Nintendo, Pull Production from China Because of the Trade War," *The Washington Post*, July 19, 2019

9. Paul Merrion, "Fellowes Makes Federal Case of Chinese Dispute," *Chicago Business & Financial News & Analysis*, April 09, 2011

10. "Google to Move Pixel Smartphone Production to Vietnam: Nikkei," *Reuters*, August 28, 2019

11. Andrea Shalal, Alexandra Alper, and Patricia Zengerle, "US Mulls Paying Companies, Tax Breaks to Pull Supply Chains from China," *Reuters*, May 17, 2020

12. Nikhil Inamdar, "Coronavirus: Can India Replace China as World's Factory?" BBC News, May 18, 2020

13. Kenneth Rapoza, "Kudlow: Pay the Moving Costs of American Companies Leaving China," *Forbes*, April 10, 2020

14. Stephanie Clifford, "US Textile Plants Return, With Floors Largely Empty of People," *The New York Times*, September 19, 2013

15. Jethro Mullen, "Western Businesses Say China Is Increasingly Hostile," CNN Money, June 7, 2016

16. Peter Navarro, "Death by China: How America Lost Its Manufacturing Base," A documentary film on Netflix, 2016

17. Hiroko Tabuchi, "Walmart's Imports from China Displaced 400,000 Jobs, a Study Says," *The New York Times,* December 9, 2015

18. Chuin-Wei Yap, "How China Built a Steel Behemoth and Convulsed World Trade," *The Wall Street Journal*, December 24, 2018

19. "How Elon Musk Built a Tesla Factory in China in Less than a Year," *Fortune*, January 7, 2020

20. "Tesla Plans $5 Billion Investment in Chinese Factory," *Industry Week*, August 1, 2018

21. Dan Flynn, "Beyond Meat Inks Agreement with Food Safety Challenged China to Produce Its Plant-Based Proteins," *Food Safety News*, September 9, 2020

22. Brendan Murray, "Apple Shifts to India Just as the Global Chips Race Heats Up," *Bloomberg*, April 10, 2024

Chapter 9 References

1. "China Is Quietly Reducing Its Reliance on Foreign Chip Technology," *The Economist*, May 14, 2024

2. Christopher S. Chivvis and Hannah Miller, "The Role of Congress in US-China Relations," The Carnegie Endowment for International Peace, November 2023

3. "Chip Technology Spending Gets $81 Billion Boost in China Rivalry," *Bloomberg*, May 12, 2024

4. Dylan Butts and Sheila Chiang, "China Remains Crucial for US Chipmakers Amid Rising Tensions Between the World's Top Two Economies," CNBC, April 12, 2024

5. Madhumita Murgia, Tim Bradshaw, and Richard Waters, "Chip Wars with China Risk 'Enormous Damage' to US Tech, Says Nvidia Chief," *The Financial Times*, May 23, 2023

6. "Fact Sheet: President Biden Signs Executive Order to Ensure Robust Reviews of Evolving National Security Risks by the Committee on Foreign Investment in the United States," Committee on Foreign Investment in the United States (CFIUS), The US Department of Treasury, September 15, 2022

7. "Fact Sheet: CHIPS and Science Act Will Lower Costs, Create Jobs, Strengthen Supply Chains, and Counter China," The White House, August 9, 2022

8. "Fact Sheet: President Biden Issues Executive Order Addressing United States Investments in Certain National Security Technologies and Products in Countries of Concern; Treasury Department Issues Advance Notice of Proposed Rulemaking to Enhance Transparency and Clarity and Solicit Comments on Scope of New Program," Office of Public Affairs, The US Department of the Treasury, August 9, 2023

9. "Semiconductors–China," Statista Market Insights, www.statista.com, assessed May 14, 2024

10. Indrabati Lahiri, "China's Semiconductor Production Challenges Could Be Boon for Europe," *Euro News*, March 15, 2024

11. Eva Dou and Ellen Nakashima, "Commerce Department Revokes More Export Licenses to China's Huawei," *The Washington Post*, May 7, 2024

12. "Huawei Is Quietly Dominating China's Semiconductor Supply Chain," *Merics*, April 9, 2024

13. Natalie Sherman, "TikTok Sues to Block US Law That Could Ban the App," May 7, 2024

14. "BIS imposes $300 Million Penalty Against Seagate Technology LLC Related to Shipment to Huawei," Bureau of Industry and Security (BIS), The US Department of Commerce, April 19, 2023

15. Daniel Araya, "Will China Dominate the Global Semiconductor Market?" Centre for International Governance Innovation, January 8, 2024

16. Diederik Baazil, Cagan Koc, Mackenzie Hawkins, and Michael Nienaber, "US Urges Allies to Squeeze China Further on Chip Technology," *Bloomberg*, March 6, 2024.

17. Alexandra Alper, David Shepardson, Karen Freifeld, Stephen Nellis, Chris Sanders, Fanny Potkin, David Kirton, and Eduardo Baptista, "US Revokes Intel, Qualcomm's Export Licenses to Sell to China's Huawei, Sources Say," *Reuters*, May 14, 2024

18. Dong Cao and Yuan Gao, "China Readies $27 Billion Chip Fund to Counter Growing US Curbs," *Bloomberg*, March 8, 2024

19. Gregory C. Allen, Emily Benson, and Margot Putnam, "Japan and the Netherlands Announce Plans for New Export Controls on Semiconductor Equipment," Center for Strategic and International Studies (CSIS), April 10, 2023

20. "Japan, Netherlands to join the US in Restricting Chip Equipment Exports to China," *Reuters*, January 27, 2023

21. Stephen Nellis, "Intel to Spend $20 billion on US Chip Plants as CEO Challenges Asia Dominance," *Reuters*, March 23, 2021

22. Gregory C. Allen, "Choking off China's Access to the Future of AI," Center for Strategic and International Studies, October 11, 2022

23. "US to Give Micron $6.1 Billion for American Chip Factories," *Techxplore*, April 25, 2024

24. "Commerce Acts to Deter Misuse of Biotechnology, Other US Technologies by the People's Republic of China to Support Surveillance and Military Modernization that Threaten National Security," The US Department of Commerce, December 16, 2021

25. "Biden-Harris Administration Announces Preliminary Terms with Intel to Support Investment in US Semiconductor Technology Leadership and Create Tens of Thousands of Jobs," Office of Public Affairs, The US Department of Commerce, March 20, 2024

26. "Intel and Biden Admin Announce up to $8.5 Billion in Direct Funding Under the CHIPS Act," www.Intel.com, March 20, 2024

27. "Micron Announces Over $150 Billion in Global Manufacturing and R&D Investments to Address 2030," www.Micron.com, October 20, 2021

28. "President Biden Announces up to $6.1 Billion Preliminary Agreement with Micron under the CHIPS and Science Act," *Fact Sheet*, White House, April 25, 2024

29. "GlobalFoundries and Biden-Harris Administration Announce CHIPS and Science Act Funding for Essential Chip Manufacturing," www.gf.com, February 19, 2024

30. "Biden-Harris Administration Announces Preliminary Terms with Samsung Electronics to Establish Leading-Edge Semiconductor Ecosystem in Central Texas," The US Department of Commerce, April 15, 2024

31. "Biden-Harris Administration Announces CHIPS Preliminary Terms with Microchip Technology to Strengthen Supply Chain Resilience for America's Automotive, Defense, and Aerospace Industries," The US Department of Commerce, January 2024.

32. Dylan Butts, "Nvidia Supplier SK Hynix Plans to Invest $3.87 Billion in US Chip Facility," CNBC, April 4, 2024

33. "Governor Holcomb Announces Generational Multi-Billion-Dollar Investment to Make Indiana Leader in Semiconductor Packaging," www.iedc.in.gov, April 3, 2024

34. "TSMC's Arizona Economic Impact," www.tsmc.com, assessed May 28, 2024

35. "Biden-Harris Administration and BAE Systems, Inc., Announce CHIPS Preliminary Terms to Support Critical US National Security Project in Nashua, New Hampshire," The US Department of Commerce, December 11, 2023

36. "Governor Abbott Announces Texas Instruments' Potential $30 Billion Investment in Sherman," www.texas.gov, November 17, 2021

37. "Biden-Harris Administration Announces Preliminary Terms with Polar Semiconductor to Establish an Independent American Foundry," The US Department of Commerce, May 13, 2024

38. "Polar Semiconductor Announces Plans to Expand Semiconductor Manufacturing Facility in Minnesota," www.polarsemi.com, May 13, 2024

39. "Biden-Harris Administration Announces Preliminary Terms with Absolics to Support Development of Glass Substrate Technology for Semiconductor Advanced Packaging," The US Department of Commerce, May 23, 2024

40. "Biden-Harris Administration Announces $420 Million Funding Opportunity to Promote Wireless Equipment Innovation," National Telecommunications and Information Administration, May 7, 2024

41. "BIS Imposes $300 Million Penalty Against Seagate Technology LLC Related to Shipments to Huawei," Bureau of Industry and Security, US Department of Commerce, April 19, 2023

42. C. Todd Lopez, "DOD Looks to Establish 'Mine-to-Magnet' Supply Chain for Rare Earth Materials," *DOD News*, The US Department of Defense, March 11, 2024

43. "US Government to Give $75 Million to South Korean Company for Georgia Computer Chip Part Factory," *US News and World Report*, May 23, 2024

44. "Biden-Harris Administration Announces Preliminary Terms with Texas Instruments to Expand U.S. Current-Generation and Mature-Node Chip Capacity," The US Department of Commerce, August 16, 2024

45. "Biden-Harris Administration Announces Preliminary Terms with HP to Support Development and Commercialization of Cutting-Edge Semiconductor Technologies," The US Department of Commerce, August 27, 2024

46. "Two Years Later: Funding from CHIPS and Science Act Creating Quality Jobs, Growing Local Economies, and Bringing Semiconductor Manufacturing Back to America," The US Department of Commerce, August 9, 2024

47. "US Department of Commerce Announces Preliminary Terms with SK Hynix to Advance U.S. AI Supply Chain Security," The US Department of Commerce, August 6, 2024

48. "Department of Commerce Announces CHIPS Incentives Award with Hemlock Semiconductor to Help Secure U.S. Production Capacity of Semiconductor-Grade Polysilicon," The US Department of Commerce, January 7, 2025

Chapter 10 References

1. James Kaufman, "US Foods Imports", USDA, April 10, 2024

2. "US-China Trade Facts," United States Trade Representative, 2019

3. "China-EU – International Trade in Goods Statistics," Eurostat (Statistical Office of the European Union), March 2021

4. "China: Evolving Demand in the World's Largest Agricultural Import Market," USDA Foreign Agricultural Service, September 2020

5. Lucia Mutikani, "US Trade Deficit Narrows in 2019 for First Time in Six Years," *Reuters*, February 6, 2020

6. Tom Polansek, "Tyson Foods Cleared to Ship Poultry to China from all US Plants," *Reuters,* December 16, 2019

7. Ryan McCarthy, "Hormel Stops Ractopamine in Pork," www.meatpoultry.com, accessed February 20, 2020

8. "US International Trade in Goods and Services," The US Bureau of Economic Analysis, December and Annual 2023, February 7, 2024

9. "US-China Trade Facts," United States Trade Representative, 2022

10. "US Trade with China," Office of Technology Evaluation, US Department of Commerce, 2021

11. "US International Trade in Goods and Services, December and Annual 2023," US Bureau of Economic Analysis (BEA), February 7, 2024

12. "The People's Republic of China," United States Trade Representative, accessed May 14, 2024

13. "US-China Trade Relations," Congressional Research Service, March 28, 2024

14. "China-EU - International Trade in Goods Statistics," Eurostat, February 2024

Chapter 11 References

1. Artavazd Hakobyan and Paavo Eliste, "Food Safety in China: Addressing Common Problems Requires Unusual Approaches," World Bank, March 30, 2015

2. Hon-Ming Lam, Justin Remais, Ming-Chiu Fung, Liqing Xu, and Samuel Sai-Ming Sun, "Food Supply and Food Safety Issues in China," Health and Human Services Public Access, June 8, 2013

3 "Organic Food Products in China," International Trade Centre, 2011

4. Fred Gale and Jean C. Buzby, "Imports from China and Food Safety Issues," United States Department of Agriculture, July 2009

5. Zhe Liu, Anthony N. Mutukumira, and Hongjun Chen, "Food Safety Governance in China: From Supervision to Co-regulation," *Food Science & Nutrition*, November 20, 2019

6. "The Most Neglected Threat to Public Health in China Is Toxic Soil," *Economist*, June 8, 2017

7. Didi Kirsten Tatlow, "Cadmium Rice, Now Lead and Arsenic Rice," *The New York Times*, April 25, 2014

8. "Report: One-Fifth of China's Soil Contaminated," BBC News, April 18, 2014

9. Yonglong Lu, Shuai Song, Ruoshi Wang, Zhaoyang Liu, Jing Meng, Andrew J. Sweetman, Alan Jenkins, Robert C. Ferrier, Hong Li, Wei Luo, and Tieyu Wang, "Impacts of Soil and Water Pollution on Food Safety and Health Risks in China," *Environment International*, April 2015

10. Tiankui Li, Yi Liu, Sijie Lin, Yangze Liu, and Yunfeng Xie, "Soil Pollution Management in China: A Brief Introduction," *Sustainability*, January 22, 2019

11. "Addressing China's Water Scarcity," World Bank, 2009

12. Deng Tingting, "In China, the Water You Drink Is as Dangerous as the Air You Breathe," *The Guardian*, June 2, 2017

13. Dianqin Sun, Maomao Cao, He Li, Siyi He, and Wanqing Chen, "Cancer Burden and Trends in China: A Review and Comparison with Japan and South Korea," *Chinese Journal of Cancer Research*, Mar 10, 2020

14. Edward Wong, 'Pollution Rising, Chinese Fear for Soil and Food," *The New York Times*, December 30, 2013

15. "PRC, Food Processing Ingredients. Industry Matures as It Caters to Demand for Natural, Healthier, and More Convenient Processed Foods," USDA Foreign Agriculture Service, April 4, 2019

16. "China's African Swine Flu Outbreak: Implications for US Food Safety and Trade," US-China Economic and Security Review Commission, May 15, 2019

17. Edward Wong, "China Exports Pollution to the US, Study Finds," *The New York Times*, January 20, 2014

18. Meiyun Lin, Larry W. Horowitz, Richard Payton, Arlene M. Fiore, and Gail Tonnesen, "US Surface Ozone Trends and Extremes from 1980 to 2014: Quantifying the Roles of Rising Asian Emissions, Domestic Controls, Wildfires, and Climate," *Atmospheric Chemistry Physics*, March 2017

Chapter 12 References

1. "China's Water Crisis Part II – Water Facts at a Glance," Chinawaterrisk.org, March 2010

2. Edward Wong, "Pollution Rising, Chinese Fear for Soil and Food," *The New York Times*, December 30, 2013

3. "The Most Neglected Threat to Public Health in China Is Toxic Soil," *The Economist*, June 8, 2017

4. Edward Wong, "China Exports Pollution to the US, Study Finds," *The New York Times*, January 20, 2014

5. Joe Zhang and Xiaoxia Lin, "Cleaning up Toxic Soils in China: A Trillion-Dollar Question," International Institute for Sustainable Development, September 10, 2018

6. "Addressing China's Water Scarcity," World Bank, 2009

7. "Latest Air Pollution Data Ranks World's Cities Worst to Best," Greenpeace, 2019

8. David Stanway, "China Soil Pollution Efforts Stymied by Local Governments: Greenpeace," *Reuters*, April 16, 2019

9. Chris Buckley, "Rice Tainted with Cadmium Is Discovered in Southern China," *The New York Times*, May 21, 2013

10. Tiankui Li, Yi Liu, Sijie Lin, Yangze Liu, and Yunfeng Xie, "Soil Pollution Management in China: A Brief Introduction," *Sustainability*, January 22, 2019

11. Haidong Kan, Bingheng Chen, and Chuanjie Hong, "Health Impact of Outdoor Air Pollution in China: Current Knowledge and Future Research Needs," *Environmental Health Perspectives*, May 2009

12. Meiyun Lin, Larry W. Horowitz, Richard Payton, Arlene M. Fiore, and Gail Tonnesen, "US Surface Ozone Trends and Extremes from 1980 to 2014: Quantifying the Roles of Rising Asian Emissions, Domestic Controls, Wildfires, and Climate," *Atmospheric Chemistry Physics*, March 2017

13. Nathan Vanderklippe, "Wealthy Chinese Are Avoiding Food Scares with Their Own Organic Farms to Avoid Food Tainted by Heavy Metals or Fouled with Pesticide," *The Globe and Mail*, May 16, 2018

14. Chris Buckley, "China Says Water Supplies Exploited by 2030," *Reuters*, December 14, 2007

15. Ana Swanson, "An Incredible Image Shows How Powerful Countries Are Buying up Much of the World's Land," *The Washington Post*, May 21, 2015

16. Shuping Niu, Emma O'Brien, Lulu Yilun Chen, Borges Nhamire, and Christina Larson, "Farming the World: China's Epic Race to Avoid a Food Crisis," *Bloomberg*, May 22, 2017

17. "A Decade of Dangerous Food Imports from China," *Food & Water Watch*, June 2011

18. Caitlin Dewey, "The Dark Side of Trump's Much-hyped China Trade Deal: It Could Make You Sick," *The Washington Post*, July 7, 2017

19. David Barboza, "In China, Farming Fish in Toxic Waters," *The New York Times*, December 15, 2007

Chapter 13 References

1. "China Says Firms Exported Tainted Protein to US," *Reuters*, May 8, 2007

2. Jennifer Pifer, "Avoiding Chinese Food Products Nearly Impossible," CNN, July 26, 2007

3. "China Imports in the Grocery Store: A Cause for Concern," Fox News Network, May 13, 2011

4. Fred Gale and Jean C. Buzby, "Imports from China and Food Safety Issues," USDA, July 2009

5. "A Decade of Dangerous Food Imports from China," *Food & Water Watch*, June 2011

6. "Shoppers Offered Few Safeguards Against Wild West Imports," CNN, July 26, 2007

7. Rick Weiss, "Tainted Chinese Imports Common," *The Washington Post*, May 20, 2007

8. David Stanway, "China Uncovers 500,000 Food Safety Violations in Nine Months," *Reuters*, December 23, 2016

9. "US Food and Agricultural Imports: Safeguards and Selected Issues," USDA, July 1, 2020

10. Zhe Liu, Anthony N. Mutukumira, and Hongjun Chen, "Food Safety Governance in China: From Supervision to Coregulation," *Food Science & Nutrition*, November 20, 2019

11. Katie Hunt, "Why Chinese Food Safety Is So Bad," CNN, January 16, 2015

12. "Potentially Unsafe Food Entering US from China," *Food & Water Watch*, June 8, 2011

13. "China's Efforts to Address Ongoing Food Safety Concerns," Congressional Research Service, September 9, 2016

14. Yuan Yuan, Rui Gao, Qiang Liang, Li Song, Jun Huang, Nan Lang, and Jing Zhou, "Outbreak Reports: A Foodborne Bongkrekic Acid Poisoning Incident — Heilongjiang Province," *Chinese Center for Disease Control and Prevention (CCDC) Weekly* 2020, accessed January 27, 2021

15. "China Probes another Report of Fake Cooking Oil," *Reuters*, January 5, 2012

16. "China's Counterfeit Medicine Trade Booming," *Canadian Medical Association Journal*, October 5, 2009

17. "Pharmacist Convicted of Purchasing Chinese Counterfeit Drugs," US Department of Justice, May 25, 2006

18. "Recycled Cooking Oil Found to Be Latest Hazard in China," *The New York Times*, March 31, 2010

19. "E. China Province Bans Sales of Contaminated Fish," *China Daily*, November 20, 2006

20. Nicholas Zamiska and David Kesmodel, "Growing Concern: Tainted Ginger's Long Trip from China to US Stores; Supply Chains Make Finding Source Tough; Lots of Small Farms," *The Wall Street Journal*, November 19, 2007

21. "Man Tried over China-Japan Tainted Dumplings," BBC News, July 30, 2013

22. David Barboza, "Tainted Eggs from China Discovered in Hong Kong," *The New York Times*, October 26, 2008

23. "Organic Food Products in China," International Trade Centre, 2011

24. Guo Nei, "Death Toll over Fake Drug Rises to 9 in China," *China Daily*, May 22, 2006

25. Chen Zeng-long, Dong Feng-Shou, Xu Jun, Liu Xin-gang, and Zheng Yong-Quan, "Management of Pesticide Residues in China," *Journal of Integrative Agriculture*, 2015

26. David J. Ettinger, Jenny Xin, and Li Eric Gu, "Breaking News: China Publishes Long-Awaited Food Safety Law Implementation Regulation," *National Law Review*, January 4, 2021

27. Ramy Inocencio and Feng Ke, "Maggots, Bacteria Allegedly Plagued China's Number One Meat Brand," CNN, May 31, 2013

28. Zhang Yan and Cao Yin, "32 Held in Gutter Oil Crackdown," *China Daily*, September 14, 2011

29. Elizabeth Brotherton-Bunch, "The US Imports Much Food from China — and You Might Be Surprised What is on the List," www.AmericanManufacturing.org, September 23, 2014

30. Didi Kirsten Tatlow, "Cadmium Rice, now Lead and Arsenic Rice," *The New York Times*, April 25, 2014

31. Ab Latif Wani, Anjum Ara, and Jawed Ahmad Usmani, "Lead Toxicity: A Review," *Interdisciplinary Toxicology*, June 2015

32. "Cancer Progress Report," National Cancer Institute, March 2020

33. Andrew Martin, "F.D.A. Curbs Sale of 5 Seafoods Farmed in China," *The New York Times*, June 29, 2007

34. "Chinese Frozen Food Firm Recalls Products Suspected of African Swine Fever Contamination," *Reuters*, February 17, 2019

35. "Tainted Milk Sickens 6,000 Babies in China," *Economic Times*, September 17, 2008,

36. "Pet Treat and Processed Chicken from China Concerned for American Consumers and Pets," US Congressional-Executive Commission on China, 113th Congress Session, June 17, 2014

37. Iris Jiang, "Toxic Shock: China Restaurant Filmed Spraying Cancer-Causing Paint on BBQ Meat Skewers," *South China Morning Post*, June 15, 2024

38. Alice Yan, "China Food Scandal: Meat Producer Exposed Using Food off the Floor and Making Staff Wear Filthy Uniforms in Undercover Report," *China Morning Post*, March 16, 2022

39. Simone McCarthy and Joyce Jiang, "China Food Safety Scandal: Cooking Oil Carried in Same Trucks as Fuel, Report Claims," CNN, July 10, 2024

Chapter 14 References

1. "China's Efforts to Address Ongoing Food Safety Concerns," Congressional Research Service, September 9, 2016

2. Chen Zeng-long, Dong Feng-Shou, Xu Jun, Liu Xin-Qang, and Zheng Yong-Quan, "Management of Pesticide Residues in China," *Journal of Integrative Agriculture*, 2015

3. Jane Parry, "Chinese Court Sentences Former Drug Regulatory Chief to Death," *British Medical Journal*, June 9, 2007

4. Artavazd Hakobyan and Paavo Eliste, "Food Safety in China: Addressing Common Problems Requires Unusual Approaches," World Bank, March 30, 2015

5. Fred Gale and Jean C. Buzby, "Imports from China and Food Safety Issues," USDA, July 2009

6. Chen Zeng-Long, Dong Feng-Shou, Xu Jun, Liu Xin-Gang, and Zheng Yong-Quan, "Management of Pesticide Residues in China," *Journal of Integrative Agriculture*, 2015

7. "China's Counterfeit Medicine Trade Booming," Canadian *Medical Association Journal*, October 5, 2009

8. Jonathan Watts, "China Sentences Former Food and Drugs Chief to Death," *The Guardian*, May 29, 2007

9. "National Food Safety Standard Maximum Residue Limits for Pesticides in Foods," US Department of Agriculture, Foreign Agricultural Service, November 18, 2019

10. Zhe Liu, Anthony N. Mutukumira, and Hongjun Chen, "Food Safety Governance in China: From Supervision to Coregulation," *Food Science & Nutrition*, November 20, 2019

11. "China's Food Laws: Looking Back on 2019, the Year of the Pig," www.lexology.com, March 25, 2020

12. "China Uncovers 500,000 Food Safety Violations in Nine Months," *Reuters*, December 23, 2016

13. "A Decade of Dangerous Food Imports from China," *Food & Water Watch*," June 2011

14. Hon-Ming Lam, Justin Remais, Ming-Chiu Fung, Liqing Xu, and Samuel Sai-Ming Sun, "Food Supply and Food Safety Issues in China," Health and Human Services Public Access, June 8, 2013

15. Katie Hunt, "Why Chinese Food Safety Is So Bad," CNN, January 16, 2015

16. David J. Ettinger, Jenny Xin, and Li Eric Gu, "Breaking News: China Publishes Long-Awaited Food Safety Law Implementation Regulation," *National Law Review*, January 28, 2021

17. Will Coggin, "Why We Should Get a Lot Less Food from China," *The New York Post*, June 10, 2020

18. "China: New and Amended National Food Safety Standards," The US Department of Agriculture, August 12, 2022

Chapter 15 References

1. China's Efforts to Address Ongoing Food Safety Concerns," Congressional Research Service, September 9, 2016

2. The Food Safety Modernization Act (FSMA), The US Food and Drug Administration, accessed January 19, 2021

3. Andrew Martin, "F.D.A. Curbs Sale of Five Seafood Farmed in China," *The New York Times*, June 29, 2007

4. "US Food and Agricultural Imports: Safeguards and Selected Issues," Congressional Research Service, July 1, 2020

5. "The Food and Drug Administration (FDA) Budget: Fact Sheet," Congressional Research Service, April 2, 2020

6. Caitlin Dewey, "The Dark Side of Trump's Much-hyped China Trade Deal: It Could Make You Sick," *The Washington Post*, July 7, 2017

7. Philip DeVencentis, "1 Million Pounds of Smuggled Pork from China Seized at NJ Port," *North Jersey*, March 16, 2019

8. Maribel Alonso, "FSIS Issues Public Health Alert for Ineligible Imported Raw Frozen New Orleans – Roasted Chicken Wings from the Peoples Republic of China," USDA's Food Safety and Inspection Service, December 19, 2020

9. "48.4 Tons of Ineligible Beef from China Caught and Recalled," *Food Safety News*, February 22, 2021

10. "The Food and Drug Administration (FDA) Budget: Fact Sheet," Congressional Research Service, June 16, 2021

Chapter 16 References

1. Nathan Vanderklippe, "Wealthy Chinese Are Avoiding Food Scares with Their Organic Farms," *Globe and Mail*, August 1, 2016

2. "Organic Food Products in China," International Trade Center, 2011

3. Mischa Popoff and Jay Lehr, "Should the Boost in Funding for Organic Farming Survive in the New Administration?" *Food Safety News*, April 21, 2017

4. "I-Team Investigate: Pesticides-Laced Organic Food Follow up," ABC News, August 5, 2008

5. "Whole Foods 365 Organic: Made-in-China, an ABC Exposé," ABC News, February 20, 2010

6. Roger Blobaum "Can Consumers Trust the USDA Organic Label on Food Products from China?" *Organic Broadcaster*, November 1, 2007

7. Melissa Allison, "Questions Remain about Organic Foods Grown in China," *Seattle Times,* January 10, 2012

8. "2010-2011 Pilot Study, Pesticide Residue Testing of Organic Produce," United States Department of Agriculture, November 2012

9. Miles McEvoy, "Organic 101: What the USDA Organic Label Means," United States Department of Agriculture, March 13, 2019

10. "China Publishes New Organic Standard and Certification Rules," United States Department of Agriculture, December 8, 2019

11. Laura Reiley, "The Organic Food Industry Is Booming, and That May Be Bad for Consumers," *The Washington Post*, March 14, 2019

12. Jon Entine, "Organic Food – What Is an Organic Label Really Worth?" *Reuters*, July 12, 2013

13. "EU Imports of Organic Agri-food Products," European Commission, June 2020

14. Peter Whoriskey, "The Labels Said Organic. But These Massive Imports of Corn and Soybeans Were not," *The Washington Post*, May 12, 2017

15. M. Jason Kuo, "Why it is So Hard to Know Whether Organic Food Is Really Organic," *The Washington Post*, May 22, 2017

16. "Importing Organic Products into the United States," The United States Department of Agriculture, accessed March 25, 2021

17. Dan Flynn, "Inspector General Again Finds Weaknesses in Organic Imports," *Food Safety News*, September 20, 2017

18. William Neuman and David Barboza, "US Drops Inspector of Food in China," *The New York Times*, June 13, 2010

19. Mike Hendricks, "Missouri Charmer Led Double Life, Masterminded One of the Biggest Frauds in Farm History," *Kansas City Star*, January 17, 2020

20. "Organic Import Oversight: Collaboration Opportunities and Technology Needs Assessment," The United States Department of Agriculture, July 2018

21. "Field of Schemes Fraud Results in Over a Decade in Federal Prison for Leader of Largest Organic Fraud Case in US History," Department of Justice, US Attorney's Office, Northern District of Iowa, August 19, 2019

22. Monique Marez, "US Organic Worldwide: New Report Analyzes Organic Imports and Exports through 2016," Organic Trade Association, August 17, 2017

23. "Country of Origin Labeling Frequently Asked Questions," www.fda.gov, accessed March 29, 2021

24. "International Trade Partners", USDA, accessed July 12, 2024

25. "2024 Organic Industry Survey," Organic Trade Association, 2024

Chapter 17 References

1. Matt Snyder and Bart Carfagno, "Chinese Product Safety: A Persistent Challenge to US Regulators and Importers," US-China Economic and Security Review Commission, March 23, 2017

2. "China Says Firms Exported Tainted Protein to US," *Reuters*, May 8, 2007

3. Terri Pous, "FDA: Nearly 1,000 Pets Sickened by China-Made Dog Treats," *Time*, May 23, 2012

4. Louise Story, "Lead Paint Prompts Mattel to Recall 967,000 Toys," *The New York Times*, August 2, 2007

5. "Mattel Announces Third Toy Recall," CNN, September 5, 2007

6. Parija B. Kavilanz, "China to Eliminate Lead Paint in Toy Exports," CNN, September 11, 2007

7. Andrea Chang, "Official: Mattel Fined $2.3 Million for Toy Hazard," *The Los Angeles Times*, June 6, 2009

8. Elizabeth Weise, "Report Backs Chinese Drywall Health Complaints," *USA Today*, May 2, 2014

9. Anderson Cooper, "60 Minutes Found that Lumber Liquidators' Chinese-Made Laminate Flooring Contains Amounts of Toxic Formaldehyde that May Not Meet Health and Safety Standards," CBS News, March 1, 2015

10. "Feds: Harmful Formaldehyde Levels in Lumber Liquidators Flooring," CBS News, February 10, 2016

11. Nicholas Zamiska and David Kesmodel, "Growing Concern: Tainted Ginger's Long Trip from China to US Stores; Supply Chains

Make Finding Source Tough; Lots of Small Farms," *The Wall Street Journal*, November 19, 2007

13. "The People's Republic of China," United States Trade Representative, accessed January 27, 2021

12. The Heparin Disaster: Chinese Counterfeits and American Failures," US Government Printing Office, House Hearing, 110 Congress, April 29, 2008

14. "Fiscal Year 2021 Performance Budget Request to Congress," Consumer Product Safety Commission (CPSC), February 10, 2020

15. "Center for Environmental Health vs. Fayeon Distributors Inc. et al.," Superior Court of the State of California for the County of San Francisco Unlimited Jurisdiction, Case number CGC-12-526396, September 2, 2014

16. Bruce Japsen, "$625,000 Judgement against Baxter in 2007 Blood-Thinner Death Case," *Chicago Tribune*, June 9, 2011

17. "Foreign Sovereign Immunity and COVID-19 Lawsuits against China," Congressional Research Service, May 15, 2020

18. John B. Bellinger III, "Opinion: Suing China Over the Coronavirus Won't Help. Here is What Can Work," *The Washington Post*, April 23, 2020

19. James Comer, "The Committee on Oversight and Accountability Is Investigating the Chinese Communist Party's Increasing Influence on Consumer Products and the Work That the U.S. Committee on Oversight and Accountability," US Congress, May 6, 2024

Chapter 18 References

1. Kenneth Rapoza, "No End in Sight to China's Food Safety Woes," *Forbes*, February 5, 2014

2. Nancy Huehnergarth and Bettina Siegel, "Chicken from China? Your Seafood Is Already Being Processed There," *Food Safety News*, March 4, 2014

3. Peter Parks, "KFC Cuts More Than 1,000 Suppliers after China Chicken Scare," *Business Insider*, February 26, 2013

4. Ramy Inocencio and Feng Ke, "Maggots, Bacteria Allegedly Plagued China's Number One Meat Brand," CNN, May 31, 2013

5. Edward Wong. 'Pollution Rising, Chinese Fear for Soil and Food," *The New York Times*, December 30, 2013

6. Tom Polansek, "At Smithfield Foods' Slaughterhouse, China Brings Home US Bacon," *Reuters*, November 5, 2019

7. "Eligibility of the People's Republic of China (PRC) to Export to United States Poultry Products from Birds Slaughtered in China," United States Department of Agriculture Food Safety and Inspection Service, *Federal Register*, November 8, 2019

8. Caitlin Dewey, "The Dark Side of Trump's Much-hyped China Trade Deal: It Could Literally Make You Sick," *The Washington Post*, July 7, 2017

9. Stephanie Strom, "Chinese Chicken Processors Are Cleared to Ship to US," *The New York Times*, August 30, 2013

10. "Avian Influenza Weekly Update Number 791," World Health Organization, May 7, 2021

11. Rick Weiss "Tainted Chinese Imports Common," *The Washington Post*, May 20, 2007

12. Philip DeVencentis, "1 Million Pounds of Smuggled Pork from China Seized at NJ Port," *North Jersey*, March 16, 2019

13. "US Food and Agricultural Imports: Safeguards and Selected Issues," Congressional Research Service, July 1, 2020

14. "48.4 Tons of Ineligible Beef from China Caught and Recalled," *Food Safety News,* February 22, 2021

15. Nicola Davison, "Rivers of Blood: The Dead Pigs Rotting in China's Water Supply," *The Guardian*, March 29, 2013

16. "FSIS Issues Public Health Alert for Ineligible Imported Raw Frozen New Orleans–Roasted Chicken Wings from the People's Republic of China," Congressional and Public Affairs, December 19, 2020

17. "FSIS Issues Public Health Alert for Ineligible Imported Cooked Duck Blood Curds from China," Congressional and Public Affairs, September 4, 2020

18. Wenonah Hauter, "Yet again, Chinese Chicken Proves Unfit, but USDA Remains Committed to Its Importation," *Food & Water Watch*, December 13, 2013

19. "Final Report of an Audit Conducted in the People's Republic China, May 8 to May 28, 2015. Evaluating the Food Safety Systems Governing Slaughtered Poultry for Export to the United States of America," The United States Department of Agriculture's Food Safety and Inspection Service, February 17, 2016

20. Chris Buckley, "Rat Meat Sold as Lamb Highlights Fear in China," *The New York Times*, May 3, 2013

21. "Chinese Frozen Food Firm Recalls Products Suspected of African Swine Fever Contamination," *Reuters*, February 19, 2019

22. "Chicken Imports from China," Congressional Research Service, March 12, 2015

23. "Who is Behind the Chinese Takeover of World's Biggest Pork Producer?" PBS News, September 12, 2014

24. "China's African Swine Flu Outbreak: Implications for US Food Safety and Trade," US-China Economic and Security Review Commission, May 15, 2019

25. Mike Ives, "Scientists Say New Strain of Swine Flu Virus Is Spreading to Humans in China," *The New York Times*, July 1, 2020

Chapter 19 References

1. "Record High Seafood Imports in 2018," USDA Foreign Agriculture Service, March 7, 2019

2. Nancy Huehnergarth and Bettina Siegel, "Chicken from China? Your Seafood Is Already Being Processed There," *Food Safety News*, March 4, 2014

3. "US Food and Agricultural Imports: Safeguards and Selected Issues," Congressional Research Service, July 1, 2020

4. "China: Continued Seafood Import Growth in 2019," United States Department of Agriculture Foreign Agricultural Service, May 13, 2020

5. Don Lee and Tiffany Hsu, "Now, China's Fish Are Suspect," *Los Angeles Times*, Dec 24, 2008

6. "The Use and Abuse of Polyphosphates," *Intrafish*, July 11, 2012

7. Alan Farnham, "Seafood from Asia Raised on Pig Waste, Says News Report," ABC News, October 17, 2012

8. Andrew Martin, "FDA Curbs Sale of 5 Seafoods Farmed in China," *New York Times*, June 29, 2007

9. "How FDA Regulates Seafood: FDA Detains Imports of Farm-Raised Chinese Seafood," United States Food and Drug Administration, June 28, 2007

10. David Barboza, "In China, Farming Fish in Toxic Waters," *The New York Times*, December 15, 2007

11. Alicia Villegas, "Atlantic Cod to Be Farmed for First Time in China," *Undercurrent News*, November 4, 2013

12. "Fisheries of the United States," United States Department of Commerce, NOAA, 2015

13. "Fisheries of the United States," United States Department of Commerce, NOAA, 2018

14. "A Tale of a Fish from Two Countries," USDA, February 21, 2017

15. Jamie Grey and Lee Zurik, "Untested Water: 99.9 Percent of Foreign Fish Goes without Testing for Unsafe Drugs-Majority of US Seafood Is Imported, the Government Fails to Keep up with Food Safety Laws," Investigate TV, February 11, 2019

16. "President Signs New Executive Order Promoting American Seafood Competitiveness and Economic Growth," NOAA Fisheries, May 07, 2020

17. "USA Fisheries Statistics: Production, Consumption and Trade," Food and Agriculture Organization of the United Nations, accessed March 12, 2021

18. Xiaolin Hou, Yonggang Li, Guojuan Wu, Lei Wang, Miao Hong, and Yongnin Wu, "Determination of Para Red, Sudan Dyes, Canthaxanthin, and Astaxanthin in Animal Feeds Using UPLC," *Journal of Chromatographic Science*, Volume 48, January 2010

19. "2018 Meeting the Sustainable Development Goals," Food and Agriculture Organization of the United Nations, 2018

20. Fred Gale and Jean C. Buzby, "Imports from China and Food Safety Issues," United States Department of Agriculture, July 2009

21. David Love, "Testing of Seafood Imported into the US Is Inadequate," Johns Hopkins Bloomberg School of Public Health, November 9, 2011

22. "The State of World Fisheries and Aquaculture," Food and Agriculture Organization of the United Nations (FAO), 2022

23. "US Aquaculture," National Oceanic and Atmospheric Administration, assessed July 16, 2024

Chapter 20 References

1. "Honey Bees," The United States Department of Agriculture, National Agricultural Statistics Service, September 2019

2. "China's Beekeepers Feel the Sting of COVID-19," *The Economist*, April 11, 2020

3. Andrew Schneider, "Asian Honey, Banned in Europe, Is Flooding US Grocery Shelves," *Food Safety News*, August 15, 2011

4. Andrew Schneider, "Tests Show Most Store Honey Is Not Honey," *Food Safety News*, November 7, 2011

5. "Center for Food Safety and Applied Nutrition 2003," Food and Drug Administration, accessed June 10, 2020

6. Norberto L. García, "The Current Situation on the International Honey Market," *Bee World Journal*, July 3, 2018

7. Alan Milner, "Honey in the Bank: China Exports Bogus Honey to the US," *Food Safety News*, February 28, 2014

8. "The Scourge of Honey Fraud, America's Taste for Honey Is Nectar for Con Men," *The Economist*, August 30, 2018

9. "Scientific Support to the Implementation of a Coordinated Control Plan to Establish the Prevalence of Fraudulent Practices in the Marketing of Honey. Results of Honey Authenticity Testing by Liquid Chromatography-Isotope Ratio Mass Spectrometry," *JRC Technical Report*, European Union, 2016

10. I. Root, "2018 Annual Honey Report," *Bee Culture*, July 2, 2018

11. Oktay Yildiz, Zehra Can, Ozlem Saral, Esin Yulug, Ferhat Oztürk, Rezzan Aliyazıcıoglu, Sinan Canpolat, and Sevgi Kolayli, "Hepatoprotective Potential of Chestnut Bee Pollen on Carbon Tetrachloride-Induced Hepatic Damages in Rats," *Evidence-Based Complementary and Alternative Medicine*, 2013

12. "National Honey Report, Honey Market for the Month of July 2020," Volume XL, US Department of Agriculture, August 29, 2020

13. "Food Detectives on a Tough Case, Savanah, Georgia," *The New York Times*, January 19, 2015

14. "Three Arrested in Jacksonville Honey Dumping Scheme," *Ice Newsroom*, Department of Homeland Security, November 29, 2011

15. "California Honey Broker Sentenced in Illinois to Three Years in Prison for Evading Nearly $40 Million in Import Duties on Chinese-Origin Honey," *Ice Newsroom*, Department of Homeland Security, September 30, 2013

16. "Chinese Honey Importer Arrested for Allegedly Evading US Import Duties," *Ice Newsroom*, Department of Homeland Security, February 17, 2011

17. "Chinese Honey Importer Sentenced to 2 Years for Evading Import Duties," *Ice Newsroom*, Department of Homeland Security, June 26, 2012

18. "Feds Announce Charges in Chinese Honey Import Case," Fox News, February 20, 2013, updated December 20, 2015

19. Paola Tamma, "Honeygate: How Europe Is Being Flooded with Fake Honey," *Euractive*, January 23, 2020

21. "Texas Honey Broker Sentenced in Illinois to Three Years in Prison for Evading Nearly $38 Million in Tariffs on Chinese-Origin Honey," *Ice Newsroom*, Department of Homeland Security, November 14, 2013

22. "HSI Chicago Seizes Nearly 60 Tons of Honey Illegally Imported from China," *Ice Newsroom*, Department of Homeland Security, May 5, 2016

23. "Proper Labeling of Honey and Honey Products: Guidance for Industry," United States Food and Drug Administration, February 2018

24. "ICE and CBP Announce Charges Linked to Major Commercial Fraud Enterprise," *Ice Newsroom*, Department of Homeland Security, February 20, 2013

25. "CBP in Houston Seize Illegally Imported Honey Valued at $2.45 million," *Ice Newsroom*, Department of Homeland Security, January 27, 2015

26. "Honest Honey Changes Name to True Source Honey to Clarify Goal of Protecting US Honey Consumers and Customers," PR Wires, July 15, 2010

27. Ananias Pascoal, Sandra Rodrigues, Alfredo Teixeira, Xesus Feás, and Leticia M Estevinho, "Biological Activities of Commercial Bee Pollens: Antimicrobial, Antimutagenic, Antioxidant, and Anti-Inflammatory," *Food and Chemistry Toxicology Journal*, January 2014

28. Esra Küpeli Akkol, Didem Deliorman Orhan, Ilhan Gürbüz, and Erdem Yesilada, "In Vivo Activity Assessment of a Honey-Bee Pollen Mix Formulation," *Pharmaceutical Biology*, January 20, 2010

29. Viveat Susan Pinto, "Leading Honey Brands Fail Adulteration Test by Foreign Lab, Says CSE," *Business Standard*, December 3, 2020

30. Matt Snyder and Bart Carfagno, "Chinese Product Safety: A Persistent Challenge to US Regulators and Importers," US-China Economic and Security Review Commission, March 23, 2017

31. Katy Stech, "Honey Supplier Groeb Farms Files for Chapter 11," *The Wall Street Journal*, October 2, 2013

32. Vidalina Abadam, "Visualization: Meeting Honey Demand in the United States," The United States Department of Agriculture, June 20, 2024

33. "U.S. Honey Imports in Metric Tons, by Country of Source, Calendar Year, Since 1989," The United States Department of Agriculture, June 20, 2024

34. Robert Perez, "Strategy for Increasing Targeted Testing of Honey Imports," US Customs and Border Protection, Homeland Security, September 25, 2020

Chapter 21 References

1. Gerry Schwalfenberg, Stephen J. Genuis, and Ilia Rodushkin, "The Benefits and Risks of Consuming Brewed Tea: Beware of Toxic Element Contamination," *Journal of Toxicology*, October 2013

2. Justyna Brzezicha-Cirocka, Małgorzata Grembecka, and Piotr Zefer, "Monitoring of Essential and Heavy Metals in Green Tea from Different Geographical Origins," *Environmental Monitor & Assessment Journal*, February 22, 2016

3. Declan T. Waugh, William Potter, Hardy Limeback, and Michael Godfrey, "Risk Assessment of Fluoride Intake from Tea in the Republic of Ireland and Its Implications for Public Health and Water Fluoridation," *International Journal of Environmental Research & Public Health*, March 2016

4. Daniel Workman, "Tea Imports by Country," www.worldstopexports.com, accessed July 19, 2024

Chapter 22 References

1. Rick Weiss, "Tainted Chinese Imports Common," *The Washington Post*, May 20, 2007

2. Don Lee, "China's Additives on Menu in the US," *Los Angeles Times*, May 18, 2007

3. Kane Wu, "China's Harbin Pharma to Buy Stake in US Health Retailer GNC," *Reuters*, February 13, 2018

4. Vinicy Chan, Cathy Chan, and Ed Hammond, "GNC's Chinese Backer to Consider Buyout of Vitamin Retailer," *Bloomberg*, October 22, 2019

5. Betsy McCaughey "The Hidden Perils of Drugs Imported from China," *Opinion*, September 3, 2019

6. "Grassley Urges HHS, FDA to Implement Unannounced Inspections of Foreign Drug Manufacturing Facilities," The United States Senate Committee on Finance, August 07, 2019

7. China's Counterfeit Medicine Trade Booming," *Canadian Medical Association Journal*, October 5, 2009

8. Sam Piranty, "Coronavirus Fuels a Surge in Fake Medicines," BBC News, April 9, 2020

9. Matt Volz, "Canadian Pharmacy Fined $34 Million for Illegal Imports," *Seattle Times*, April 13, 2018

10. Chuin-Wei Yap, "Pandemic Lays Bare US Reliance on China for Drugs," *The Wall Street Journal*, August 5, 2020

11. "2019 Report to Congress of the US-China Economic and Security Review Commission: Section 3, Growing US Reliance on China's Biotech and Pharmaceutical Products," US Congress, 2019

12. Ryan W. Miller, "More Blood Pressure Medicines Recalled over Possible Cancer-Causing Impurity," *USA Today*, September 23, 2019

13. Dave Sebastian, "FDA Asks Five Companies to Recall Diabetes Drug Metformin," *The Walls Street Journal*, May 29, 2020

14. Senator Tom Cotton and Congressman Mike Gallagher, "China Stole US Capacity to Make Drugs - We Must Take It Back," 116th Congress (2019–2021), March 25, 2020

15. Ken Dilanian and Brenda Breslauer, "US Officials Worried about Chinese Control of American Drug Supply," NBC News, September 12, 2019

16. Mark Abdoo, "Exploring the Growing US Reliance on China Biotech and Pharmaceutical Products," US-China Economic and Security Review Commission, July 31, 2019

17. Denise Roland and Jared S. Hopkins, "FDA Cites Shortage of One Drug, Exposing Supply-Line Worry," *The Walls Street Journal*, February 28, 2020

18. David Lazarus, "China Makes Many Drug Ingredients, Sparking Coronavirus Worries," *Los Angeles Times*, February 28, 2020

19. "Pharmacist Convicted of Purchasing Chinese Counterfeit Drugs," The US Department of Justice, May 25, 2006

20. "The Impact of Counterfeit Drugs in South and South-East Asia," *European Pharmaceutical Review*, Accessed March 22, 2021

21. Huileng Tan, "China's Pharmaceutical Industry Is Poised for Major Growth," CNBC, April 19, 2018

22. Douglas Hebert, "Opioid Crisis X Attracts Foreign Counterfeit Pharmaceutical Drugs," *Arizona Capitol Times*, June 27, 2019

23. Marius Schneider and Nora Ho Tu Nam, "Africa and Counterfeit Pharmaceuticals in the Times of COVID-19," *Journal of Intellectual Property Law & Practice*, May 1, 2020

24. "Department of Health and Human Services Fiscal Year 2021, Food and Drug Administration," US Food and Drug Administration, January 2020

25. Henry I. Miller, M.S., M.D. and Wayne Winegarden, Ph.D., "Fraud in Your Pill Bottle: The Unacceptable Cost of Counterfeit Medicines," Pacific Research Institute, Center for Medical Economics Innovation, October 2020

26. Yuron, "China Considers Tougher Law Against Counterfeit Drugs," *Xinhua Headlines*, October 23, 2018

27. Ian Sample, "Fake Drugs Kill More than 250,000 Children a Year, Doctors Warn," *The Guardian*, March 17, 2019

28. Liu Zhihua, "Generic Drug Approvals Boost Pharma Firms' Global Ambitions," *China Daily*, March 7, 2019

29. Anna Edney and Peter Robison, "Dozens of CVS Drug Recalls Expose a Link to Tainted Factories in China and India," *Bloomberg*, Jun 11, 2024

30. "Combating Counterfeit Medicine," www.pfizer.com, accessed July 1, 2024

31. Wenyi Zhang, "Pharmaceutical R&D Expenditure in China from 2014 to 2019," www.statista.com, January 27, 2022

Chapter 23 References

1. "Documenting Genocide: The Extrajudicial Killings of Prisoners of Conscience for Organs in China and the Campaign to Eradicate Falun Gong Factual Findings and Analysis Report," China Organ Research Center, September 2019

2. Hollie McKay, "Survivors and Victims on Shocking State-Sanctioned Organ Harvesting in China," Fox News, October 26, 2019

3. "Investigates the Horrific Practice of Forced Organ Harvesting in Chinese Prisons," *Health Europa Quarterly*, January 29. 2020

4. Lily Kuo, "China Transferred Detained Uyghurs to Factories Used by Global Brands," *The Guardian,* March 1, 2020

5. Elizabeth Paton and Austin Ramzy, "Coalition Brings Pressure to End Forced Uyghur Labor," *The New York Times*, July 23, 2020

6. Eva Dou and Philip Wen, "Admit Your Mistakes, Repent: China Shifts Campaign to Control Xinjiang's Muslims," *The Wall Street Journal*, February 6, 2020

7. "China Uyghurs Moved into Factory Forced Labor for Foreign Brands," BBC News, March 2, 2020

8. "The Uyghurs and the Chinese State: A Long History of Discord," BBC News, July 20, 2020

9. Chris Buckley and Austin Ramzy, "China's Detention Camps for Muslims Turn to Forced Labor," *The New York Times*, December 16, 2018

10. Antonio Graceffo, "China's Crackdown on Mongolian Culture," *Diplomat*, September 4, 2020

11. "China's Repression of Islam Is Spreading beyond Xinjiang," *Economist*, Sep 26th 2019

12. Eva Xiao, "China Cracks Down on Mongols Who Say Their Culture Is Being Snuffed Out," *The Wall Street Journal*, September 4, 2020

13. Wang Xueqiao and Tom Hancock, "Overdoing It: The Cost of China's Long-Hours Culture," *Financial Times*, January 17, 2019

14. "Islam in China (650-Present)," BBC, February 2, 2002

15. Steven Lee Myers, "Crackdown on Islam Is Spreading Across China," *The New York Times*, September. 21, 2019

16. "Tiananmen Square Fast Facts," CNN, Mon May 25, 2020

17. "Timeline: Tiananmen Protests," BBC News, June 2, 2014

18. "Undermining Freedom of Expression in China, the Role of Yahoo!, Microsoft and Google," Amnesty International UK, July 2008

19. Benedict Rogers, "The Nightmare of Human Organ Harvesting in China," *The Wall Street Journal*, February 5, 2019

20. "United States Senate Resolution 274 on Falun Gong," 116th Congress, 1st Session, July 11, 2019

21. "UK Accuses China of Gross Human Rights Abuses against Uyghurs," BBC News, July 19, 2020

22. "2020 Annual Report—Executive Summary Congressional," Executive Commission on China, December 2020

23. Nicole Gaouette and James Frater, "US and Allies Announce Sanctions against Chinese Officials for Serious Human Rights Abuses against Uyghurs," CNN, March 23, 2021

www.ingramcontent.com/pod-product-compliance
Lightning Source LLC
Chambersburg PA
CBHW071319210326
41597CB00015B/1284